VIRGINIA SEASE was born in the United States. Her study of German literature led to a PhD from the University of Southern California in 1969. She has been a member of the Executive Council of the General Anthroposophical Society since 1984, and served from 1991 to 2001 as leader of the Section for the Arts of Eurythmy, Speech, Drama and Music of the School of Spiritual Science at the Goetheanum in Dornach (Switzerland). Her current responsibilities include liaising between the Executive Council and English-speaking anthroposophists around the world, and directing the English Anthroposophical Studies Programme at the Goetheanum.

MANFRED SCHMIDT-BRABANT was born in Berlin, Germany. He became a member of the Executive Council of the General Anthroposophical Society at the Goetheanum in 1975 and served as Chair of the Council from 1984 until his death in 2001. His service during those years included leadership of the Social Science Section of the School of Spiritual Science, and lecturing around the world on many subjects. English editions of his books include *Paths of the Christian Mysteries*, *The New Mysteries* and *The Archetypal Feminine* (with Virginia Sease), and *The Spiritual Tasks of the Homemaker*.

D1561753

By the same authors:

Paths of the Christian Mysteries, From Compostela to the New World
The New Mysteries and the Wisdom of Christ
The Archetypal Feminine in the Mystery Stream of Humanity

THINKERS, SAINTS, HERETICS

Spiritual Paths of the Middle Ages

Virginia Sease and Manfred Schmidt-Brabant

TEMPLE LODGE

Translated from German by Marguerite V. Miller and Douglas E. Miller

Temple Lodge Publishing
Hillside House, The Square
Forest Row, RH18 5ES

www.templelodge.com

Published by Temple Lodge 2007

Originally published in German under the title *Denker, Heilige, Ketzer, Geisteswege des Mittelalters* by Verlag am Goetheanum, Dornach 2005

A catalogue record for this book is available from the British Library

ISBN 978 1 902636 90 0

Cover by Andrew Morgan Design
Typeset by DP Photosetting, Neath, West Glamorgan
Printed and bound by Cromwell Press Limited, Trowbridge, Wiltshire

Contents

Preface to the English Edition

For this third volume of lectures, which were held in Paris in August 2000 and were published in German in 2005, I again wish to express my deep gratitude to Marguerite and Douglas Miller for their fine and careful translation. Out of their own familiarity with aspects of the subject matter they were in a position to assess sensitively and accurately various passages which demanded not only literal translation but also interpretation. In view of their translations of the two previous books, *Paths of the Christian Mysteries: From Compostela to the New World* and *The New Mysteries and the Wisdom of Christ*, this third volume manifests a similar unity of style and diction which captures the spirit of the original lectures.

As this lecture cycle was the last that the authors could hold before Manfred Schmidt-Brabant's death six months later in February 2001, I welcome the fact that these themes will now be accessible for the English reader. Many people in English-speaking countries remember fondly his lectures from his visits.

Virginia Sease, Ph.D.
Goetheanum, Switzerland, August 2007

Preface

The current book follows on the earlier publications, *Paths of the Christian Mysteries: From Compostela to the New World* and *The New Mysteries and the Wisdom of Christ*. As with these first two volumes, this book is a series of lectures we gave during August 2000, at the invitation of Manfred Kraus at the Studienhaus Rüspe.

With this volume, I am, once again, very grateful to Elisabeth Bessau for reviewing and editing the transcripts, particularly as the necessary references were often not to be found in the estate of Manfred Schmidt-Brabant. I am enormously indebted to Manfred Muhler at the Goetheanum for transcribing the texts from the recordings and for the various corrections to them.

There have been many enquiries from participants in this conference about the possibility of publishing this series of lectures as well. This is the last lecture cycle given by Manfred Schmidt-Brabant († 11 February 2001). I am particularly pleased that—almost five years later—these lectures are now being published.

Virginia Sease
Goetheanum, Dornach, July 2005

Historical Symptomology—Mystery Impulses in the Middle Ages—In Search of the Light of the Soul

Manfred Schmidt-Brabant

Why do people in our time look back with such interest at the Middle Ages? Isn't all that in the distant past, a vanished world whose remnants—paintings and cathedrals—we still enjoy? How does what happened then have anything to do with the present, with our problems of globalization, genetic engineering, and so forth? Our self-awareness, our existential sense of self—and thus the value of our biographies, our lives, for us—depends on whether we can create a right relationship to the present age; depends on whether, as is so often said, we can be people of our time in the true sense of the word.

If we really want to stand fully in the present time—if this is what we want—then we also have to develop an understanding for its roots. Substantial and significant roots of the present time are to be found in the Middle Ages. They were the origin of many impulses that continue to stream into our time and help to determine our thinking, our feeling and our actions. Knowledge of who we are in the present is quite important for an understanding of our own biography; so much in life depends on this. And it is just as important that we have at least some understanding for the biography of our modern Europe. As human beings, we have biographies that we can examine—the impulses of childhood, youth, education, our parents, perhaps the preparation for a career, and so on. These impulses can help us understand much about what affects us in the moment—what we suffer and what makes us happy. Time also has a biography—our present time has a biography. It goes beyond the Middle Ages, of course, but looking to the Middle Ages is one important step to take. Europe today is largely determined by what people of the High Middle Ages thought, endured, considered and fought over. All of this emerges today in the individual and the community. Let me give you an example.

Jan Hus

Vaclav Havel, the former president of the Czech Republic, wrote a book entitled *Die Wahrheit sagen* [Say the truth] which was quite important during the period of Soviet repression. It has been translated into many languages. Vaclav Havel caught the attention of the world through the impulse that permeates the book, and he gained an extraordinary reputation as a result. However, his book actually places him in a stream that originated in medieval Bohemia. There was a significant individual at that time—significant in Rudolf Steiner's estimation as well—by the name of Jan Hus. Hus worked in Prague during the fifteenth century as a great preacher, as a theologian, as a leader, even as an official of the university there. He fought a battle we will want to examine in the course of our discussions here, a battle against the corrupted official Church, the corrupted clergy, and the degenerate monastic system. Neither the Church, the clergy, nor the monasteries were very pleased about this. This battle led to a practice that was peculiar to the time. He was lured to the great Council of Constance under false pretenses and imprisoned there upon his arrival. The Council engaged him in long disputes in an effort to persuade him to recant. When this proved to be of no avail, Hus was burned at the stake in 1415. Thus he became the great national hero of Bohemia (the area known today as the Czech Republic). Jan Hus is a kind of national saint and what arose from him strikes a chord in us even today.

This impulse reappears in a book like Vaclav Havel's. Hus wrote some things—but not many. In *Grundlage des Glaubens* [The foundations of faith], he writes:

> ... Thus pious Christian, seek the truth, hear the truth, learn the truth, love the truth, speak the truth, hold fast to the truth, defend the truth unto death, because the truth liberates you from sins, from the devil, from the death of the soul, and finally from eternal death ...[1]

We will frequently examine what lived in these so-called heretics of the Middle Ages, but we do so here only to take note of them. We could point to many such streams as moral impulses or impulses for knowledge arising from the battles at that time. These impulses from the past enter our present age as though on moving waves of time, shaping modern human beings even down into our politics, our arts and our economics; in fact, they continue to shape all aspects of the present.

Priest and King in One Person

These lectures will deal with a certain period of time—the period between 1000 and 1500. Today, of course, we will be looking further back—at King Arthur and what flowed through him into Europe. We will also consider the historical precursors of what later made its way into Europe. In mainstream histories, 1500 is felt to be the end of the Middle Ages. The period between 1000 and 1500 is important for us as the time of great controversies and disputations that continue to exert a still fresh and vital influence on modern human life through politics, philosophy and theology even today.

The first point we will consider—always emphasized in the written history of this period—is the enormous antagonism between the emperor and the pope, between secular power and spiritual power. This is shown pictorially in the image of two swords—the sword of the spirit and the sword of secular power. We will see it later with the Templars in the symbol of the cross and the eagle: eagle, secular power; the cross, spiritual power.

In the great old Mystery cultures, there was only one unified structure. There was the priest-king, the Pharaoh; this means that secular power and spiritual power were united in a single person. It would have been impossible to have imagined it otherwise; a polarity was completely unthinkable and unimaginable. As the old Mysteries gradually came to an end, something like uncertainty arose concerning this principle. The forms became decadent. We see in the Roman Caesars how Augustus or Julius Caesar still represents this in a noble form; they are, at the same time, *Imperator* and *Pontifex Maximus*, the highest priest. Then we see how very quickly after them the decadent Caesars' claim of spiritual and religious sovereignty also degenerated. This was the case in Byzantium as well. The Byzantine emperors interfered in Church councils in a quite dishonest and unjustified way. The old principle of the priest-kings fades away.

Next comes the time of Charlemagne when this problem reaches a critical juncture. With Charlemagne a period ensues during which the emperor places himself in opposition to the spiritual power of the pope— in full consciousness and with self-confidence. This was absolutely the case with Charlemagne. He and his Franconian theologians acted without the consent of the pope, occasionally even in opposition to the pope. He was responsible for abolishing the veneration of images. Adoptionism— the view that God only adopted Christ who was, until the adoption, a human being—was rejected by Charlemagne and his theologians. The most significant factor was the so-called *Filioque* formulation.

Filioque—The Holy Spirit

The great question at that time was: Does the Holy Spirit proceed only from the Father, or does the Holy Spirit also proceed from Christ, from the Son? *Filioque* means 'and from the Son'. The pope was not in favour of this *Filioque* being accepted into the confession of faith. Charlemagne pushed it through authoritatively, with all the now-familiar consequences. The Eastern Orthodox Church arose as a result of this *Filioque* decision in the West; the East never agreed to this formulation.

Within the polarity between the emperor and the pope, Charlemagne placed absolute sovereignty in the hands of the emperor. The popes were weak, hesitant, more or less reluctantly yielding. Then the Carolingian Empire, under Charlemagne's rather inept successors, decays into the three states of France, Germany and Italy. They appear because there was no longer any authority in evidence to maintain the old realm, the Carolingian Empire.

The most disastrous events were also taking place. The Saracens force their way in from the south, destroying Italy; the Hungarians come from the east, destroying and murdering; the Normans were particularly terrible, the Vikings, coming with their boats up the Seine and other rivers, laying waste to everything. Paris, which was smaller than it is today, was repeatedly burned. The Île de la Cité was Paris; the Latin Quarter was a kind of suburb. The power of the emperor is broken during this time. On the other hand, the counter-pole of papal power ascends during this period.

Pope and Emperor

One hundred and seventy years later, we find one of the greatest and most powerful popes in Rome—Gregory VII. We will come to know more about him later, because both the origin and foundations of his power and authority are interesting. Everything changed with Gregory. The pope is now the one who makes all decisions. He sets forth the thesis that the pope is the lord of the world. Every prince must kiss the pope's feet. He has the power to dismiss the emperor.[2] A historical event familiar to many of us from our schooldays took place during this period. The German king Henry IV is so enraged about all the pope's claims, he declares the pope deposed. But Henry was not Charlemagne. The pope hurled Henry's fulminations back at him, and excommunicated Henry. As a result, Henry's vassals forsake their allegiance to him, and the pope deposes Henry. Now something takes place that has a certain appeal. Henry IV decides to make a clever move. At the time—it was winter— the pope is in residence in his castle at Canossa in central Italy. According to legend, the king goes there in the robes of a penitent and, for three days, stands barefoot before the castle. The pope was under pressure from the cardinals and bishops to do something; they tell him that this much penitence and repentance is enough. The pope had no choice but to repeal the excommunication and absolve Henry.

These are great images of a battle that begins here and continues down through the centuries. It was not long before the power of the pope again weakened. A schism arose that led to two popes; the imperial, secular side gained the upper hand once again. Meanwhile, sides were being taken across Europe, in even the smallest cities and communities. The followers of the pope were called Guelfs and the supporters of imperial power were called Ghibellines. We will find this battle affecting the destiny of figures like Dante, Brunetto Latini and others. Their whole lives were brought into confusion because they belonged to one or the other side. Later, the popes went into the so-called exile in Avignon.

Heretics

That was one of the great controversies running through the medieval world, particularly during the period between 1000 and 1500. Another great controversy is the one between heretics and the organized Church. The odd thing is that heresy actually began in Europe in the year 1000. A great standard work, the eight-volume *Lexikon des Mittelalters* [Lexicon of the Middle Ages]—a collection of research on the Middle Ages—was completed a few years ago. These volumes offer a reliable view of the Middle Ages supported by hundreds of scholars. There we read that aside from earlier isolated phenomena, 'medieval heresies begin exactly at the turn of the millennium as an almost constant accompaniment to Western religious movements and thought'.[3] What is known in Europe as the heresies, the heretical movements, began with the year 1000. We will see how the Church's retaliation through the Inquisition is part of this picture.

Nominalists and Realists

Yet another great contrast also arises during this period—actually after the year 1000: the distinction between nominalism and realism. The question was: What are concepts? The realists said: Concepts—like 'wood' or 'tree'—have an independent existence in the spiritual. All phenomena come from this independent existence of concepts—universals (*uni-*

versalia) as they were called. The nominalists said: No. Concepts are names we create. We see wolves and create a name—'wolf'—for similar things. We do the same for the name 'tree', and so on. There was a lot at stake here because the feelings people had about such a question were anything but cold and abstract. It struck a nerve in them, affected them right to their core: Which one is it? Does the spiritual have its own reality beyond what I can see? Or does everything I think consist only of names for an extant world?

Then there is another matter that brings us closer to our theme—the great contrast between the Platonists and the Aristotelians. The Platonists, the School of Chartres and everything connected to it up to the present time; and the Aristotelians, the high point of scholasticism, Thomas Aquinas, Albertus Magnus, and everything that flows from it today.

A final contrast we will encounter again and again is the one between observation and thinking. There was a stream that said: What is spiritual can be seen only through faith. The other stream said: No, what is spiritual has to be thought if it is to be recognized. These were also controversies that cut deeply into people's feelings about life, into their souls. Summing up, we could say: The great controversies concerned the spiritual world and the earthly world. Where does the human being stand in this tension between the spiritual world and the earthly world?

Paris and Chartres

Martin Luther and the historical Faust, Georg Faust, both lived around 1500. Paralleling this circumstance in Europe, America was discovered in 1492. The year 1000 and the year 1500 are great turning points for the world; during each, an evolution into something new takes place. These dates create a formal framework for our observations here.

Permit me to add something here about the cities of Paris and Chartres, the great centres of spiritual life in the Middle Ages. The influence of the School of Chartres radiated across all of Europe for two hundred years; then came the University of Paris with Thomas Aquinas, Albertus Magnus and the Scholastics. Paris becomes the centre of things. It was also the centre of the Templars and their vast infrastructure: an enormous Templar church with the familiar, mysterious design of Templar churches—a round church with a long, rectangular church attached. All this is destroyed in the end, during the French Revolution. Today, there is only the Temple Métro station in the area where the Temple once stood. Dante was also in Paris and had quite significant experiences. Brunetto Latini, as well. During these five hundred years, Paris and Chartres—more than Rome and other cities—were the spiritual centre of Europe.

The Symptomatological Method

Now a little more about methodology. These lectures will not proceed by following events chronologically. We will look instead at what came before and what followed, so that a lecture may go back in time to events that preceded what happened in the immediate past or forward beyond events that follow. This is because we are using a certain historiography indicated by Rudolf Steiner—which means we will not describe history causally but will instead treat it symptomatologically. I quote here:

> ... not a causal history and also not a pragmatic history, all the lovely things that are sometimes so admired. What then is causal history? ... It assumes that what follows always arises as the effect of what went before. But when we look at the surface of a body of water and see the waves one after the other—can we really see every subsequent wave as the result of the one that went before it? Shouldn't we then look into the depths of the water for the cause, the common cause, for the succession of the waves? It is no different with history. We overlook what is most significant if we look only at the connection between cause and effect. We overlook what prevails deep in the forces of human evolution and brings individual phenomena to the surface in the course of time so that they cannot be described merely from the standpoint of cause and effect. What happens during one century is not just the effect of what happened in the century before; it is brought to the surface independently—only secondarily as an effect—it is brought independently, I would say, to the surface from deep in humanity's evolutionary stream.[4]

We will see many such phenomena—human phenomena, above all— and we will be led back by the phenomenon itself to something loftier.

For this series of lectures, we have chosen the title 'Mystery Impulses of the Middle Ages'; we will be looking at Mystery themes, the effects of which reach even into the present. Because we are dealing with a portrayal of the Mysteries, we will turn to the observational methods and vocabulary of anthroposophical spiritual science.

Five Historical Impulses

I would now like to make clear what is implied in the passage just cited from Rudolf Steiner. We have five great impulses of history to consider. On the one hand, we have—throughout history—the *causal stream*. If I have an event 'B' here in the stream of causality, we can be certain that something is also at work in this event that was present earlier as an 'A'.

But when human beings are involved there is a *second* element. People come from a past earth life, bringing with them impulses that cannot be explained in terms of what occurred in the external history immediately preceding them. Whether it is a talent for good or evil or something else entirely, people bring an element from a previous earthly life that took place previously in history; and then they enter into a subsequent earthly life. This is *reincarnation*.

Active throughout history is also something we can identify as the streams of various Mystery traditions that have been handed down. They have somehow been active behind the scenes of outer existence: the Grail stream, the Templar stream, the Rosicrucian stream, and much else that developed out of the ongoing life of the old Mysteries that continued into the Middle Ages. They exert their influence, and their effect must be sought out when I look at a particular event. This is a *third element*.

A *fourth element* looks to a further level of activity—the level of spiritual beings. In anthroposophy, we speak about the fact that the ages of time stand under the various impulses of the archangels so that, during a certain period, an archangel is active and colours events as it were—often by working through one person. Then another archangel is active in the period that follows. Impulses from this level enter into events and must also be discovered.

There is a *fifth* element in our considerations—the great impulses of time. Archangels are not the only spiritual beings; there are other beings as well. Mystery streams make themselves visible in external life through all sorts of *secret societies*, and so forth.

Thus, when we look at historical events that seem relevant for the present time, that continue to have an effect, that are in some way connected to us, we must also examine what is at work in addition to the causal nexus which, of course, cannot be overlooked.

The period of the Middle Ages is like a differentiated, complex spiritual amalgam. Everything I am presenting here in these introductory remarks is intended to set aside conventional ideas about the Middle Ages, a period that remains veiled for certain reasons. The Catholic Church's version of history is not interested in presenting these matters with an eye to reality.

The Protestant Church's view of history—counter to Rome's, naturally—has no inkling of the spiritual element. Common materialistic historiography cannot do more than take account of points that go from A to B, from B to C. I am not saying this with disrespect—there are great Church historians. But their work is inadequate if we want to arrive at the reality of the Mystery impulses of the Middle Ages, at what actually led from the Mystery impulses to a wondrous work like Chartres Cathedral.

Everything flows into everything else. There is exoteric and esoteric Christianity; there are the mystics; Islam streams in (exoteric Islam and the esotericism of Sufism); Judaism streams in—with the Torah but also with the Cabbala. Everything swirls together, as it were. If we look at medieval thinkers, at whether they were more theologically or philosophically inclined, we find that they were familiar with all these things, they were affected by it all. They also knew that the ancient contents of the Mysteries from India, Persia, Egypt, Greece and Rome were cargo being brought in, so to speak, aboard the ship of Sufism, of the Cabbala or mysticism. The whole milieu is like a mighty vessel, in constant motion, always receiving anew what we call the life of the medieval Mysteries.

Pico della Mirandola

A brilliant Italian by the name of Pico della Mirandola lived at the end of the period we have been discussing. He came from a landed noble family and received an excellent education during his youth. He spoke all the important languages—Hebrew, Aramaic, Arabic, and so on. He did not live to be an old man, dying at the age of 31. He was the epitome of an idealistic, young, striving Renaissance man. He developed a theory proposing that everything he read and knew from Islam, Judaism, Christianity, and so on, is actually a unity containing an ancient wisdom. He wrote nine hundred theses in order to prove it. Since he was financially well off, he invited the most significant European scholars to Rome to discuss these nine hundred theses with him. This whole matter displeased the Church enormously, and it was not long before a portion of the theses—and eventually all nine hundred—were declared heretical. Pico della Mirandola had to flee. In Lorenzo de Medici, Pico della Mirandola had a powerful patron who held a protective hand over him and assured him that he would not become a victim of the Inquisition. But, as I said, Pico della Mirandola died quite early, at 31 years of age. His friend, Savonarola, the Dominican, gave the funeral address; and soon after Savonarola was burned at the stake for heretical thoughts.

Rudolf Steiner makes significant statements about Pico della Mirandola and his attempts to describe this entire spiritual cosmos as a whole and to understand it as a unity. He says: Had this attempt succeeded, Europe would have received a Platonically free Christendom. But, as it turned out, this attempt was buried under other ideological strata.

The Mystery of Mirroring Millennia

Three millennia that mirror three others; this thought brings us a step closer to what gave these lectures their subtitle. Let us turn our attention to characteristics Rudolf Steiner described for six of the great millennia. He characterizes the hue, the motif of the three millennia before the Mystery of Golgotha, and the three millennia following that turning point in time.

The third millennium BC—which Rudolf Steiner calls the Age of Abraham after the ancestral father Abraham—was marked by a historical fact in the development of the human being. Up to this millennium, the consciousness of the human being was as though excarnate, as though still outside the physical body. Consciousness lived as though at the periphery; it lived with the spiritual world, lived in the clairvoyance of an age that could still perceive spiritual beings. Beginning with the third millennium BC, human consciousness connects itself to the brain; human beings gradually develop the kind of brain-bound thinking we have today. This is characteristic of the third millennium.

The second millennium follows, characterized by the figure of Moses. After consciousness was, we might say, anchored in the physical body—but more so, concretely, in the brain—human beings began to grasp the ego being in nature. They looked outside themselves, and could perceive the I AM in the world just as Moses had in the imagination of the burning bush. This sounded towards them in the world of nature, but not yet within them. It was present there, as though speaking to people from a general spirituality in nature. We could also say: The I AM comes into being.

Then there is the final millennium BC, exemplified by the figure of Solomon. It was a time when humanity moved in the wisdom of the world. This is characteristic of Solomon in both tradition and legend; he was so wise that he could know all the architectural secrets of the universe. Through Solomon and later events, people of this last millennium before the turning point in time lived in the knowledge, the perception of the wisdom of the world. This wisdom of the world was still external to the human being. This brings us to the turning point in time, the Mystery of Golgotha.

Something then takes place that is extraordinarily interesting. If we examine it historically, the truth of it is confirmed. The millennia invert; they are mirrored around the Mystery of Golgotha, but in such a way that what came before, what was more general, more objective, enters into the personal subjectivity of human beings. This means that, once again, we have a Solomonic millennium after the turning point in time. However, wisdom is now no longer outside, sensed and known through instinctive clairvoyance. Instead, the wisdom of the world begins to light up in the individual human being. The wisdom of the world shines in the Gnosis, in individual people, in the great Church fathers, in Origen, Clement of Alexandria, Augustine, and others we will also come to mention later because they bring their light into the School of Chartres.

After this comes the second millennium AD. This is the period of interest to us, a period when the human being no longer finds the I AM in the outer world, in the burning bush, but now inside himself, within his own soul. This is the great theme that begins around the year 1000: the human being begins to seek the I AM, the inner light, in his soul. He begins to insist that he must seek the inner light in his soul. This leads to the emergence of certain nuances that are reflected in our theme. This turning inwards that slowly arises through a great impulse of the age can be investigated beginning around the year 1000. People say: I think. But what does that actually mean? People pose this question and thus, for example, the whole problem of nominalism and realism arises as a reality of life. What does thinking mean? What value do concepts have?

Thinkers

Rudolf Steiner points to the fact that the ancient Greeks had been constituted quite differently in relation to philosophy. A Greek received thoughts and had no doubts about them whatsoever; he doubted them as little as we would doubt whether a plant is green or the sun golden. Thoughts arise and some people receive these thoughts more easily and more fluidly than others, depending on the physical constitution of the person. Those who received them more easily and fluidly were the philosophers. Now this changes completely. The human being has the impression: I create thoughts through my thinking. I don't receive them; I create them. Immediately, a scepticism and questioning arise that were unknown to the Greeks. How is it with thinking? Now, for the first time,

Scholasticism and the dialectics of Scholasticism—a self-examination based on the truth in the content—arise.

Thus the impulse active from the year 1000 onwards introduces what we have identified as one of the three concepts of our theme: the thinker. We in no way mean just the professional philosophers, the Scholastics in Chartres and in Paris whom we know through their books. Instead, this life of thinking takes hold of all people. Even the simple man suddenly has the feeling: How is this, in fact? You hear this and that from the pulpit; you think about it. But what value does your own thinking have? During these centuries, humanity was impelled towards being thinkers. On the other hand, it was impelled by the human perception: I think in order to experience and emphasize the independent activity of the individual. Heresy arises.

Individuality Reveals Itself

Heresy arose because a stand was taken for the independence of individual conviction in the face of all the group pressure from the Church and dogmas. Some clever historians note that everyone was really a heretic at that time; only those dumb enough to speak it aloud were burned at the stake. The others were shrewder and more careful to remain silent. Because they were silent, the Church came up with the idea of making inquiries, of asking what a person is really thinking. The Inquisition—which had been unnecessary previously—now arose. What had existed as heresy in the first millennium was spoken aloud and then the Church persecuted or condemned it. Now there was the suspicion that something was occurring within human beings that seemed eerie to the Church; under certain circumstances it even contradicts the Church. Thus it becomes necessary to interrogate people in an inquisition. Actually, a constant interrogation must be conducted to ascertain whether a person believes what is correct, because every human being is considered a heretic. The clever representatives of the official Church of the time knew this.

When we read the records—from the trial of Jan Hus, for instance—we see what an effort they made! We must also come to see the following. Today we say: The inquisitors were all evil, rabid people who used torture. That is not quite the case. They often tried with enormous patience—also in the case of Hus—to get the prisoner to recant. They tried patiently to say to him: Admit that this has been a mistake, that the Church is right. But Hus resisted: No, I insist on the truth. This went on for weeks. When he failed to recant, the Church had lost the battle. They knew with certainty that when a person insists so much on his own individuality that he willingly faces being burned at the stake, a force is arising in humanity against the pressures of the group and of dogmas. Hus knew he would be burned as well. Everything that seems universal is counterbalanced by the individual.

Joan of Arc

We also have the trial records of the Maid of Orléans preserved in their entirety and in print. Just think: there stands a 19-year-old girl before a whole group of theologians, bishops, scholars, Church scholars, and so forth, all trying to convince her. Listen! The Church is correct. You cannot be right; you are a young girl in opposition to everyone else. She says: I know that I will be burned at the stake. But the truth for me is what St Michael and St Margaret told me. Then Master William explained to her that she must submit to the Holy Mother Church. In the name of several authorities and passages from the Holy Scripture, they admonish her to obey them. She replies, no; she will not bend.

> Then she was warned, admonished, and advised to take the good advice of these priests and famous doctors, and to have faith in them for the sake of her soul ... And the last answer she gave to the question of whether she wanted to submit in her deeds to our mother, the Holy Church, was: 'Whatever may happen to me as a result, I will say nothing ... but what I have already said.'[5]

Here the force of resistance becomes clear in this young girl who had inner experiences. We can imagine that aged heretics went courageously to the stake. But this fundamentally gentle shepherdess defied a whole company of inquisitors. St Michael, St Catherine and St Margaret spoke to her. It was repeatedly claimed that it was the devil who spoke to her, but she countered: No. She knew better, and stood by these voices.

This second concept—the heretic—will accompany us here, because it emerges in various forms throughout all the centuries.

Saints

Now, the saints, the third concept we have used—these people also lived during the Middle Ages. We do not mean only those simply declared saints by the Church and canonized. This is a problem for the Church: first it burned these people at the stake and then it canonized them. The Church claims that both acts were correct: We burned them because they opposed the Church; and we canonize them because they turned to God. The Church not only has a big belly,[6] but also a wide range of explanations and interpretations.

I do not mean this disrespectfully. We can read, for example, how some were concerned with such souls and fought for them. I often point to George Bernard Shaw's play *Saint Joan* which reveals an oddly concise grasp of this whole situation. He describes in thrilling terms how a young Dominican struggles and says: Dear Joan, be reasonable at last; we want the best for you. That is what we really want. If you recant, we will drive away all the Englishmen, and no one will burn you at the stake.

There were many saints. The tendency to what is saintly—self-sacrifice, devotion to the divine element people sensed in themselves—was as normative during these centuries as the disposition to be a thinker or a heretic. We will encounter the great ideals of voluntary poverty and asceticism in streams that were viewed as heretical as well as in streams that escaped heresy with great difficulty—like the Franciscans. The whole practice of judging someone as a saint or a heretic is questionable. Even Thomas Aquinas was almost declared a heretic. We will see how people would have preferred that a pope suspected of practising magic be burned at the stake; but he was pope, and this did not happen. Thus we see that the tendency to saintliness, to a deep and humble devotion to God, was characteristic of this century.

This was a manageable world. Everyone knew everyone else. If we look out at the modern world today, it is compartmentalized and closed off. Our so-called flow of information actually isolates everything. The University of Paris, located in several buildings in the Latin Quarter, was already known as a quite advanced centre of learning. Among others, an Alanus ab Insulis, a Thomas Aquinas lectured there. People knew one another, knew about one another, and accompanied one another; and people were astonishingly mobile.

Wanderers

We give ourselves a lot of credit for travelling across Europe with modern means of transportation—cars, planes, trains. If we look at the biographies of these medieval colleagues, they were at least as mobile as we are—and did all of it on foot! The famous Bishop Malachi of Armagh (AD 1095–

1148) was constantly on the road from Ireland through Europe to Rome, and back again from Rome to his home in Ireland—back and forth frequently. In the end, he died while visiting St Bernard of Clairvaux; the two were friends and so this was a frequent stop along the way. When Albertus Magnus was quite old, he once again set out for the University of Paris to defend his pupil, Thomas Aquinas, who had died in the meantime. After lengthy deliberations, the friars had approved an ox cart for Albertus—he was 80 years old—in which he could jolt along not too comfortably between Cologne and Paris. Otherwise, it was customary for people to travel by foot.

We will point out how the Cistercian Order spread. Part of their rule said that once a year a general synod took place in Cîteaux where all the abbots of the Cistercian monasteries had to be present. There were monasteries in the far north on the Baltic Sea or far to the east. Thus an abbot was on the road for two or three months to arrive in Cîteaux, and two or three months on the way home. He could take care of a little business and then had to be back on the road to the next synod. There are many, often quite funny stories that could be told about how these men wandered back and forth. We think: How did they manage this? The road conditions were often disastrous; they ran through morass and woods. But a kind of industriousness moved people within this medieval cosmos. An exchange of ideas and knowledge of everything that was going on flowed with the movement of people through this cosmos.

Bernard of Clairvaux

People at that time had a different consciousness. Anthroposophy again and again calls our attention to this: people of that time were not as abstract, intellectual or removed as we are today. They lived with what is spiritual, above all, with a spiritual perception of other people. When a saint appeared—a real saint, no matter whether a Church had declared him one—people shared in the saint's aura as it radiated far and wide. Bernard of Clairvaux preached in the Rhineland—no one understood him, yet everyone followed him. They perceived something else entirely. The story of St Bernard is quite significant.

Bernard preached the Second Crusade at the church in Vézelay, standing behind the church on the edge of a cliff. The cliff drops off sharply into the valley below where a few thousand people were assembled. Above them stood Bernard, preaching. The acoustics at that time were not that much different than they are today. The words died

away; only those standing in immediate proximity heard them. Nevertheless, it is reported that all the thousands assembled there were deeply
moved by what they perceived radiating from Bernard of Clairvaux.
They were filled with enthusiasm for the Crusade and everything associated with it. We will find the emanation of a far-reaching spirit-aura in
many other events as well. Rudolf Steiner mentions them as characteristic
of that era.

This consciousness resulted in a perception that rose above the level of
time. People perceived something in the spirit that took place somewhere
else—not as a medium, not prophetically, but simply because they still
had an expanded capacity to sense these things. In the Compostela lectures,[7] I spoke about events surrounding the discovery of the grave of the
apostle who was the brother of Christ. In the meantime, ecclesiastical
history has shown conclusively that the relics of the true brother of Christ
lie in Compostela. This was presented in a massive volume by an
American church historian. Shortly after, people began to set forth on
pilgrimages from the North Sea, from Slovenia, even from what is today
Turkey. They struggled to get to Compostela because they understood
that something had happened there. This kind of supersensible appre-
hension of events was maintained for a long time; it was especially active
during the centuries we are discussing.

The Network of Destiny

We need a certain spirit awareness and spiritual consciousness to look at
this period of time. And we ourselves need to be clear it is present today as
a factor regardless of whether we were incarnated in that era, whether we
lived during one of these centuries—which is actually true for many
people who are concerned with spiritual questions of the present time—
or whether it was a more peripheral experience. Situations exist in which
events from a previous earthly life play a role. When we find ourselves in a
present-day situation, we must recognize that events may play a role in it
that we ourselves participated in during the Middle Ages.

Part of this is to look a bit at a peculiarity of human nature. We say: I
exist now in the present time, but I might have been incarnated during
the Middle Ages. We like to think as a knight, perhaps. Or we experience
antipathies towards another person and say: I am certain he burned me at
the stake and that is why I cannot stand him. If we do this we are making a
mistake because the ego is not such a concentrated point within the
human being; rather, the real human ego-being exists at a certain

periphery. Rudolf Steiner demonstrated this philosophically and episte-
mologically already in 1911. The human ego actually lives at the periphery, not within the skin; only its reflection is there. We knock there at
the door and say 'I', but we are not there at all. Where are we then with
our consciousness? Everywhere outside, but not within our skin—unless
we hurt on the inside and then there is a sense of pain. Otherwise, our
consciousness is always at the periphery. Above all, it resides in the
relationships of destiny that we have with the people connected to us.
That is where our ego is really at home. It resides in the network of
destiny made up of people with whom we are connected.

This was also the case in the Middle Ages. One might say that the
interweaving threads of destiny have come down to us from that time.
We could also say the destiny threads of the human and social world. We
must also take into consideration the situation of the human environment
when we look at the Middle Ages. Suppose that someone thinks or even
says, based on certain inner experiences: I once lived as a monk, as a
Cistercian, as a Dominican, as a Franciscan. That certainly did not unfold
in isolation. He would miss something significant if he only looked at an
isolated life in the cloister. That is just a point of reference. At that time,
the world around him played an active part—the world of the cloister
community, the social community of the Church with all the tensions
and problems that have been described. All of this influences the present
time. We see the extent to which all these questions continue to affect us:
questions of the nominalists, the realists, as well as all the questions about
heresy, and about the over-arching order of a community that binds
everything together; the questions about who has the right to decide—a
secular or a clerical authority? We experience how that continues today in
relation to abortion and other such questions. The pope says this; secular
authority says something else. What is right? How does it live in people?
What am I obliged to do as a human being? The state says: You are free to
do as you will. The Church says: You are not at all free and cannot do
whatever you wish. Do I act only according to what I agree with? Are
there ways to know the right path?

At the cathedral in Chartres there is a famous, large labyrinth. There
were many such labyrinths in other cathedrals and in antiquity. The
labyrinth is an inner spiritual situation of a person on the path to
knowledge of the spirit. There is forward movement and backward
movement, and there are dead ends. In one of Rudolf Steiner's great
Mystery Dramas, the second drama, the spiritual leader Benedictus says:
Only he can find the truth in the spirit who 'with patience, can wander
through labyrinths'.[8] That is the primal experience of all Mysteries. The

search for the spirit exists only for those who 'with patience, can wander through labyrinths'.

Thus, what has come down to us from the Middle Ages and into our spiritual present as well is an image of the paths to the spirit that people can tread in freedom. Today, we must walk them differently than in the past. But the course of the present has been shaped by the past.

Anthroposophy

I want to close by noting that Rudolf Steiner draws attention to the fact that people on a spiritual path today can be differentiated into souls who are Platonically inclined and those inclined towards the Aristotelian. He says that many people who have found their way to anthroposophy were, during their previous incarnation, Platonists in the vast environs of the School of Chartres; or they were Aristotelians who participated in the cultivation of thinking, of Scholasticism, and belonged to the equally wide circle of Dominicans moving throughout Europe.

What we take up today as a modern spiritual science was prepared at Chartres. Anthroposophy does not represent itself as a religious persuasion or a persuasion of any kind; it actually intends to be something like natural science on a spiritual plane, an objective science that anyone can apply.

We held a large conference at the Goetheanum on the Esotericism of World Religions.[9] Representatives from Islam, Shinto, Buddhism and other religions spoke. They were all anthroposophists. They demonstrated how anthroposophy as a spiritual science is capable of bringing forth and illuminating the kernel of truth, the esoteric kernel of every religion. The youthful ideal of Pico della Mirandola—nine hundred theses that united everything, drawn up out of a youthful inspiration that led, in a way, to his downfall because the time for them was not yet ripe— can today find full expression through anthroposophy. The more anthroposophy understands how it is inwardly nourished by the great spiritual forces of the Middle Ages, the more effectively it will be able to pursue its objective task.

I will close with a somewhat complicated remark by Rudolf Steiner that will lead into our next presentations. He says:

> We can see this anthroposophy arising in a living way like a being that had to be born, but which rested—as though in a mother's womb—in what had come from the first Christian centuries, been prepared on earth in the School of Chartres, then found its continuation in the

supersensible, and in collaboration with what endured on earth in the defence of Christianity coloured by Aristotelianism.[10]

What had worked into the School of Chartres and streamed out towards Paris in the Aristotelian defence of Christianity was resting as though in a mother's womb.

Lecture 2

King Arthur and the Celtic Mysteries

Virginia Sease

In his comprehensive introduction, Manfred Schmidt-Brabant addressed vast areas of our theme. I will now enter into the old Mysteries, specifically those around King Arthur.

A Pre-Christian Mystery School

Rudolf Steiner often spoke about King Arthur and the Round Table. He begins early on to speak of these Mysteries around King Arthur and this continues right on through to his very last lectures. Rudolf Steiner shows how a great mass of people found its way across Africa to Asia with the folk migration that came from Atlantis, and how another group came over to western and central Europe and settled there. Some of this group remained behind in a region of western Europe. Its leaders are those individuals we experience as a faint echo through history when the story of King Arthur and the Round Table is told. This Round Table was the first European Mystery school situated in a region of what is Great Britain today.

For centuries and millennia, many stories and legends have streamed out of this Mystery school. Often there is no agreement among the accounts. But the initiates intimately involved in this Mystery school were its leaders. As was always the case in the early Mysteries, they guided everything in the lives of the people connected to them. Whether it was knowledge about plants, or cattle breeding, or human community—all of it fell under the guidance of the wise priests, the Mystery teachers.

According to Rudolf Steiner, everything belonging to this first Mystery school was concentrated around a kind of spiritual monarchy because there had to be leadership at a spiritual centre on the earth. This spiritual centre was in Wales and the south of England. It radiated from there over into western Europe, towards central Europe, and further into eastern Europe.

As Rudolf Steiner describes it, people spoke throughout the millennia

in occult language—a secret language—about the great white lodge.
These were highly advanced individuals who had developed themselves
earlier than the rest of humanity so that they could lead humanity. The
primal Arthur-figure was sent out from this great white lodge.

Over time, various leaders of humanity were designated as 'Arthur'. At
that time it was a rank. This rank was sustained at various levels until the
early Middle Ages, that is until the time before AD 1000. As I noted just
now, it existed before the Mystery of Golgotha. Many legends and stories
tell about an Arthur—and these various Arthur stories flow into one
another.

Arthur had the task of forming a group of twelve men around himself;
this is a spiritual law we often encounter. Naturally, we think here of the
twelve apostles; the Grail community was another community of twelve
people. The Arthurian community has twelve members; the thirteenth is
the centre around which the twelve form.

The Celts

The Arthurian legends are deeply embedded in the Celtic tradition—
known in the Celtic language as the Cymraeg or Kymrish tradition—or
in the Welsh tradition. Research about this tribal people—later called the
Celts—has its earliest external source in reports by the historian Herodotus who was born in 484 BC. He says the Celts occupy the area between
the Greeks and the barbarians. He describes battles and says two settlements have to be considered when these people are discussed—a settlement at the source of the Danube and a settlement beyond the Pillars of
Hercules, which means beyond the Iberian peninsula. Herodotus'
descriptions of these two places were probably based on reports from
sailors who had visited them.

The territory defined by Celtic culture was quite extensive, even
though other peoples also lived there. Even from clan to clan it was not
uniform but made up of many and varied parts. As a whole, however, it
was Celtic culture, and it covered the regions of central Gaul, upper Italy,
the area bordering the Rhine, the Pyrenees, the Alps, the Mediterranean
and the Atlantic, as well as England and Ireland.

During the last two centuries, many artefacts of the Celtic people
have been unearthed in Europe, and it can be truthfully said that
Europe is a treasure trove of such objects. One example is an archaeological site on the banks of the Seine in France. Excavations have been
conducted there and, in 1953, astonishing things were uncovered.

These are known today as the Treasure of Vix. A female body—likely a queen or priestess—was found at the site, along with a wooden burial chariot with four wheels. Gold jewellery was also found, for example a chain weighing 14.11 ounces. And the largest vessel from antiquity was also unearthed at this site; called the Vix Crater, it is made of bronze and can hold 290 gallons.

Why was this container there? This is a question even for science. It was probably imported from Egypt, but some documents maintain it was Greek or Etruscan. In all likelihood, it was used for cultic activities—as was the gold jewellery. In the museum at Châtillon-sur-Seine where the Vix Treasure is housed, for example, there is a diadem, a hairband-like gold object that is worn behind the ears. There is a decorative spiral of gold with a small winged horse on both sides where the ear would be. If we take into consideration the symbolism of horses in relationship to humanity, its cultic purpose is clear.[1]

Alesia

Not far from Vix is a place called Alesia where a faint echo of this period of time can be found. In Alesia, in the department of the Côte d'Or, there was a large precinct of approximately 247 acres where the last great uprising against Caesar took place. The Celts, under their leader Vercingetorix, fought this battle. Alesia sits on a hill between two rivers with a large moat and a wall surrounding it. Its position is quite exposed but also very protected. The Celts were besieged and starved out by Caesar there in 52 BC. Rudolf Steiner spoke about Alesia, and asked his audience to note how he described it: 'Caesar was a destroyer of what had existed as the centre of the old Celtic-Druid culture. It was an enormous institution of learning ... tens of thousands of Europeans studied there in the way people of that time pursued science.'[2] Tens of thousands of Europeans studied there in this Celtic-Druid educational institution—which offers an idea of how widespread Celtic culture was outside England and throughout all of Europe.

Arthur and the Round Table were also embedded in this Celtic culture as it fulfilled its special task. This task is also connected with the geography of a certain part of Wales. To gain a better sense of why Rudolf Steiner made such decisive statements about Arthur and the Round Table in 1924, I would like to add something here. We believe—although we have no proof that confirms this—that Rudolf Steiner may have visited Alesia in May 1906. There were a couple of days before the big Theosophical Congress in Paris during which there were apparently no lectures scheduled, so the possibility would have existed.

Tintagel and the Arthurian Circle

In August 1924 Rudolf Steiner visited Torquay, which is also located in the south of England. By today's measure, Torquay is about two hours by car from Arthur's royal seat, Tintagel; the roads are quite good. Rudolf Steiner made a relatively demanding day trip there along with others who were there for his lectures. As a result of this visit to Tintagel, he had quite significant experiences—quite spiritually enhanced experiences. This visit opened certain levels of the Akasha to him that previously had not been as accessible. A visit to Tintagel is strenuous under the best of circumstances. The ruins of a castle are situated high up and the climb is steep. Although there are stairs now, it is doubtful that such stairs existed during Rudolf Steiner's time; there is a handrail on the side that can be used for support. And yet Rudolf Steiner climbed to the top four weeks before he found it necessary to stop all his activity. This is certainly something of a riddle.

Afterwards Rudolf Steiner describes how Arthur and his knights experienced the sun in a quite specific way, and how they had experienced the Christ on the Sun before He had left it in order to descend to earth. The Arthurian knights had taken up this experience of the Christ on the Sun in their own ether bodies. There was a direct effect from the Christ in the Sun that entered into their own ether bodies. They took the Christ into themselves. This created a foundation for their mission. I will cite a few lines here because this mission is a very special one; it was quite decisive for Europe and for western, middle European and eastern civilization.

> Thus, before the Mystery of Golgotha and starting with Arthur's Round Table, the knights of the Round Table took the Sun Spirit into their own being, by which is meant the very essence of the pre-Christian Christ. Then they sent their emissaries out across Europe in order to battle the wildness in the astral bodies of Europe's population, as well as to purify and civilize it. This was their task. And we see just such people—the knights of the Arthurian Round Table—coming from this western point of what is today England; we see that what they received from the Sun is carried by them throughout all of European humanity at that time, purifying, cleansing the astrality of the untamed

European population—at least the quite untamed population of central and northern Europe.[3]

That was their task. They could fulfil this task because they had undergone that sun experience. They also experienced how the Christ had died for the sun itself, one might say, as He came to the earth. This death on the sun, however, left something behind on the sun. A part of the Being of Christ, Spirit Man, remained on the sun. With the completion of the Mystery of Golgotha, with the crucifixion and resurrection, the Life Body of Christ remained in the surroundings of the earth. In relation to the human being, we find that the normal person has the physical body, the ether body, the astral body, the ego, and then, in an undeveloped, rudimentary form, the Spirit Self, the Life Spirit and the Spirit Man. Later, we will evolve the last three members to the degree that we have been able to transform the lower members through the power of our ego. In the case of the Christ, Spirit Man remained on the sun; and after the Mystery of Golgotha the Life Spirit remained in the surroundings of the earth. The Life Spirit could be seen in the Hibernian Mysteries of Ireland and the Arthurian Round Table. They saw it. From this observation of the Life Spirit, they were then able to have an effect on this untamed humanity.

The Celtic Folk Spirit

Why did the Celtic culture disappear? Mainstream scholarship explains that the Romans conquered the Celts, battle by battle, up to Alesia and beyond. That is what is said in the exoteric indications, and it is correct, but there is an even deeper reason. The Celtic folk spirit, the spiritual being connected to the Celtic culture, could have ascended when its task was complete; it could have risen from its existence as an archangel-being to an archai, a spirit of personality. But there are also spiritual situations in which spiritual beings renounce a further development which—to use earthly words—they had earned. This is the case with the folk spirit of the Celtic culture when it withdraws from this culture. Instead of ascending, he accepted another task: he became the inspiring spirit of esoteric Christianity. This new task arose soon after the Mystery of Golgotha and the centuries that followed. The Celtic folk spirit became a source of inspiration for esoteric Christianity and influenced evolution for a long, long time.

This inspiration passes through the Grail community, through everything connected with the Grail community, and then continues further into Rosicrucianism—thus through the thirteenth and fourteenth centuries—and right into our own time where the life of esoteric Christianity continues to have a relation to esoteric Rosicrucianism. The task that began for the Celtic folk spirit in these early centuries continues and, even today, we experience the results of this being's renunciation.

In these early times, the question was: In the future—when humanity comes to the age of the consciousness soul beginning in 1413—how can the individual person arrive at independent experiences? We have come to know about examples of independent experiences—Jan Hus and the Maid of Orléans, for instance, had independent experiences based on the ego itself. For humanity generally—humanity of the fifth epoch, the epoch during which we now live—a prerequisite for independent experiences is a type of repetition of the Egyptian and Chaldean Mysteries, thus the third epoch.

Aspects of the Zodiac

This repetition occurs when people can experience cosmic secrets, all the secrets of the cosmos expressed through the different aspects of the zodiac and the planets—when the secrets of the whole cosmos are organized into the relationships of zodiac and the planets. The people who were able to do this very early on, the predecessors of modern humanity, were called 'Knights of King Arthur's Round Table'. They brought cosmic wisdom in from twelve directions. These twelve knights who surrounded King Arthur in the legends represent various qualities of the zodiac. Here the problem is that the same individualities do not always hold each of the twelve positions in the knighthood. At one time it is a certain individual, then another—depending on the Arthurian legend. There are some who are always mentioned, but others who vary in the accounts.

Geoffrey of Monmouth Concerning Arthur

The legends about Arthur were summarized by several historians—early historical scribes, tellers of legends. These histories are primarily based on Geoffrey of Monmouth who lived in the first half of the twelfth century—this core period we are looking at—exactly at the time, for example, that the School of Chartres flourished. He was an Englishman, a historian. He also became a bishop shortly before his death around 1154.

He wrote *Historia Regnum Britanniae*, the history of the kings of Britain, which culminates in the story of Arthur and his Round Table, but ends there. He recounts something like summaries of various sources, a spider's web of threads, relationships, and so on. I will simplify this quite a bit and give a somewhat sketchy recounting of it so we can identify where some of the main emphasis was placed. We will begin with the birth of Arthur.

While visiting the royal court in London, King Uther suddenly developed a passion for Ygerna, the wife of Count Gorlois of Cornwall. The count soon noticed the king's passion, and immediately rode away with his wife to their castle in Cornwall, to Tintagel. This enrages King Uther; first because he had fallen passionately in love with her; second, because Gorlois had not received permission to leave the court before he rode away. Thus King Uther arrived in Cornwall with his army, intending to lead a battle against Count Gorlois. While Count Gorlois is occupied on the field of battle, a great magician—Merlin—comes to the aid of King Uther. He manages for King Uther to be transformed into an exact copy—in every detail—of Count Gorlois. King Uther, in the form of Count Gorlois, walks into the castle at Tintagel completely unhindered. He comes to Ygerna and thus Arthur is conceived. The real Gorlois dies in battle so that Uther can appear in his own form and marry Ygerna. The child Arthur is born but, according to an old law of the Celtic period, an illegitimate child cannot be raised by its mother. The magician Merlin appears immediately and takes Arthur as a newborn infant into his care. He is raised as a knight by a foster family, but ignorant of his parents' identity. When Arthur is a young man—18 or 19, according to Geoffrey of Monmouth—King Uther dies. Since there are no other children, Arthur would actually be his heir—which he learns from Merlin. The Archbishop of London calls together all the knights who might have a claim to the throne, and Arthur goes there to see whether or not an heir will step forward as a result of a divine sign. They go to mass, and Arthur also attends. After mass, they assemble in the plaza before the church where a sword has been embedded in an anvil atop a stone step. The sword has an inscription: 'The divinely appointed heir will be the one who can remove the sword'. All the knights try, but only Arthur accomplishes it. He has now to prove through all kinds of tests and adventures that he really has what it takes to be a king. Behind this tradition, however, there is some confusion.

A sword that can be removed only by the rightful king, by the right person, is actually connected to deep spiritual secrets. The confusion about Arthur's sword ought to be resolved. Arthur's own magic sword was not actually the sword he pulled from the stone—the sword he removed was there only as a sign: He is the one. His own sword is the sword widely known as Excalibur, but in Celtic tradition it is known as *Caledwich*. Excalibur is a compound word: *ex* from the Greek/Latin meaning 'of', and *chalybs* meaning 'steel'. There are also other etymological attempts to explain this word, but I believe this is probably the most scholarly one. Arthur receives this sword from supersensible worlds, as a gift to him from the other world, from the *Dame du Lac*, the Lady of the Lake. He received it as an aid for his mission on the earth. This is the mission I just mentioned in relation to the task for the Sun-Christ within the ether body of Arthur's knights who could understand it—and for the taming, the humanizing of people in middle Europe. For this, he needed what can be called a supersensible instrument.

The story continues through the activity of Merlin. There are legends that say Merlin himself founded the Round Table in memory of Christ and the Last Supper—that is also a tradition. Rudolf Steiner refers to Merlin as the protector of Arthur and the Round Table. Arthur—I will not tell of his life, but will turn quickly to his death—enters into a battle with his own son, Mordred. Arthur is killed and Mordred also dies. In the short time after he was mortally wounded, Arthur asks a comrade-in-arms to hurl Excalibur into the water, into the lake. He cannot persuade his comrade to do this; twice his comrade fails him. He hides the sword—but Arthur sees what he has done. The third time, his comrade hurls the sword in and sees that a hand comes out of the water to take the sword. This, again, reveals a strong connection to the supersensible world, especially to the elemental world. Everything surrounding King Arthur and the Round Table, everything in the whole of Celtic culture, is connected with the elemental world—with the water spirits, the undines; with the air spirits, the fairies; with the earth spirits, known in the Irish tradition as the leprechauns, the cobolds. It is all bound up in these secrets. Arthur dies. Women—among them his sister, Morgan le Fay—come and take his body aboard a ship. After a few days, the ship comes to shore; the body is taken off and brought to a grave in an abbey. These are a few steps in the life of Arthur.

Merlin

We can indeed say that Rudolf Steiner shed some light on the secret surrounding the figure of Merlin who belongs intimately to this group of legends and appears in it frequently. There is an old tradition connected with the birth of Merlin that remains incomprehensible without Rudolf

Steiner's interpretation. The tradition has it that Merlin was born to a nun who was overshadowed by the devil. As Rudolf Steiner describes it, the devil's intent was for Merlin to have been the antipode, the counter-pole to the Christ. While Mary had been overshadowed by the Holy Spirit, the nun was overshadowed by the devil. But the nun was so pious—the overshadowing took place while she slept—she was so pious and upright that the Merlin she brought into the world was not evil enough to become the counter-pole to the Christ. He was not evil enough—he had other magical tasks through which he always had to serve the good in some way or another. Legend and history, of course, flow into one another here.

Merlin helped Arthur in a substantial way with his task. Perhaps something should be mentioned here, but considered with caution; it comes by word of mouth from a number of sources in the early days of the Anthroposophical Society. It is said that Merlin, who is so surrounded by magic, reappeared in the individuality we know as Richard Wagner. This is an unsubstantiated oral tradition, but we might take such oral traditions into account.

The Grail Knights

There is also another group of twelve besides Arthur's Round Table—the Grail knights. Rudolf Steiner looked at both groups. Rudolf Steiner sat in on a history lesson given by Walter Johannes Stein during 1923 at the first Waldorf School in Stuttgart. Walter Johannes Stein reports in his book *Das neunte Jahrhundert* [The ninth century] that he was speaking about Parzival and working with eleventh-grade students when Rudolf Steiner made some remarks to the class. Walter Johannes Stein immediately wrote them down. In speaking to the children directly, Rudolf Steiner brought something with a different nuance about the Grail community. He said the following about the Middle Ages:

> They were bloody times. People were accustomed to live with blood. At that time, wild forests covered the land. People fought in them; bloody sacrifices were made everywhere there. From time to time, bright, glittering figures with flashing armour travelled through these woods. When they came upon places where people lived in the woods, they put their heads together and talked with one another, no longer setting out for battle or to loot. These travelling knights who appeared from time to time in their flashing armour were those who in this

bloody time imposed a bloody order. At the centre of this knightly order which was scattered everywhere were the Arthurian knights or, as they can also be called, 'the knights of the sword'. They had their centre in northern France, in England. But there were other knights at that time. Think for a moment, the Arthurian knights were the knights of the sword. What kind of knights would the other knights have been?—The children guessed what that might be, and came to the conclusion: Knights of the word. 'Yes, truly,' said Rudolf Steiner, 'that's quite right; the others were actually knights of the word. The word is also a sword, but not the usual kind of sword. The word that is a sword is the one that comes from human mouths. And, you see, it is this sword that is being discussed here in *Parzival*.'[4]

They are called the knights of the sword and the knights of the word. There are various meetings between these two companies of knights, groupings of knights, in Wolfram's *Parzival*. I will mention only one so that you may feel how all this comes together. It is said that Parzival was also an Arthurian knight, and that he went on the search for the Holy Grail like the others. Some of the others were named Gawain, for example—also Lancelot or Galahad. He was the most perfect, the most complete knight. Now, about the encounter. We see the young Parzival having left his mother and wearing the comical clothes of a fool. He finds Sigune, in her lap her bridegroom who had just died. And in this moment Parzival learns his real name.

The morning after this shock he sets out and meets a knight who appears entirely in red. This is Ither of Gahevies, Ither the Red Knight. His hair is red, his armour, his horse, his sword—all are red. He tells Parzival about how he stole a golden goblet from the Round Table in such a hurry that the wine in the goblet spilled on the lap of Arthur's queen, Guinevere. Ither explained that he was doing this because he wanted to challenge the Arthurian knights to recover the goblet as a sign of his claim to a particular piece of land. He asks Parzival to look for Arthur and to relay his request for a meeting between himself and the Arthurian knights. Parzival continues on his way in his comical clothing and arrives in Nantes where Arthur and his knights are. In his childish way, he poses the question: Who is Arthur? He says: 'I see many Arthurs here. Which one will make of me a knight?'[5]

This is an especially important passage in Wolfram von Eschenbach. Are they knights or is it King Arthur? He has not yet been trained well enough to know. Who is supposed to make him a knight? From whom shall he receive his destiny? He states the request from Ither and brings yet another request of his own. He wants to fight Ither, and hopes that he himself will then become a knight. This is permitted him. Parzival has a small lance in his hand which he thrusts between the helmet and the visor—Ither dies as a result. Parzival takes the red armour and rides away, only he does not dare take the lance with him because he is not yet a knight. He thus comes to Gurnemanz where his real education begins, and it is here that two paths cross—Parzival's and the path of the Arthurian knights. There are also other encounters; it can be observed in each encounter that something happens belonging intimately to Parzival's karma.

During Rudolf Steiner's visit to Torquay—after he had been in Tintagel and had spent time up on the mountain—he said, '. . . this host of twelve under the guidance of King Arthur' was 'a Michael host . . . from the time when Michael still administered the Cosmic Intelligence . . .'[6] Thus, this was before the time in the middle of the ninth century when the descent of the Cosmic Intelligence took place. The Round Table surrounding Arthur was a Michael host.

The Grail stream around Parzival came from the opposite direction, from the south, from the region of Spain. It was not the task of the Grail stream to try to protect the Michael authority over the Intelligence. It was the task of the Arthurian circle to protect and secure this Intelligence that came from Michael, from the Sun Spirit—thus the Sun Intelligence. The Grail stream had the task of allowing this Intelligence to develop on the earth. These were two great tasks for different periods of time, of course.

Rudolf Steiner indicates a great spiritual fact, a decisive one: the School of Chartres actually brought both of these streams together. The School of Chartres mediated between the two streams. Something of the Sun-Christianity brought into the world by the Michael knights of the Arthurian Round Table as an impulse hovered above the School of Chartres. However, the School of Chartres also brought in the principle of the southern stream as a Christ-principle. Coming together, touching, they meet one another in the School of Chartres.

Francis of Assisi and the Colchian Mysteries— The Mission of the Franciscans

Virginia Sease

The theme of these presentations is *Thinkers, Saints, Heretics*. We will now turn our attention to a saint—Francis of Assisi.

The Middle Ages is a period of a few centuries in which we find a number of quite special incarnations. Francis of Assisi is one of these many extraordinary people. It seems as though this period—from AD 1000 to approximately four to five hundred years after the turn of that millennium—was a time when important incarnations take place in order to contribute to the development of humanity and especially to the development of Christianity.

It may have been modesty that prevented Rudolf Steiner from mentioning that quite significant people will incarnate around the turn of the current millennium, or that there were significant incarnations during Rudolf Steiner's lifetime at the beginning of the last century. There is a parallel in the fact that many significant personalities were also present on the earth around the time of the turn of the last millennium. We see that what occurred at the turn of the first millennium is reflected in events nine hundred to a thousand years later.

Francis of Assisi is famous in the European tradition. He is a figure who has remained unconnected to any one Church, someone who belongs to all the people—at least in western and eastern Europe. In our considerations concerning the name Arthur, we found that it is an overarching concept representing various people who have held the office of Arthur although, according to indications by Rudolf Steiner, a real Arthur also existed. The situation with Francis of Assisi is different. His name does not indicate a rank; he carries the honours of his office, but from a wholly inner perspective. He is a great individuality, singular in his configuration.

The Birth and Childhood of Francis

Francis of Assisi's life is well documented by his first biographer, Thomas of Celano, and a second biographer, Bonaventure. Rudolf Steiner has confirmed that many of the stories and legends surrounding Francis are based on fact; they are not wild fantasies, but can be understood as factual. The stories that swirl around his birth are an example. Francis's father, a cloth merchant, was on his way to France at the time his son was to be born. Francis's mother was visited by a mysterious personality who brought her a visionary revelation: she could not give birth to the child at home, as was customary. Instead, the baby was to be born in a stable. Right from the beginning, this incarnating individual had the capacity to imitate Christ Jesus down to the smallest detail. According to tradition, this was how Francis was born. Strange events took place after the birth; for example, invisible birds sang and bells rang that no one could see. There is a whole body of legend surrounding Francis's birth.

Francis of Assisi was born there in 1181 or 1182. Assisi was not a big city at that time, but more like a village. A foreigner in a small place like Assisi attracted a lot of attention. Suddenly a man arrived and proclaimed loudly that this child—Francis—would possess a great moral power. That became Francis's entry into this incarnation. His father then returned from France. The child was to have been christened Giovanni Baptista after John the Baptist, but his father chose the name Francis, Francesco, because his recent business transactions in France had been successful.

Even in childhood this individuality is said to have possessed all the virtues of the Middle Ages: he was warlike, brave, loved adventure, the leader of his playmates. At 19, he and his comrades were taken prisoner during a war between Assisi and Perugia and held for a year, something typical of the many disputes between various towns at that time. In these details we see the human side of Francis; although we often focus on quite lofty things, there are also more day-to-day life circumstances that we need to take into account. It is important to pay attention to these various levels if we are to achieve balance in our discussion.

A Life-changing Vision

Francis of Assisi's warlike side emerged again when he planned to go to Naples to join a Crusade. But then, when he was 24, he heard a voice in a vision. The voice advised him against seeking worldly service through knighthood; instead, he was to transform all his forces so that they could awaken as love, sympathy, empathy, mercy. This is what the voice and the vision told him. Like Pico della Mirandola, Francis died early—at the age of about 35. Thus he had just eleven years left to live after he had this vision. All that took place in his life, all the impulses he brought, and so on, occurred during these eleven short years.

This vision naturally had a life-changing effect on Francis of Assisi. He immediately set out to transform his life; he gave away all that he possessed. He had been a spendthrift, especially when it came to his friends, and his rich and proud father had been understanding and supportive of this—but now that changed. There were also others who failed to understand why he stripped his life of everything and sought out only poverty. People called him 'Povorello' (the poor one) because he had set out to serve Lady Poverty. It is noteworthy that the forces he had earlier devoted to his comrades—knightly virtues of strength, courage, trustworthiness—quickly transformed into very strong moral forces, thus fulfilling the prediction by that unknown pilgrim who had come to Assisi shortly after Francis's birth. Rudolf Steiner called Francis a spendthrift of moral forces—a beautiful description.

How did this express itself? Francis felt no fear, only love. He tended to the lepers. During the Middle Ages there was a church ritual when someone was afflicted with leprosy; the person was given a blessing from a distance, and then expelled from the city—far from the city. Lepers lived alone with the blessing of the Church on their heads until they died, also alone. Francis of Assisi went out to these people and—according to legend—even kissed them. This occurred at the beginning of his work; later he did other things, met other challenges. However, he had actually taken up the being of the disease, of leprosy; he met the being of the illness without fear. This had the effect of alleviating the suffering of these victims.

The Founding of an Order

There were others who joined Francis; they too wanted to take up poverty, give their possessions away, and share in his ideal. Thus Francis unintentionally became the founder of an order. He had not planned to do this, but he needed to bring form to what was developing as other people gathered around him. All this was in keeping with the character of the age.

He formed the Order with a quite simple rule which he then brought to Pope Innocent III. He asked for a sign that this rule had received the pope's approval. The Church tried to avoid acknowledging any special groups at that time because it did not wish to allow heretics—people who turned even the slightest bit from the Church—a chance to organize.

Nonetheless, the acknowledgement Francis sought was received from the pope. Francis wanted to work wholly within the Church. Later we will see that other streams were created within this Franciscan Order, but Francis of Assisi's own initiative was embedded within the structure of the Church.

Frances did not actually intend to become a preacher; it was widely thought that heretics spread their views by preaching. They undertook long preaching journeys—Peter Waldes, for instance, the founder of the Waldensians. Francis of Assisi also preached, but it was not his main intent. His aim was not teaching based on words, but teaching based on an exemplary life. He was more moved by the deed than by the word—by the word as deed.

Journeys

We learn that between 1213 and 1215 Francis set out for Morocco, first by foot and then by ship when he reached the Mediterranean. He began by travelling across Spain. It has not yet been shown through scholarship, but the legend is that he visited Santiago de Compostela while there. If true, it is a significant fact—and not just because he would have witnessed everything to be seen there at the time, things we described in detail during our lectures in Compostela.[1] It would be significant because this man who possessed quite special qualities had been there—and because these qualities live on. Later we will show how something streamed from Compostela to France, and especially to Chartres.

Then legend says that Francis's journey took him to Egypt in the company of a Crusader army: this would have been in 1219. There he separated from the group and went off to visit the Sultan. The Moorish, Arabian culture was present in Europe and there were battles against the Moors; we think especially of Spain in this regard. Francis of Assisi, however, sought out the Sultan in order to convert him to Christianity—an impossibility from our perspective. He could have been thrown in prison! But the Sultan greeted him and welcomed him with great kindness. Although the Sultan was not converted, Francis and the friar who accompanied him—Brother Illuminatus—were given a lovely, friendly reception. Why is this important? Not merely because it is a striking moment, but because we can experience how two great representatives of their own religions and cultures meet one another—the Islamic Sultan on the one hand and Francis of Assisi as a bearer of Christianity on the other. They meet in this moment on the earth.

A Second Vision and the Appearance of the Stigmata

I am now coming to the end of this admittedly sketchy biography. When Francis was just 33—two years before his death—he wanted to withdraw with his closest brethren, the Fratres Minores, or lesser brothers, as they called themselves. They wanted to retreat to a hermitage in the Alvern Mountains where they would pray and fast between the Ascension of the Virgin, 15 August, and Michaelmas, 29 September. During this time, Francis of Assisi had a great vision. There are two differing reports of this vision, one of them by Thomas of Celano. We can suppose that Thomas of Celano was present because he belonged to the inner circle around Francis of Assisi. The second, somewhat more objective report is by St Bonaventure.

According to Thomas of Celano, a man who looked like a seraph and was crucified on a cross appeared to Francis of Assisi. According to Bonaventure, Christ in the form of a seraph was gazing at Francis of Assisi. This is a somewhat different nuance. But that this actually took place is confirmed by the fact that the story is always handed down in the one form, a crucifix with a seraph affixed to the cross, or in the other form, a vision of Christ as a seraph. Seraphim are the loftiest hierarchical beings, and below them in the uppermost hierarchy are the cherubim and the thrones. As Rudolf Steiner describes it, the seraphim look out upon the Trinity; they continually gaze upon the Trinity. In addition, they have the special task of mediating among the various galaxies—a very lofty task. And it was through such a figure that Francis of Assisi experienced the Christ gazing at him.

In January 1999, there was an exhibition in Paris of seventeenth-century Brazilian art from a private collection. Among these works was a picture that depicted this event. On the left side, Francis of Assisi is looking at another figure who is Christ with a halo. But Christ also has the wings of a seraph—a seraph always has six wings—and one wing extends in a gesture as though to take the outstretched hand of Francis of Assisi.

As Frances came to himself after the vision, the wounds of the Crucified One appeared on his hands and feet. This was how he received the stigmata which he carried until his death.

The Ether Body of Sem

Now I come to a rather difficult chapter in spiritual science. But without it we cannot actually understand what lived on in Christianity after the

Mystery of Golgotha. We must try to understand this chapter; we turn back again and again in order to take it up and grasp it through our thoughts. It is a fact that, in keeping with the spiritual intent of the earth, particularly valuable attributes are preserved. This has been the case all the way back to the beginnings of humanity. These attributes do not disappear, but instead are carried forward.

For example, during the pre-Christian era a quite lofty being was incarnated in the ether body of Sem, one of Noah's sons. This means that Sem is physically present while a very lofty being is also incarnated in his ether body—not down into his physical body, but in the sheath above. For the spiritual leadership of humanity it was a fact that this ether body would not be dissolved; the special ether body of Sem where this lofty being had incarnated, incorporated, gave rise to many, many replicas or copies of itself with these attributes. For this reason, Sem is called the 'Father of the Semites', because the Semites continue to carry these attributes, in part as replicas.

The ether body of Sem was not dissolved after death. It remained intact and replicas were formed. Then it was passed on—one might say, donated—to Melchizedek who offers bread and wine to Abraham. According to Rudolf Steiner, Melchizedek was the Light Purifier before the time of Christ, a very lofty task. These replicas were passed on in pre-Christian times as a gift—but only to blood relatives. They were not distributed to others. This principle of the blood relationship was set aside at the Mystery of Golgotha, and the development of Christianity is quite connected with this fact. Today, every person has pieces of other replicas, replicas of great ether bodies, great astral bodies, in his own ether body, astral body, and even in his ego—which, if we really think about it, is rather astonishing. This is the situation today. It explains many phenomena of our time. For example, a quality manifests at a certain time in the biography of a well-known person; this quality makes it possible for that person to do something extraordinary. But later it is as though this quality, this talent, this possibility or this capacity completely disappears again. We ask: Where did it go? A person may do something in youth that later fades away, or a capacity or quality suddenly and unexpectedly appears in old age. This is connected to these replicas, and is a normal process today.

Replicas of the Bodily Members of Christ

The greatest replicas are the replicas of the ether body, the astral body and the ego-organization of Christ Jesus. There are, of course, no replicas of greater significance. In tracing the development of Christianity, we find that early on—in the first or second century—Christianity was spread through the story told about it, a story passed down by the apostles and their pupils. Stories that came by way of the apostles' followers possessed an enormous power. Someone like Irenaeus, Bishop of Lyon, in the second century after Christ—c. 177—was still able to tell of these stories that came from the apostles' pupils. Augustine lived a short time later, in the fourth century. It was during this period that the wonder, the mystery, of the replicas began. Rudolf Steiner explains how Augustine was the recipient of one of the replicas of the ether body of Christ Jesus.

How did this take place? This replica ether body was woven into Augustine's own ether body. Augustine's ether body is still present, but this special ether body appears and interweaves with it. Because of this Augustine was able to find the source of his mysticism within himself, for the ether body is the bearer of memories. With this replica of the ether body of Christ Jesus within him, Augustine found memories arising of the events surrounding the life of Christ Jesus and the Mystery of Golgotha. Later, from the twelfth to the fifteenth centuries—and this is particularly central to our considerations—replicas of the ether body of Christ Jesus are present, but there are also many replicas of His astral body, organized into sentient soul, intellectual soul, consciousness soul. With the inclusion of these replicas of the astral body, we find a certain quality of differentiation in this age, although the qualities of the sentient soul and the astral body are quite closely related.

Francis of Assisi lived with a replica of Christ Jesus' astral body and sentient soul qualities in his own astral body. Rudolf Steiner said that this was not just the case for Francis of Assisi, but for many of his brethren as well. We might assume it was the case with Thomas of Celano, for example.

Thomas of Celano is not only known as a disciple of Francis of Assisi, but also as the author of the words we hear in many requiems, the words sung when the human being has died. We hear them, for example, in Mozart's *Requiem* and in every requiem composed in this form; this occurs right into the nineteenth century. These words are:

Dies irae, dies illa,
Solvet saeculum in favilla,
Teste David cum Sybilla

Day of wrath,
O day that leads this world epoch to ashen ruin
According to the testament of David and the sibyl.

These are the words that accompany the one who has died when, immediately after death, he begins to look back over his life. That was the great deed of Thomas of Celano—he could experience this path so precisely that he was able to bring it into words. These words are also found in Goethe's *Faust*, in the Gretchen scene in the cathedral.

When we speak of Francis of Assisi and this astral body woven into him, we are speaking about a part of the astral body of Christ Jesus. We have yet to speak of the replica of the intellectual soul that occurs in Thomas Aquinas; and Meister Eckhart and Johannes Tauler, for example, bear within them qualities of the consciousness soul. Based on the power of the astral body he had received, Francis of Assisi worked with ardour and mercy. His path was one of suffering. He had chronic malaria and an eye disease that led to periods of blindness. During one of these episodes he wrote his famous 'Sun Song' where he praises the sun, the moon, the animals, the elements, the plants, all as his brothers and sisters.

Francis of Assisi died on 3 October 1226, two years after the onset of the stigmata. Although it was evening, an exaltation of larks sang. Thomas of Celano mentions this and says it was in anticipation of Francis's canonization. Francis of Assisi was canonized, but not until a few years later.

The Mystery School in Colchis

In order to come to a true understanding of Francis of Assisi, we can look at the replica within his astral body and then trace that individuality back in time on the basis of remarks made about him by Rudolf Steiner. We find Francis of Assisi at the Black Sea around the seventh, eighth century in a Mystery school, a centre where the Mysteries were taught. In this Mystery school which was not far from Colchis—it is called the Colchian Mystery School—those pupils who had been admitted were already advanced. They had two kinds of teachers: physically incarnated Mystery teachers and teachers who were present only spiritually. In this school was a great teacher, the Gautama Buddha, one of those who were present only spiritually; he was the individuality who had been elevated to the rank of Buddha in his previous incarnation. Before that, he had been a bodhisattva, which is a preliminary stage; and then, approximately a half millennium before the Mystery of Golgotha, this individuality was elevated to the rank of Buddha.

Buddha indicates an individuality who has achieved the rank of Buddha and no longer has to incarnate; the incarnations are already completed.

The Gautama Buddha, however, decided not to move further away from the earth's evolution—which he could justifiably have done—but to remain instead with humanity.

The Gautama Buddha was always intimately connected with the Christ-being. He had received tasks from the Christ-being long before the Mystery of Golgotha; during the separation of the planets he was an emissary to Venus where he had to tend to Venusian souls and provide impulses for their well-being. After he had achieved the rank of Buddha, he shone down from out of his spirit body upon the birth of the so-called Nathan Jesus Child; he was present there. In anthroposophy, it is described how, as the great radiating Gloria, he overshadowed the host of angels. He was present spiritually at the most important events throughout the incarnation of Christ Jesus: for example, at the awakening of Lazarus when Christ Himself performs the initiation for Lazarus-John. The Buddha was also present at the Mystery of Golgotha, and afterwards when—according to tradition—the Christ returned following His liberation of the souls in the underworld. Then, seven or eight centuries later, the Gautama Buddha was a teacher at this Mystery site at the Black Sea, in the Colchian Mysteries.

This area of the Black Sea is an interesting region. Markus Osterrieder has compiled a good deal of information about it; in his book[2] he describes it from the seventh century before Christ—which we have mentioned in connection with the Celts—to the third century after Christ, almost four centuries before the Colchian Mystery School attended by Francis. When Francis was there as a pupil with the other brethren, this Mystery school was not new; it had existed earlier. During that earlier time, the Scythians, a people widely spread across the steppes of eastern Europe, lived there. The Scythians are known to have undertaken long migrations, travelling far into the west of Europe; art historians have shown that the Scythians travelled as far as England and Ireland. And, from the west, the Celts came from England, Ireland, France, central Europe, southern Europe, and travelled as far as the Black Sea. These east-west, west-east connections are spoken of as the Celto-Scythian migrations, and they resulted in an interpenetration of cultures. The Celts left behind the qualities of their culture in the etheric realm around the Black Sea, and the Scythians had a similar effect in the west. This Colchian Mystery site is the place where the Celts made their furthest penetration into the region.

The pupils there were divided into two groups. The one group was able to experience the Buddha face-to-face in the spiritual world; they found the Buddha clairvoyantly. This group continued to have a full experience of the Buddha through clairvoyance, and afterwards carried the teachings of Buddha out into the world. They did not always use the name of Buddha in their later incarnations, but they brought teachings of compassion, love and the equality of all people out into the wider world.

The pupils belonging to the other group—and Francis of Assisi and his brethren were among them—fully experienced the Buddha clairvoyantly and took up his teachings, but their experience of this came through the Christ impulse. For the second group the experience of Christ was direct; what they experienced had a Pauline immediacy. They impregnated, penetrated the teachings of the Buddha with the Christ impulse and then brought it back into their next incarnation. Rudolf Steiner describes Francis of Assisi as having overcome all passions. His ego had completely transformed his passionate nature so that when he entered into his incarnation as Francis of Assisi he was fully able to take up the sentient soul quality of the astral body of the Christ. Rudolf Steiner calls Francis of Assisi a 'pupil of the Buddha'.[3]

Christian Rosenkreutz

The relationship between Francis of Assisi and the Buddha continues. This is one of the greatest mysteries of Christianity—we might even say of modern times or of the last five hundred years. It is connected with the Lazarus-John individuality who was called Lazarus before his initiation through the Christ, and who later came to be called John, John the Evangelist, the Apocalyptist. After several quiet incarnations, this individuality underwent two more initiations so that, beginning in the fifteenth century, he was enabled as Christian Rosenkreutz to carry a task related to the future of humanity. We ourselves are part of this future, and this is a significant factor for us.

This individuality, Christian Rosenkreutz, saw what happens when human beings go through the various planetary spheres after death. Each of us makes such a passage after death. We have tasks after death, and we traverse the planetary spheres where we of necessity undergo certain experiences. Christian Rosenkreutz perceived that the circumstances in the region around Mars were so disastrous, so riven with battles, that human beings could only become materialists after passing through that sphere. This coincided with a great development of materialism through inventions, the emerging scientific view of the solar system, and so forth during the consciousness soul age. Christian Rosenkreutz experienced how this leads to the deepest sort of materialism.

The Buddha on Mars

If human beings who had died wished to avoid this materialism in the region around Mars, there was only one other possibility and that was to withdraw from life, not fully engage with life, to live as human beings within their own soul, although not necessarily by joining a religious order. As a result, in time, the creation of two groups of people would become unavoidable. Therefore, in 1604, after deliberation among the great leaders of humanity and at the behest of Christian Rosenkreutz, Gautama Buddha—whom Rudolf Steiner calls 'the most intimate pupil and friend of Christian Rosenkreutz'[4]—goes to Mars where he carries out his task, his mission as the Prince of Peace. Gautama Buddha went there to calm the conflict in the region around Mars. 'And since that time the Buddha impulse is to be found on Mars in the same sense that the Christ impulse is to be found on earth since the Mystery of Golgotha.'[5]

Working with the Buddha is the individuality of Francis of Assisi. During the time after his incarnation as Francis, this individuality had a short, interim incarnation in which he died as a child. He has been working since 1604 with the Buddha so that, today, when the human being goes to the region of Mars after death he is, for a while, a pupil of Francis of Assisi. This means that in our time and in the future every human being can meditate, can become a meditant if he wishes. His external life can unfold in accord with the needs of his karma, but he can also become a meditant in the midst of life.

As a result, the human being—or humanity—now has the task of fully taking hold of the teachings of the Buddha during the next three millennia which means, for example, every person becomes a master of the eightfold path. Every person will become a practitioner of love, of compassion—not as a teaching in the way Buddha brought it, but permeated by the Christ impulse. In this way the Buddha and the Christ work together so that 'Francis of Assisi is a pupil of the Buddha'. This is the path for humanity in the future, and Francis of Assisi is there, far ahead of us.

The Franciscan Order

As for the Franciscan Order, it fell on hard times after the death of Francis of Assisi. There were difficulties and divisions. When a leading individuality dies it often happens that a relationship tends to drift apart. This resulted in crises and splits within the Order. St Bonaventure—we will return to him later—became the General of the Order, leading it from 1257 to 1274. He is often referred to as the second founder of the Order. Almost 25 years after the death of Francis of Assisi, the brothers, the monks, broke up into splinter groups.

One group, still called the Spirituals as they were at that time, was utterly radical. They only wanted to practise the most extreme poverty and to own absolutely nothing; this became difficult because there were issues that concerned more than the individual person. How can the Order have a centre of learning? How can it provide housing for its pupils? The Spirituals were in favour of the extreme poverty of Francis of Assisi as they understood it. One representative of this interpretation was Petrus Johannis Olivi. That was the one group.

The other group, the so-called Conventuals, was also in favour of poverty. They did not want to accrue a vast property, but they did want the Order to remain vital and acquire a certain status. The second half of the thirteenth century was a turbulent time, especially in regard to the history of the Order. The division between the Spirituals and the Con-ventuals became ever more serious and determined the further course of its history.

Alanus ab Insulis, the Inner Teachings of the School of Chartres, and the Esotericism of the Cistercians

Manfred Schmidt-Brabant

I would like to begin our discussion by mentioning a few important texts that are generally still worth reading today. First of all, the oldest book on our present theme is Karl Heyer's *Das Wunder von Chartres* [The wonder of Chartres]. It first appeared in 1926 and since then new editions have been published again and again. It remains relevant even today. Soon after, a book appeared by Gottfried Richter about the cathedral and its art impulse. The third book is by Frank Teichmann, and appeared later—1991—in the series *Der Mensch und sein Tempel* [The human being and his temple]: *Chartres, Kathedrale und Schule* [Chartres, cathedral and school]. The final book, *Chartres* by Michael Ladwein, has only recently been published; it is a convenient and handy guide to almost everything you would want to know on the subject. Anyone whose library contains a lot of literature on cathedrals knows that these books are often as big as hams, making them impossible to take along when you visit the cathedral itself! This small book is to be highly recommended since it provides in a very concentrated form everything there is to say about the cathedral and its surroundings.[1]

Chartres as a Mystery Centre

Chartres has always been a Mystery site; these sites, the geological-geographic areas where the Mysteries take place, create a living unity with human history. The location of the great cultic sites of humanity is never accidental; the places where the Christian cathedrals were built had once been megalithic cultic sites. Thus it is understandable that all the guide-books—even this small one by Mr Ladwein—tell us that Chartres has a cultic history reaching back far into megalithic times. Beyond that point of agreement there are differences of opinion because the artefacts found are naturally ambiguous when we come to the millennia before Christ. However, this much can be said: there were Celtic and Druid sanctuaries

and cults in Chartres. We know that a legend, an image, from this period
and a later period before the turning point in time was handed down; it
indicates that the *virgo paritura*, 'the Virgin who will give birth', was
venerated there.

Here I would mention a book I referred to during our lectures at
Compostela, the book by Kaminsky. He is the director of the observatory
in Bochum and chairs various scientific societies. Interestingly, this book is
called *Sternstraßen* [Star routes].[2] I did not take that phrase from him,
although he might have borrowed it from me. In it, he points out that
there are long vertical and horizontal geographic lines—in Europe and
the Middle East at least—and that all important cultic sites are situated
along these lines.

There is a mighty line that goes diagonally through Europe, and along
it lie both Chartres and the Odilienberg in the Alsace. This can be
considered significant because the way cultic sites are situated also indicates whether they were actually related to one another as Mystery sites.

Again and again, we will come across the fact that the existence of the
Christ-being was known in the Mysteries prior to the Mystery of Golgotha. We need only think of Zarathustra who proclaimed the great Sun
Spirit. Human beings have looked upon the great divine Being of the Sun
in various ways. It was taught in the loftier Mysteries that this great divine
Being of the Sun would one day descend to the earth; this was further
connected with the image of this Sun Being becoming a human being
through a virgin birth. In this way, the image of the *virgo paritura* also lived
in the Celtic-Druid sanctuary in Chartres. It is said that the Black
Madonna venerated in the crypt when the great cathedral rose in the
thirteenth century is an image—whether as an object or an idea—handed
down from this early Celtic Mystery.

The French Revolution radically destroyed everything, even the crypt.
Today everything has been renovated to some extent, and a new
Madonna—so to speak—now stands where the original had been. And
yet a magic still stirs in this crypt even after innumerable desecrations,
including use during the French Revolution as a wine cellar and an
arsenal. At the end of the crypt is a stairway leading up to a closed door;
even today it is possible to experience that the pilgrims entered through
this door when they stopped at Chartres on their way to Compostela—
through it they were led into a long room where they were given a bed
and a meal.

Now I want to turn to the period that begins in the year 1000. Chartres
stands on the ground of the ancient Mysteries. The history of the School
at Chartres begins with one of the most fascinating figures, a Bishop

Fulbert of Chartres who constructed a Romanesque church on the site following a fire. Fulbert worked at Chartres from 990 until 1028. According to Heyer, 'the "Golden Age" … of Chartres begins' with him.[3] It is likely that Fulbert originally came from Italy and had been a pupil of Gerbert of Aurillac at the cathedral school in Reims. We now stand at a decisive moment in our history. We can grasp the significance of Gerbert of Aurillac if we take seriously something Rudolf Steiner said, namely, that there is a very close connection between the Mystery sites of Compostela and Chartres.

Peter of Compostela

Rudolf Steiner says, 'It was at Chartres, where today those wonderful architectonic masterworks still exist, that the living wisdom of Peter of Compostela, who had worked in Spain, who had cultivated in Spain a living Mystery-based Christianity, came radiating in … the teaching of Peter of Compostela radiated into the School of Chartres.'[4]

A question naturally arises when we meet such a statement in Rudolf Steiner's work. How are we to understand this? What is possible in way of an inner understanding? Who, in fact, was this Peter of Compostela? Let me respond briefly to this last question. There were three men who could be the Peter Rudolf Steiner mentions: a Bishop of Compostela from 995 until 1002; a bishop in the next century who was immediately deposed when he came into conflict with Rome; and finally a Magister Petrus who wrote *De consolatio rationis*, The Consolation of Reason, which deals with the being of Natura. Inasmuch as Rudolf Steiner speaks about this being, we can sense that it may have been this Peter and his book whom he meant. However the most current research shows that this book was not written in the twelfth century but sometime later, around 1317 to 1330, and thus after the two-hundred-year history of the School of Chartres had come to an end. This book also cites Alanus ab Insulis and Bernardus Silvestris, two of its great teachers.

Gerbert of Aurillac

Gerbert of Aurillac—who later became Pope Sylvester II—was in Spain for a number of years at a great monastery I have often mentioned, the monastery at Ripoll, before he went to the cathedral school in Reims to teach. Virginia Sease and I have noted that there were two great monasteries there, San Pedro de Roda and Ripoll, both situated on the road between Spain and France. The whole of Arabic knowledge was known to these two monasteries. Today, we can still see evidence of what developed out of Arabism in Spain and entered into the West; that is one important aspect. The other is that Ripoll is one of the most important stops on the pilgrimage path to Compostela.

We must not imagine it is a classic monastery with a cloister, a church and cells for the monks. Instead—and this can still be seen in Ripoll today—it was a whole university town, a campus with a variety of facilities for sciences, scriptoria, libraries, and so on. Pilgrims passed through, were cared for and supplied there. Among these pilgrims there were, of course, still many who had initiate knowledge and knew precisely why they were going to Compostela, this Mystery site. On their return from Compostela, they again stopped at Ripoll where they spoke about their experiences and discoveries. Thus it is quite natural that a person like Gerbert of Aurillac—a great scholar as well as someone initiated into the treasures of wisdom, initiate knowledge—would converse with the Compostela pilgrims who knew where they were going and where they had been. He then went on to Reims where he became a teacher, with Fulbert as one of his pupils.

It is thought that when Mystery sites are connected with one another like this, something spiritually overarching is also present. But Rudolf Steiner often draws attention to the fact that there must always be a physical connection as well. Like the laying on of hands, so to speak, this connection must be established in the physical world so that the spiritual element can accompany it. For various reasons, it is obvious to me that Fulbert had heard of the cathedral school at Chartres and its Mystery secrets from his revered teacher, Gerbert of Aurillac, in Reims.

Odilo of Cluny

With this another problem becomes clear, which we will encounter later in various places. If we imagine how Peter of Compostela worked, we see that two lines of development emerge from him. One leads to Fulbert of Chartres, and the other leads directly to a third member of this circle of friends. I like to refer to these three individuals as the three great friends at the turn of that millennium. This third friend is Odilo, the great Abbot of Cluny. With this background we can understand an assertion by Rudolf Steiner that has been corrected in the latest edition of the karma lectures. There Rudolf Steiner says that the teachings of Peter of Compostela enter the School of Chartres, 'and, with inspiring power, the essence of what was taught in this way in the School of Chartres was also transplanted into the Cluny Order...' This sentence previously made no sense; the 'also' was missing, so it merely said that what had been taught in the School of Chartres was transplanted to the Cluny Order. Then it continues: 'and was secularized through what Hildebrand, the abbot of the Cluny Order who became Pope Gregory VII ... decreed...'[5] Previously this made no sense at all. How could Gregory VII, who was pope from 1073 to 1085, have received anything from the School of Chartres which actually flourished in the twelfth century? This was not what Rudolf Steiner meant, and it has now been corrected.

Two impulses radiate from Peter of Compostela: the one—around the year 1000—towards Chartres to Fulbert; the other directly to Odilo who was Abbot of Cluny around the same time, from 994 to 1049. Correspondence from this time survives; Fulbert and Odilo corresponded with one another, and there were all kinds of connections between Compostela and Odilo. Cluny was also a place where people stopped during their pilgrimages to Compostela. I, too, will pause here for a moment because this touches on something extraordinarily interesting.

Gregory VII

What does it mean that the Mystery wisdom that once flowed towards Chartres was secularized by Hildebrand who then became Gregory VII? I have already mentioned something about this Gregory, the greatest pope of that time. He drew up 27 theses for himself, for the papacy. There we find:

> He alone can use the imperial insignia. The pope is the only human being whose feet all princes kiss... He is the only one whose name is spoken in churches. His name is unique in the world. He can depose emperors... His judgment cannot be altered by anyone; and only he can alter the judgment of everyone. He may be judged by no one...[6]

We can say that we recognize this as language of the eleventh century. How does it sound? It has the ring of language used by a powerful dictator: 'his name alone'— he is the supreme individual. Without intending to cast aspersions on Gregory VII's moral integrity, these words suddenly lead us to understand an ancient law. When Mystery wisdom is secularized, it leads to an abuse of power. This is an eternal law that prevails throughout history. Rudolf Steiner points to it again and again. It is true in the recent past and especially so in the present time. When Mystery knowledge is used for secular matters, that knowledge becomes decadent and it leads to an abuse of power.

Let us return to Gerbert of Aurillac who had learned much from Arabism in Ripoll. At that time, Arabism also meant magical capacities and arts of all kinds. Gerbert of Aurillac becomes Pope Sylvester II. Not even the pope could avoid suspicions of being a heretic, and this is what happens to Sylvester II. Because he knew about so many dark arts and Arabism, and had taken up all manner of things, the orthodox purists always suspected him.

The Cathedral School of Chartres

Let us now return to Fulbert. He comes to Chartres and takes over the Cathedral school. The Cathedral school had always existed there as shown by evidence from the fifth century on. If we go back even further into the pre-Christian era, we find Druid schools had existed there. Caesar mentions that the Druids have a centre of wisdom in Chartres similar to the one in Alesia that Virginia Sease mentioned. There were, of course, many such centres of wisdom, even smaller ones. One of them was in Chartres. Thus the ancient tradition of a school of wisdom, a Mystery school, forms the foundation of Chartres.

Fulbert

Naturally, all this cannot be compared to what now begins with Fulbert—the golden age of Chartres. Fulbert became the Bishop of Chartres in 1006. As I mentioned earlier, an old wooden church there burned down, and in 1020 Fulbert begins construction of a new, Romanesque cathedral. At first just the exterior exists. Then Fulbert supports the acquisition of a significant library for the church which immediately makes him a sympathetic figure for us. Because of Fulbert's deed, Chartres becomes the great western centre of learning for the next two hundred years, not least of all because of its valuable collection of books. And with him what will characterize the next two hundred years also begins—the connection between Platonism and Christianity.

Just what are Platonism and Aristotelianism? We can use a simple image that is nonetheless powerfully expressive. Platonism is the observation of ideas; Aristotelianism is the thinking of concepts. Idea and concept are only qualitatively different. With *idea* we understand a larger context, while *conceptualization* often reaches down into specifics. Rudolf Steiner spoke about a great painting by Raphael, the *School of Athens*; he says there have always been disagreements about the identity of its two central figures—whether they represent Plato and Aristotle or Paul and Peter. Rudolf Steiner says that this is not the way to look at them. This image portrays primal gestures of human spiritual conduct. The older man of the two points upwards: like Plato, you must look at the ideas. The younger figure points downwards: like Aristotle, you must penetrate the earth with concepts and thereby find the spirit. We will touch upon this again when we consider the Aristotelianism of Thomas Aquinas and the Dominicans.

An old Mystery Sun-Christianity lived in Platonism, the perception of all that connects the human being through ideas with the Sun and the Sun-being. Thus Plato was obviously one of the shining stars in this School of Chartres. A second was Boethius who lived in the sixth century and was the first to have written a work on the *Consolation of Philosophy*.

Medicine was taught in Chartres, and Fulbert, Bishop of Chartres, was a much sought-after doctor. We must set aside modern preconceptions that only theology and philosophy were taught at a cathedral, that the bishop just walked around with his stout crosier. These are, in part, mundane pictures from the last centuries. The bishops of that time were actually rather like rectors of a university, like the heads of an academy. I once had an argument with someone who did not understand why I said that the greatest opponent of Christianity taught in Gondishapur; he was a Christian bishop. At that time, Gondishapur was Christian, although the Arabs had occupied it. Only the day-labourers and the slaves had taken up Islam. The elite of Gondishapur were Nestorian Christians, and the academy of Gondishapur was led by bishops just as Peter of Compostela was a bishop but also leader of an entire Mystery school.

Fulbert was much sought after as a doctor, not merely a medical theoretician; he, along with others, taught medicine. He was a spiritually gifted teacher and pedagogue; his pupils called him Socrates. Frank Teichmann rightfully points out that all the subsequent teachers at Chartres were also highly gifted pedagogues. Instruction was not given abstractly through textbooks and so forth; texts were also used but, as Rudolf Steiner says, they look like abstract catalogues. Platonic instruction was given in conversation from human being to human being— actually through the effect the teacher had on the pupil.

Fulbert was highly learned and, at the same time, profoundly pious; he was a counsellor of princes and bishops in France and Europe, and when he died all of France mourned. It is said there was hardly a church in

France that did not have a pupil of Fulbert as a teacher. Teachers and pupils from the School of Chartres exerted an influence from England to Sicily, and even into the Islamic region. Thus Rudolf Steiner also says that what characterized the School of Chartres was not so much a teaching, but a soul-spiritual aura that spread out from it. It spread in much the same way as a conversation between a teacher and a student; the student absorbs much more than what was said in words during a soul-level exchange. This is in large part how the aura of Chartres worked its way into Europe and effected spontaneous initiations here and there.

Nevertheless, the end of Chartres is already approaching during Fulbert's time; the whole School of Chartres is like the twilight of a great Mystery period of the past. This is why Fulbert repeatedly stressed holding to the Church fathers. He warned about overestimating the dialectic in approaching theological questions, and said that the depth of divine secrets alone—not human knowledge—opens the eyes of faith. This is not merely an allegory; people actually experienced it in the following way. True faith unlocks the capacity to view ideas; the eyes of faith are supersensible organs of perception which, according to Fulbert, we can only develop when we cling in faithfulness to what our elders have bequeathed to us. Later, another teacher at Chartres, Bernard, will say: We are dwarves who stand on the shoulders of giants and therefore we can see further than they; but without them we would not exist.

Thus, from the beginning, something like a tragic cloud hangs over the School of Chartres. Rudolf Steiner describes it this way when he speaks about Alanus ab Insulis—the last of the great teachers—and Bernardus Silvestris: 'A hint of a tragic mood rests upon the countenance of these people—something that said: we live in a time that has lost much. Something tragic and mournful that came from their immersion in knowledge, I would say, lived in the countenance of those people.'[7]

A certain calm sets in with the mighty first note struck by Fulbert. During the last decade a number of worthy books about Fulbert have appeared which describe, for example, his renewal of the whole veneration of the Virgin Mary; he composed hymns to Mary.

There is only one more individual who falls within the eleventh century—Ivo of Chartres [1040–1115]. It is not until the twelfth century that the whole list of greats we hear so much about begins: Bernard of Chartres, Thierry of Chartres, Bernardus Silvestris, Gilbert de la Poirrée, John of Salisbury, and lastly Alanus ab Insulis who died in 1203. He was the culmination of this entire school; nothing else comes after him. Writers about the School of Chartres formulate this as follows. After

Alanus ab Insulis, Chartres sinks into unimportance as a school. The city of Paris emerges—the Sorbonne, the University of Paris. Chartres is again a small and insignificant town. However, only as the School of Chartres comes to an end does the marvel of the cathedral arise. This is a peculiar imagination. For two centuries Chartres is the centre of learning with an aura that radiates out into all of Europe. Pupils from all over the world leave the School of Chartres and spread out across the globe; as bishops, they manage cathedrals and so forth. Then, suddenly, it comes to an end. There is no one there to carry on any more; Alanus ab Insulis is the last one. In its stead, this marvel that is the cathedral—perhaps the greatest work of art in Europe—gradually rises after 1203.

This is one external exoteric point I have noted. The other point, of course, is that Chartres offered an inner, esoteric Mystery teaching. All historians—including our friends—cite a letter from a certain Adelmann, Archdeacon of Liège, to his friend Berengarius of Tours. Both had been pupils of Fulbert. After Fulbert's death, Adelmann needed to write to Berengarius of Tours about a serious matter. According to the Church, Berengarius of Tours was the first great arch-heretic because he challenged the transubstantiation of the eucharist in the Holy Communion. Now Adelmann writes to his dear childhood friend: 'We remember our dear Fulbert; doubtless he thinks more of us, loving us even more fully than when he still made his pilgrimage in this mortal body. And he guides our will to him through wishes and silent requests, calling upon us in those secret evening colloquia he often led in the small garden by the chapel; there he told us of that realm in which he, by God's will, lingers as a senator.'

This has always been a clue, particularly for anthroposophical historians: there were secret evening colloquia! I cite this passage from the book by Heyer because he states the following in a footnote: This is a significant bit of information. If we read Catholic translations of this letter, nowhere are colloquia mentioned; instead we hear of 'marvellous evening hours'. Heyer justifiably notes that it is impossible for the Catholic Church to acknowledge the existence of what is hidden; hence in its rendering there are 'marvellous evening hours'. But the Latin text unmistakably indicates: there were secret instructions.[8]

What was the actual great Mystery impulse that came from Compostela and then flourished and continued in a new, metamorphosed form in Chartres? The impulse had two great aspects. The one aspect was centred on the goddess Natura, which Virginia Sease will discuss. And then there was the aspect of Urania, the being connected with the heavenly spheres. In order to understand the sources of that impulse, we must look back at a well-known figure, the famous Dionysius the Areopagite mentioned in the Acts of the Apostles.

Dionysius the Areopagite

We know that Paul came to Athens on one of his long journeys and that he preached on the Areopagus; Areopagus means 'Hill of Ares'. There was an institution there that was also called Areopagus; it was the highest-level assembly that addressed all religious and educational matters as well as questions of morality. There were always some among its members who continued to possess Mystery knowledge. One of them was initiated in the Eleusinian Mysteries; this was Dionysius the Areopagite. He understood the preaching of Paul, and he knew from the Mysteries that the Sun God would come. Dionysius becomes a pupil of Paul, and it is through him that Paul founds the great school of esoteric Christianity in Athens, the school of Dionysius the Areopagite.

Writings surfaced in the sixth century that appeared to stem from Dionysius the Areopagite. These documents portrayed the heavenly world of the gods, the hierarchies, and the inner, mystic path to these hierarchies through the planetary spheres. However, scholarship says the author could not have been the Dionysius from Athens because it can be shown philologically and in other ways that these writings were not produced until the sixth century. Rudolf Steiner says that, by tradition, this teaching was passed along by word of mouth until it was written down at a certain point. This was the point at which the School of Athens was closed and its non-Christian scholars went to Gondishapur.

During the Middle Ages, these texts were accepted and attributed to Dionysius the Areopagite, the pupil of Paul. But they did not arrive in the main centres of the West until later because they were in Greek and it took a while before they were translated by Scotus Erigena in the ninth century. They became the most read texts in the West among scientific minds; Thomas Aquinas, Albertus Magnus and the entire School of Chartres lived with these texts.

There was something else that took place at the same time. Legend tells that around 250 three bishops were sent to Gaul in order to spread Christianity. One—Dionysius or Denis—was sent to Paris where he suffered a martyr's death. Afterwards, the names were confused with one another; these two identities merge into one. It is said that Dionysius the Areopagite suffered a martyr's death in Paris on 'Mont Mars' which means 'Hill of Mars'. Ares and Mars are the same. Because he was executed as a martyr, this hill was also called 'Mont Martyr', which remains today in the name 'Montmartre', 'Hill of Martyrs'. Then, it is said, because he was such a powerful saint he stood up after the beheading, took his head in his hands, and went to the spot where the present-day cathedral of St Denis, St Dionysius, was built . . .

Emil Bock, who also discusses the story, says that behind these legends is hidden the reality that Athens and Paris were connected in mysterious ways. The cityscape of Paris is connected with Athens by way of historical and destiny secrets which are partly revealed and partly concealed in the images of the legends.

The first Gothic choir was created in Saint-Denis, and what is more the kings of France are interred there—more or less ugly in stone, plaster and marble. Among them is Philip the Fair with his satanically beautiful face; it was he who destroyed the Templars. Saint-Denis became the national shrine of France, and the abbots of Saint-Denis—like the famous Suger of Saint-Denis—were the most influential people in France.

In reflecting on this esoteric teaching, we find the familiar hierarchies described in these writings by Dionysius: the angels, the archangels, the archai; then the elohim, i.e., the exusiai, the dynamis (spirits of move-ment), the kyriotetes (spirits of wisdom), the thrones, cherubim and seraphim. There is also an indication that the whole rises up through these choirs to the realm of the fixed stars: the angels connected with the moon sphere, the archangels with Mercury, and so forth. Then there is the connection of the elohim to the sun, the dynamis with Mars, the kyriotetes (the spirits of wisdom) with Jupiter of course; and the super-earthly already begins with the thrones in the Saturn sphere.

At that time, thoughts, nature and the world were a unity for human beings—which remains true for the centuries that followed and even for Albertus Magnus. Looking up to the planetary spheres was also an act of perceiving how these planetary spheres worked their way into human existence and nature. This was actually the origin of Mystery medicine, the true core of Mystery medicine. At that time, Mystery medicine was an etheric astronomy which told about how human beings were affected by celestial events. Today, when we inject Aurum D_{20} or Argentum D_{12} we are reconnecting with this ancient knowledge in a new and completely different way—with how silver and gold work in the bile, nerves, blood, and so on. From this, we can understand why Fulbert's services as a doctor were in high demand; at that time, astronomy, philosophy and theology—which we separate today—were a unity in this academy.

Thus the people in the academy were like initiates. Rudolf Steiner says of them that they were 'personalities who . . . with the characteristics of initiates went among other people'. They were 'the type of people who know much about the secrets of existence'.[9]

The Odilienberg

Why does Chartres lie along the same Mystery line as the Odilienberg? What, in fact, was the Odilienberg? Certainly, it was a pre-Christian Mystery site. I am not referring to the individuality of Odilie, who also accomplished a lot, but to that Mystery site surrounded by a mighty wall, the so-called Heathen's Wall, which can still be seen today. Such walls were used to define Mystery precincts, a large area. But a very simple fact is also visible here. When a person stands on the hilltop above, with the Rhine valley down below, it is possible to see two depressions in the ground protected by a small latticework. They are said to be graves, but they are not. The one is a box with its cover lying beside it. The other is formed differently. Anyone who knows about initiation recognizes that these are two forms of the old initiation brought over from Atlantis—the initiation of the northern stream and the initiation of the southern stream.

During the initiation of the northern stream, the neophyte was laid inside the box which remained open. Then he was left out for days, exposed to nature, to the weather; he lay there regardless of rain or lightning. It can be said that he excarnated into nature. That was the northern initiation. In the southern initiation, the human being would be packed into the box and the box covered. We might say that he suffocated, but at that time they did not suffocate; just as in the case of a fakir, breathing ceased or decreased to a point where it was hardly present. And in seclusion, in the darkness of this box, the soul departed, not into nature but into the world of the stars. Natura and Urania met one another. These two initiation depressions in the earth—which can still be seen and understood—are a sign that the northern and southern initiation streams came together and connected at this Mystery site on the Odilienberg.

The Cathedral at Chartres

Quite a bit later—during the Christian age—an interpenetration of Urania and Natura also became a reality at Chartres. Here, the harmony of the spheres connected with the hierarchies was interpenetrated by the qualities of the goddess Natura. This impulse came from Compostela where, on the one hand, what had entered from the north, from the

Celtic Mysteries, was already present; and on the other hand, the Grail Mysteries from southern Europe were also present. To a certain extent, Compostela represents a turning point in the history of the Mysteries. It is interesting that Peter of Compostela—about whom there is a very detailed biography—is called the last of the six glorious Gothic fathers and the first of the medieval saints. Something ends, a Christianity imbued with the Mysteries; at the same time, it changes and develops in Chartres as the twilight of the Mysteries. This is a development that radiates out into all of Europe and leads even further.

The cathedral itself arises out of the disappearance of the School of Chartres. When we look at such a cathedral today, we have to realize that people at that time experienced things in a completely different way. We stand before these wonderful draped figures, before the windows, before the traceries and geometrical relationships as though they were abstractions. But someone from that time—the thirteenth century when they were created, or even the fourteenth century—looked through what came to meet him there, penetrating directly to the spiritual reality. The figures from the Old Testament, from the New Testament, approached him—the Queen of Sheba, Solomon, Melchizedek, John, and so on. When people of that time stood before such a figure, something was loosened within them. These figures were also carved in a very wonderful way. By means of their inner observation, their eyes of faith, these people were able to pass through the statuary, one might say, to the spiritual realities expressed in the Old and New Testaments.

For decades I have had a very large and good quality reproduction of an image of Melchizedek hanging in my study. When I pace back and forth there while preparing an article or a lecture, I look again and again at this face, this figure, and never grow tired of it because it always speaks to me anew. I know that this is only a fraction of what people at that time experienced. But I also know that people today can still find traces of that earlier experience by looking at such a leader of humanity and how he is represented with a vessel in one hand, bread and wine—or even the Grail, an experience which is simply harder to discern. Observing such a figure can lead again and again to something new that comes through the figure itself. This is one of the mysteries of Chartres Cathedral. I have already touched upon the second; it is found in something like the labyrinth, an image of the soul's path. Ladwein correctly points out that the Chartres labyrinth has no blind alleys. We arrive at the goal by moving forwards and backwards, right and left. The remark by Rudolf Steiner is appropriate here: Only he will find the spirit who can patiently wander the labyrinth.

What did people experience in the cathedral's windows at that time? Although the soul was guided on a path that passed through all the statuary, people had the feeling the spiritual world spoke to them through the windows. The oldest glass windows there were created out of an alchemical knowledge so that there is no way to imitate them today. The colouring that streamed through the old windows along with the light and passed into human beings held cosmic secrets for these people.

Thus we can understand how something was brought to revelation through the cathedral itself, something that had previously lived invisibly in the imaginations of the School of Chartres. This is a well-known process. Elsewhere, I have drawn attention to the fact that the pilgrim route to Compostela is marked by countless churches with many, many capitals. In fact, these churches were not built until the first great spiritual phase of the pilgrimage route was fading away; then the clairvoyantly gifted artists expressed in stone what the people had received earlier in imaginations. It is the same with the cathedral at Chartres. What lived in imaginations—and also in higher forms, like inspirations—as Mystery teachings in the School of Chartres appears in a revelation of form and colour, measure and distance.

Alanus ab Insulis

Towards the end of his life, Alanus ab Insulis entered the Cistercian Order. The legend is well known, so I will recount it only briefly. He was planning to hold a big lecture in the Latin Quarter on the Trinity, and went for a walk along the Seine. I am telling the story as I know it; you will sometimes hear it told in other ways. There he came upon a small child who had dug a hole and was spooning water from the Seine into it with a small spoon. The good Alanus says to him quite affably: My child, what are you doing there? The child answers: I am spooning the Seine into the hole I made. Still affable, Alanus responded: but you will need a long time to do that. The child beams at him and says: I will be done here long before you are finished with your explanation of the Trinity. And the child disappeared. Alanus knew who had spoken. He returned to the Latin Quarter, ascended the speaker's podium, and said: Dear friends, today it will have to suffice that you have seen Alanus. Goodbye. And he leaves. As a result of that encounter he was so ashamed that he went to the Cistercians and became a swineherd, entering the Order at the lowliest level.

Rudolf Steiner said about Alanus ab Insulis that '. . . as a teacher at

Chartres he could only go so far in his own earthly development; the result was that he put on the garb of the Cistercian Order and became a priest of that Order. What remained of monastic practices at that time had taken refuge in the Cistercian Order so that it could awaken Platonism, a Platonic world-view, together with Christianity... There was ... something noteworthy ... that came over the Cistercian Order when Alanus ab Insulis ... became a Cistercian priest.'[10] In another place, Rudolf Steiner said that throughout the entire twelfth century, most of the pupils at Chartres were Cistercian monks.

The Cistercians

Thus we inevitably come to this unusual Order. During that time there was a struggle to reform the monastic orders. The Church was run down, had become decadent; the bishops, the pope were venal. Many of the monasteries—the Benedictine monasteries—had gone completely to seed. And so the reforms began. One of the great reforms was the one at Cluny. A second great reform was the one that led to the founding of the Cistercian Order. A small group of reformers had gathered around the person of Robert of Molesmes. In 1097, Robert of Molesmes moved with his followers to Cîteaux; thereupon he was not only ordered to give up his office but recalled as well. Thus he had to return to Molesmes, his monastery. The others, among them Stephen Harding, remain in Cîteaux. After a brief time, the work of Stephen Harding begins to have an effect there, and he is considered to be the true great founder of the Cistercian Order. In 1109, at the beginning of the second century of the School of Chartres, he became the Abbott of Cîteaux. All these people knew about each other—it was an easily manageable world. The teachers from Chartres, the schools, were over here; the Cistercian Order arises over there. Soon monks are going back and forth to participate. It was *one* world.

Stephen Harding brings something into this that leads to all the things Virginia Sease described. He was, after all, an Englishman and still very connected with the Celtic Mystery traditions. As a younger man he had taken part in the Battle of Hastings in 1066, where he saw the victory of William the Conqueror. William the Conqueror put all his forces into holding back the ancient British-Celtic religious and Mystery life. He was a Norman; I have spoken elsewhere about the Normans who sailed up the Seine and burned Paris. In the end, these Vikings—they were, in fact, Vikings—settled in northern France in what is known today as Normandy. William the Conqueror came from Normandy as a Teuton, a Viking, and repressed this Celtic religious element.

Stephen Harding had experienced this as a shock. He was, at first, in a number of other monasteries in England and Scotland, then in France; he studied and, after a pilgrimage, he went to Rome and Molesmes, joining the group of reformers there. Later he became the first great Abbot of Cîteaux and an actual founder of the Cistercian Order. He was an eminent scholar, a lover of illuminated manuscripts; beautiful manuscripts with illuminated letters and so forth from the first period of the Cistercians still exist. Then he experienced the arrival of the person commonly considered the father of the Cistercians—Bernard of Clairvaux.

Bernard of Clairvaux

Bernard made his appearance with an army of associates, entering the monastery with 30 friends. The monastery at Cîteaux was soon filled to overflowing, and eventually the four great 'daughters', as they are called, grow out of Cîteaux: Potingny, La Ferté, Clairvaux and Morimond. Each of these four daughter monasteries made an enormous effort at colonizing Europe. Bernard became the abbot of Clairvaux at the age of 25, a possibility at that time. During his century, he becomes the great figure in the development of theology.

What was the original purpose of the Cistercian Order? They wanted to take up Benedict's old rule again, the original rule of the Benedictine Order that had fallen into decadence. It was a simple formula: *Ora et labora*, pray and work. This can also be shown in a circle so that what is written and read is O-R-A-E-T-L-A-B-O-R-A. Sceptics and cynics say that this then reads: *Ora et labora et labora et labora* ... prayer happens only once, and then there is just work. But a profound image stands behind this. *Ora*: You lift your soul to the spirit. *Labora*: You turn to the earth; you serve the earth. This is the primal image in the Christian Mysteries that continues in the School for Spiritual Science founded by Rudolf Steiner. Attention to the spiritual world through meditation, representation of the impulse right into the world—*ora et labora* survives essentially unchanged.

A humanization of the earth lives in this turning towards the world. This is the goal—to form the earth so that it becomes human. What did the Cistercians do? Whenever possible, they went to the most desolate, empty, inhospitable places that could be found. If a valley was such a muddy morass that even the wild boars avoided it, the Cistercians went to

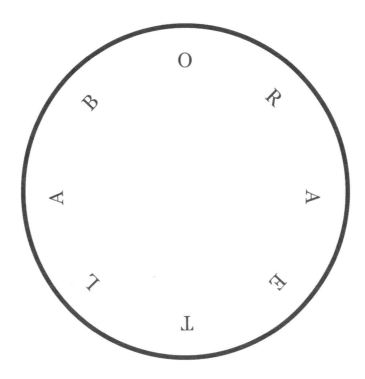

work there. The fourth great daughter monastery, Morimond, is found near Langres because behind it there was a sloping valley criss-crossed by flowing waters of every kind that made the land swampy, inaccessible, and so on. What did the Cistercians do? Today we can still see what they did; they built an enormous rampart and dammed the flowing water so that wonderful lakes were created up above. The valley then became dry, and they built their buildings, their monastery, and so forth there. A church and a monastery arose in this valley, but also a whole city with workshops, scriptoria and all manner of gardening projects, and so on. This was and remains today the most identifiable characteristic of the Cistercians.

One might say they sought to recreate Genesis: 'the earth was without form, and void'.[11] There are some who know that this has secret meanings. In Hebrew it says, 'the earth was *tohu wa bohu*'. *Tohu* and *bohu* are cabbalistic concepts. They indicated: We want to begin just as God began with an earth that was formless and void; and then we want to humanize the earth. We have the Cistercians to thank for the cultivation of Europe. Without them, we would have no agriculture, no orchards, no fisheries, no cheese production as we know them today. For all practical purposes, they created a cultural landscape from the vast, empty primal forests and muddy morasses of the European continent. That is the first thing they did.

A second deed was to set forth the principle of filiation. As soon as a monastery was too full, it sent monks off to found a new one. The monastery was kept to a manageable size by founding a new monastery when too many monks had been admitted. How did they do this? The monastery was not to become bigger and bigger; instead, filiation was practised. The practice was to send off twelve plus one; this was the rule established by Benedict, and later Stephen Harding reintroduced it. Stephen Harding prescribed this arrangement in the so-called *Charta Caritatis*. Twelve plus one go off and create a basis for the new monastery. What do we know about the twelve? One was the music master who brought with him all the sheet music he had written out; another was the master gardener who brought all the seedlings with him; another was the master builder. This shows how all the skills of the monastery were replicated—a wonderful image. And then, when the new monastery became too large, it would be further replicated through this practice of filiation; it was a system of unending filiations. By the time Bernard of Clairvaux died, there were already 351 monasteries; and a hundred years later there is evidence that Cistercian monasteries were scattered across Europe.

The inner spirituality of the Cistercians is not at all connected to the *ora* of *ora et labora*. Instead it was based on attention to the person close at hand. Love thy neighbour was their principal commandment, and next came the strict commandment to practise poverty. The Cistercians created their own church buildings; during the age of Gothic cathedrals these buildings were simple and without decoration, but with a wonderful proportionality in which nothing blocked the way. Bernard of Clairvaux banned any sort of decoration or embellishment. Today these churches have often been cleared out, and in their emptiness we can experience the simplicity of spirit, the human spirit in relation to God.

A third deed can be found in the Cistercian development of mysticism, a mystical path that led to an experience of God and His love. Bernard of Clairvaux stands on the foundation of *ora et labora* as perhaps the most important figure of the twelfth century. Rudolf Steiner has spoken frequently about Bernard of Clairvaux; for instance, he characterized him as 'the ... most significant personality of that age when the fourth post-Atlantean cultural epoch was approaching its end'. And that is followed by something Rudolf Steiner never tires of emphasizing:

> ... this personality has a soul structure that is no longer possible in Europe after the fifteenth century. What the interior of such a human soul looked like is extraordinarily difficult to describe for people today

because, in fact, all the prerequisites needed for coming to such imaginations are lacking.

Rudolf Steiner continues with a note about the immense power of faith at the time:

> This should not be confused with piety. It does not indicate piety—which was also there; it indicates the power of faith.[12]

The way Rudolf Steiner depicts this makes it clear that faith is something like a magical power. Faith is so strong that it can literally move mountains. Rudolf Steiner often refers to what I have just mentioned; when Bernard of Clairvaux preached, people were moved whether they heard him or not. The glowing fire of his preaching, his speech—all this moved people like a mighty astral aura. Eighty-six of his extant sermons are solely concerned with Solomon's Song of Songs; scholars of the great Cistercian histories or of Church history in general assert that they are the greatest, most profound mystical treatises ever written. Bernard of Clairvaux is the most important phenomenon of that century, as well as the great mystic of love.

The next lecture will again touch on the image of Natura, and on the great preaching of the Crusades, something that also concerns Bernard of Clairvaux. People across Europe were fired by the sermons preached by Bernard of Clairvaux for the Crusades. But how the Crusades actually came about, what they meant, and their consequences, will be taken up in our next discussions.

Lecture 5

The Seven Liberal Arts as the Path of the Soul to the Spirit—The Goddess Natura and Her Retinue

Virginia Sease

Right into the Middle Ages there was a tradition that the human being who had prepared himself on earth for a deepened wisdom could one day be allowed to undergo an experience on the far side of the threshold of the physical world. In this situation on the other side of the threshold, the individual was not left alone; instead there were angels who would accompany him so that he would not set out to wander aimlessly in an unknown land.

The Greeks called these angels 'guardians'. A question arises: Who are these angels, these guardians? In pre-Christian times, they were more or less identified with the arts, later more precisely with the Seven Liberal Arts. There was already an understanding in pre-Christian times that every art is a gateway, a window into the spiritual world. Every art is a path of schooling; even today, such a path can lead the human being deep into the spiritual world.

Martianus Capella

To begin, I would like to turn back to a very early text about the Seven Liberal Arts by Martianus Capella, a heathen who lived in Africa during the fifth century. Heathen is not meant derogatorily; at that time, all those who had not found a path that led in the direction of the Christ were called heathens. He wrote a work called *De Nuptiis Philologiae et Mercurii et de Septem Artibus Liberalibus libri novem* [On the wedding of Philology and Mercury and on the Seven Liberal Arts, in nine books]. In antiquity and into the present time, the first of the Seven Liberal Arts are the grouping of three called the trivium—the three roads or ways—comprised of Grammar, Rhetoric and Dialectic. Later, Dialectic was often replaced by the concept of logic. In addition, there is a second grouping of four referred to as the quadrivium—the four roads or ways—comprised of Arithmetic, Geometry, Astronomy and Music. The last two, Astronomy and Music, were frequently cited in reverse order. There is a lovely summary of Martianus Capella's account of these Seven Liberal Arts in Michael Ladwein's book. A marriage between Mercury and Philology was to take place—a marriage that points figuratively to supersensible processes. Mercury wants to marry; the problem is that he has already received three refusals because he has a reputation of being a bit unstable—who would want to enter into a union with Mercury? His brother, Apollo, suggests Philology. She is said to be the most learned maiden in the world. Mercury is successful, but there is still something that has to be corrected. Mercury is a god but Philology is not yet a divinity. It remains for her to be elevated to the level of goddess which means that she has to strip away everything earthly. Martianus Capella describes in the most wonderful way how, when she opens her mouth, many, many books in all sorts of languages stream from her. In this way, she rids herself of everything that belongs to the earth.

Now the question arises: What should Mercury bring as a dowry to this special occasion? Apollo recommends that the seven noblest maidens, the seven noblest serving girls of Mercury, should come along as a worthy dowry for this special marriage. These are, of course, the Seven Arts. This is where Martianus begins. In the book by Karl Heyer mentioned earlier, there is a quite lovely and detailed description of this. In addition, there is an article by him in the March 1925 *Die Drei* [The three].[1] The Seven Liberal Arts arrive as a dowry. How do they appear? The description here is quite wonderful.

First comes Grammar who is an ancient woman. She came into the world under the rule of Osiris in Memphis and lived hidden for a long time. Then Hermes found her and raised her. She appears as an old, dignified helper, a servant. She also has an interesting attribute—she brings with her a kind of scalpel. Why? In order to perform corrective surgery on the tongues and teeth of people so they can speak better. In this text by Martianus, she sets forth a number of grammatical principles, and Heyer draws attention to a significant fact about them: the principles go on for 40 pages. But back to the matter of this scalpel, to tongues and teeth. Rudolf Steiner mentioned to the teachers at the Waldorf school that if consistent grammar instruction begins in the schools when students are nine years old, this becomes an enormous help for their understanding of language and for their facility with language later in life. Thus this picture of Grammar is not at all absurd.

The second figure is Dialectic. Here we also see that Martianus changes the order of Dialectic and Rhetoric. She enters as a pale woman with a quite severe look, wearing a black gown. She holds a snake in her hand.

Then she makes her presentation at such length and in such detail that everyone else begins to yawn and fall asleep; this is really brain-bound thinking, and for that reason she holds the snake in her hand.

Things are different with Rhetoric. She enters as a majestic figure to the blare of trumpets and accompanied by Cicero and Demosthenes. She wears a robe covered entirely with embroidered flowers and designs, finely made and colourful in every detail.

Geometry comes next in Martianus' description. She enters as a land surveyor and has good, strong limbs; she criss-crosses the earth, measuring and also making her own discoveries. She has a geometric instrument, a compass, in her left hand; and in her right hand she holds a sphere. She also has the task of explaining to the gods what it is like on the earth—the lakes and the forests, the mountains, and so on.

Then Arithmetic appears. Pythagoras carries a torch ahead of this servant in order to light the way. She is a beautiful, stately older woman. When this was noted in the ninth century by St Remigius of Auxerre, he writes in his 888th commentary that she appears this way because 'number comes from eternity'.[2] This work by Martianus Capella was thoroughly studied and frequent commentaries were written on it; it was really a fundamental study for many, many centuries. Thus it is quite natural that Remigius wrote a commentary, even though it comes much later. Rays are also extending from Arithmetic's forehead; they radiate in all directions. But then they radiate back and are taken into her forehead again. The rays emerge from unity and divide; then they return to the unity. Oneness is unity.

Then Astronomy makes her appearance. The gods at this wedding see a wonderful ball of light and colour enter. This ball is also fiery. Within sits a maiden decorated all over with diamonds and wearing a crown of stars. Her golden wings have crystal feathers. In one hand she holds a book made of various metals. In this book she can see the movements of the stars and the heavenly bodies, how they progress and regress, and so forth.

Finally, Music arrives. She is announced by a symphony and accompanied by the Graces who go before her with song and the playing of harps. This appearance of Music is well balanced, has a wonderful harmony about it, and every movement of this sublime figure resounds. We could think here that Martianus might have had a presentiment of the birth of eurythmy. But it would have been a very early presentiment because Rudolf Steiner said that, even for him, eurythmy appeared as a surprise.

Rudolf Steiner points out that these seven goddesses are no longer seven creative beings for Martianus Capella; the period when the arts were creative beings has already passed. They appear to him now as allegories. Rudolf Steiner makes a witty remark about this—he calls them Martianus Capella's 'ladies' who 'have already become quite thin'. But, right into the Middle Ages, they carry people into the spiritual world, haggard though they may be. Rudolf Steiner also said that Martianus could have called his description 'The sevenfold Feminine leads us on high'.[3] For a long, long time Martianus was a fundamental element of study in the Middle Ages.

Isidore of Seville

There was also another fundamental work, this one originating in the early seventh century with Isidore of Seville, one of the most learned individuals of the seventh century, the period before the Arabs' military advance on Europe. Isidore wrote much that is important, but I am going to speak about his extensive etymology, a work that exerted a certain influence on education. The first three books are dedicated to the Seven Liberal Arts, but he loved grammar so that 40 per cent is dedicated to Grammar. Thirty per cent is dedicated to Dialectic and Rhetoric; and only 30 per cent remained for the other four arts. It is also a characteristic of this time that lasted into the period of Chartres that the four mathematical arts were more or less neglected. They were always included, but not emphasized to the same degree as the literary arts.

In his etymology, Isidore of Seville attempted to show the origins of words. He correctly identified many origins but also drew on his fantasy when he asserted that words are put together through a reduction of other words. For example, he interprets the word 'cadaver' in this way. He said that the first syllable, 'ca', comes from *caro*, flesh; 'da' comes from *data*, 'given'; and 'ver' from *vermibus*, worms. Thus he claimed that cadaver means 'flesh given to the worms'. This is not quite correct—but certainly very original.

The School of Chartres

The School of Chartres actually led to a humanistic Christianity. As we noted, the four mathematical arts were somewhat neglected during the Middle Ages From the time of Boethius in the fifth and sixth centuries, the arts connected with literature had played a much, much more important role. On the other hand, the teachers in the School of Chartres emphasized that the seven arts should work constructively in balance. Raymond Klibansky writes, 'Together, the Seven Liberal Arts offer human beings knowledge of the gods and, simultaneously, the power to express it ... and they also fulfil yet another purpose. They serve *ad cultum humanitatis*, the cultus of humanity, which means they particularly support human deeds, revealing to the human being his place in the universe and teaching him to value the beauty of the created world.'[4]

The Seven Liberal Arts then reach their culmination in the School of Chartres. We have pointed out how something like a break, an end, occurred in connection with this school when Alanus ab Insulis died in 1203. The School of Chartres—and, I believe, the School of Compostela—cultivated the Seven Liberal Arts in particular. When we look at the School of Compostela, we see how especially revered the art of music was. We see the 24 elders wonderfully depicted in stone on the Pórtico de la Gloria. Beginning with the Book of Revelation, these elders have served as a profound image of the ideal of humanity. Every figure is shown with a musical instrument. These instruments were made in Compostella and it is quite clear from this that the musical arts were cultivated in a particular way in this school.

When we come to the High Middle Ages and look at the Seven Liberal Arts, not as allegory but more in the sense of how they were interpreted during the Middle Ages, then we see that the arts divide themselves somewhat into sets of instructional material or instructional levels.

Grammar was understood to be the foundation for all the others; this was how it was perceived. In a tract from the Middle Ages, it says:

> From the spring of the seventh year to the end of the fourteenth, when the light of reason begins to radiate forth, the pupil should make grammar the main object of study. Grammar offers the power by which we can learn everything else.[5]

According to the view held during the Middle Ages, none of the other arts would have been achievable without Grammar.

Above all, Rhetoric offers modalities, models, the possibilities of expression. It was thought that she had five aspects to be considered, and then the pupils, the students, had to use rhetoric to present what they had learned. The five modalities are: first, structure; second, invention (what is the idea?); third, presentation; fourth, style; and fifth, memory (whether it can actually be remembered). On a personal note, when I was in school in America—it was a regular public school—we had to practise these five steps throughout the seventh and eighth grade. It was called elocution—a subject profoundly disliked by all of us!

Dialectic—later also described as logic—actually provides the coherent framework for thinking. It was already clear during the Middle Ages that wonderful grammatical structures can exist, a wonderful rhetoric; but if dialectic, logic, is missing, it is all for naught.

Boethius called the quadrivium the four-part path. This is the principle of number not only as size but also as entity. Rudolf Steiner stressed in Waldorf pedagogy that small children have to develop a sense for the differences among numbers, for their qualities. What is a one like? What is a two or a three or a four or a five like? A grasp of this kind of quality begins to lay the foundation that leads to what we are discussing here. In the Middle Ages, people did not think about mathematical operations or processes like addition, subtraction, multiplication or division; these were certainly not the point of mathematics at that time. They were a matter for tradesmen, a manual skill that went back to the abacus. Arithmetic was much, much more sublime. Additionally, arithmetic finds expression in music. Arithmetic and music are intimately connected with one another—music gives expression to arithmetic right into the relationship of the tones. Music is experienced as a further development of arithmetic.

Geometry is to indicate how harmony arises through equations, through proportions; that was the task of Geometry. When people in the Middle Ages came to Astronomy, it was viewed as a matter of proportions, equations, harmony, geometry. Based on these foundations, people could then turn to the study of heavenly bodies, stars, planets, to the relationships of the heavenly bodies.

Martianus Capella describes music as the highest principle. It is thus the case that music as the highest art brings people into connection with the harmony of the spheres. The harmonies of the spheres are nothing other than the relationship to the divine world. Boethius divided music into three categories: *Musica mundana*, cosmic music; *Musica humana*, human music, everything connected with speaking and singing; and *Musica instrumentalis*, music played with instruments. In this conceptualization, the harmonies of the spheres were a music through which people could experience first, how all of creation sings a song of praise for the Creator; and second, how the planets express themselves to one another in tones. The cosmos was sounding; it was impossible then to imagine the cosmos in any other way.

Later in the Middle Ages, a change in the sequence of these Liberal Arts took place: first came Arithmetic, Geometry, then Music and, finally, Astronomy. This was accompanied by the conviction that if someone has a good command of music and comes to astronomy through music, then develops a command of astronomy, he can enter into metaphysics. There were seven levels of metaphysics. We recall hearing the indication in the letter about secret evening lessons; those were lessons on metaphysics.

The Cathedral at Chartres

The Seven Liberal Arts are depicted on the south portal of Chartres Cathedral's west façade. Construction of this cathedral was begun at the time of the School of Chartres, and continued after this school closed. It is evident in everything we find there that the whole tradition of the school remained alive—the sculptures, the windows, and so on. From our perspective, we see the Seven Liberal Arts.

Let us now imagine that we are standing before this portal, the *Portail Royal*, as it is called. If we stand to the left of the portal, we see a goddess, an art; and then, just below, there is another figure. Each art is accompanied by a figure which is an expression of the art itself. Thus, below on the left is Dialectic and, of course, Aristotle. Grammar, the sixth art, is on the right side.

Then Rhetoric, number two, is above on the left, again a feminine

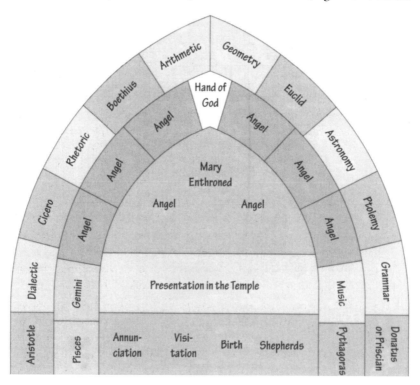

figure; and below her is Cicero. Above and to the right is Geometry with Euclid. Number four is Arithmetic with Boethius.

Geometry is depicted adjacent to Arithmetic at the top of an arch; they are positioned in relationship to one another on the arch so that the two are head to head. We might well question what is meant by this. Descending from above, number five is Astronomy. She is easy to recognize because she looks upward and is accompanied by Ptolemy. Somewhat to the right is Grammar who can easily be recognized because she has two children with her. There is a question about who is below her—whether it is Donatus or Priscian remains unclear. Right next to Grammar is Music with Pythagoras, of course, because he was the first to establish the relationships of the intervals.

Some of the figures are portrayed with attributes. Dialectic has a scorpion in her right hand which is important because it refers to the serpent—to wisdom, but wisdom of the brain. Grammar with the two children has a rod, a switch in her right hand, and a book in her left hand. Music carries a harp and a glockenspiel which she strikes with a hammer.

The Path of Schooling at Chartres

Now I come to something different, but something intimately connected with the Seven Liberal Arts. Until around the fourteenth century, the spirit was not conceived of in concepts but through experiences. This is not very easy for us to reconstruct today. Of course we have experiences of a soul nature; but whether we have experiences of a spiritual nature is a completely different question. We could say that while many people today have a wide range of soul experiences they require a spiritual schooling in order to achieve spiritual experiences. People today, our contemporaries, sense this, and that is why there are so many different possibilities for such schooling today—from both eastern and western perspectives, beginning with shamanism and extending to eastern disciplines, for example, Zen Buddhism. Anthroposophy itself is a decidedly Christian-Rosicrucian path of schooling.

During the Middle Ages, people had experiences of a spiritual nature, just as they did in the Mystery centres—for example the Mystery centre at the Black Sea, in the Colchian Mysteries. Nature, the sea and the steppes were to be found there but none of the great features of civilization. Impressions of nature were spiritual experiences for the people who lived in such surroundings. A goddess, a splendid spiritual figure, appeared to them as an experience; then, over time, they came to call this spiritual being 'the goddess Natura'. The seeker of knowledge tried to connect with her because he experienced her in the minerals, in the plants, in the animals, in the clouds, the wind and the rain. The human being experienced the goddess Natura everywhere. By turns, he experienced her as a goddess in winter and as creating in summer. Later we will look at this successor of Proserpina in connection with Joachim de Fiore.

At that time and until the fourteenth century, a seven-step initiation was possible by way of Natura herself; many people undertook this initiation. At first, the individual came to know nature in general, the living forces of the world, and to look up to them. Naturally, this was done from childhood onwards and formed something like a foundation for everyone since it was an unavoidable part of life.

Then the individual achieved the second step. In this step, the individual came to know the nature of the four elements—earth, water, air, fire—on a more intimate level, and how these elements live in the earthly realm. There was an intensification of these experiences in the third step. The individual no longer experienced himself as standing apart in relationship to the elements, but instead experienced his own ether body as woven into the elements. The ether body experienced the weight of the earth, the enlivening forces of water, the air as something that awakened him; and fire was where he came to himself, to his ego organization. Fourth, the pupil experienced that everything originated from the elements; this was like a gift from the goddess Natura, and he felt gratitude towards this goddess. In the fifth step, after cultivating this feeling of gratitude, the pupil was led out into the planetary system. These experiences in nature also had their counterpart in the planetary system; there the human being could perceive his own human soul more and more through these experiences. He became, so to speak, awake in his own soul through the planets.

Then the path led to the 'Great Ocean', as it is called. The Great Ocean indicates what in the spiritual world leads from the planets to the fixed stars and binds everything together. In the final step, he comes to know the secrets of the fixed stars. These secrets then led him back to the secrets of his own ego. That is a path of schooling through the goddess Natura.[6]

Rudolf Steiner said that what came through Peter of Compostela was like a ray out of the west. It is in this context that Rudolf Steiner also speaks about these goddesses, the Seven Liberal Arts, the seven hand-maidens connected to Natura:

In Chartres ... what entered, above all else, was a ray of the still living wisdom of Peter of Compostela who had worked in Spain, had cul-

tivated a living Mystery-related Christianity in Spain that still spoke of
the handmaiden of Christ, Natura; still spoke about the fact that only
when this Nature had led the human being into the elements, into the
planetary world, into the world of the stars, only then would he be
prepared to know by way of his soul . . . the seven handmaidens; these
handmaidens, did not appear before the human soul in abstract theoretical chapters in a book, but as living goddesses: Grammar, Dialectic,
Rhetoric, Arithmetic, Geometry, Astronomy, Music. The pupil came
to know them in a living way as divine spiritual figures.

It was about such living figures that those around Peter of Compostela spoke. The teachings of Peter of Compostela rayed into the
School of Chartres. It was in this School of Chartres that the great
Bernardus of Chartres taught, for example; he filled his students with
enthusiasm. Although, of course, he could no longer show them the
goddess Natura or the goddesses of the Seven Liberal Arts, he still spoke
with such liveliness about them that imaginative images were at least
conjured before these pupils and, in every hour of instruction,
knowledge became a luminous art.[7]

Alanus ab Insulis

We have heard a great deal about Alanus ab Insulis. Rudolf Steiner
describes how '. . . in an idealistic inspiration, [he] taught at Chartres the
secrets of the Seven Liberal Arts in their relationship to Christianity'.[8]
Along with many other texts, he wrote two of particular interest to us
here. One text he called *The Complaint of Nature*, and another concerned
the Seven Liberal Arts. There were others who also wrote about the
Seven Liberal Arts; for example, Henri d'Andeli who wrote *The Battle of
the Seven Liberal Arts* around 1236. We think here, as well, of the Hep-
tateuch, an encyclopedia of the Seven Liberal Arts by Thierry of Chartres.
We look at Alanus and later at a significant work by Brunetto Latini, *Il
Tesoretto* [The little treasure], that portrays his great vision of the goddess
Natura with the goddesses of the Seven Liberal Arts.

In his work about the complaint of nature, *De planctu naturae*, Alanus
describes Natura not only as a goddess but as a *pro dea*, which suggests that
she took part in the process of creating the world. She was, so to speak,
commissioned by God to assist in the creation, and she is responsible for
the *creatio continua*. Natura appears to Alanus in a dream; she appears as a
lovely, shining woman, sensuously beautiful, in a wondrous gown. The
description of her beauty takes up a third of the text, and her gown is truly

fantastic—embroidered with flowers, with birds and with butterflies in the most varied iridescent colours, bejewelled as well. However, a portion of the garment is not beautiful but torn and a bit dirty. This is where the human being is portrayed. The problem for Natura is that the human being had actually not fulfilled his task of loving and caring for Natura— that is his crime—and she complains about these human beings. Alanus writes another text that is a supplement or—as this second step is called in Alanus scholarship—a restitution. This is the text that comes somewhat later (1184), *Anticlaudianus* or the *Books on the Heavenly Creation of the New Human Being*.

In the work of Alanus, Natura is seen as a co-creator. She is mistress of the universe, the sovereign, the light bringer. She is all of these things at the same time; she has attributes that we later find in the depiction of the heavenly virgin, Mary. At the same time she is *puella*, a young maiden, she is also *virgo*, a virgin, and a *mulier*, woman or wife. She is *mater*, mother; *mediatrix*, mediator. And she is the earthly representative of God Himself. In *Anticlaudianus*, she calls a council, calls all the Virtues together to complain about the unsuccessful creation of the human being who is now inhabiting the world; she asserts that this must be corrected. A *homo novus et perfectus* has to be created, and that is her purpose. However, the Virtues point out to her that there is a problem. They could rightly concern themselves with the body of the human being, but how does this human being acquire a soul? Natura cannot exceed the boundaries of her power—she can create the body, but not the soul. They confer among themselves and it is determined that a great Virtue, called *Prudentia* in Latin, would be prepared to enter the heavenly world in order to ask God to create the soul.

Prudentia is most often translated in German as cleverness. In English, the word 'prudent' remains virtually the same and is used more as an adjective; it is not just clever, but appropriately clever. The German word *Vernünftig*—sensible, reasonable—is too intellectual; in English there is more of a soul meaning. There is even the noun prudence, but it is seldom used today—although it was a popular girl's name a couple of centuries ago. *Prudentia* is a genuine cleverness, deeply related to the soul. She is sent to heaven as an emissary. However, she must be accompanied on this journey. A cart is prepared for her journey, and the Seven Liberal Arts take part in its preparation. Grammar makes the thills, the shafts to which the animals will be harnessed; Rhetoric decorates them. Dialectic makes the axles; and the four more mathematical arts—Arithmetic, Geometry, Astronomy and Music—each form a wheel. In this way the cart is completed.

The arts build a carriage for Prudence, for Prudentia.
Vigilant and clever and beautiful are the seven related maidens—they who, with seven faces, present to us a single countenance. No matter the outer shape, lineage, form, age and capability, these who are filled by a single faith and ensouled by a single will, stand by the side of Prudentia, Prudence, and obey her commands.[9]

The carriage has five horses which are the five senses. Unfortunately, four of the five fall away during this journey. Only one sense remains, the sense of hearing. It remains actively at work.

Now Prudentia sets out on her journey. She must go through all the spheres up to the highest empyrean. Of course, Natura has to stay at home on the earth and wait. Prudentia has all manner of experiences. She faints and *Fides*, Faith, comes to her aid, encourages her, and they achieve her goal; they approach God and bring Him their request. I have, of course, summarized this a good deal. There are nine books.

We must approach interpretations cautiously, but when we think of who and how Alanus ab Insulis was, there are some things we can nevertheless say. God asks the so-called *Nous* or *Nus* to create a model of a soul; *Nus*—usually translated as 'spirit'—was to create a perfect idea of a soul. Naturally, the question arises: Could that also mean for Alanus that the Holy Spirit was asking about the idea of a perfect soul? *Nus* then does what he is asked, and from it arises a soul. God finally carries out the idea, and the perfect soul is brought to the cart.

Next comes the return trip with this perfect soul; Natura then creates the body for the *homo novus* out of the four elements. Concordia, Arithmetic and Music unite the body and soul. In the meantime, the Furies attempt to wage battle against this new, perfect human being; but the Virtues win the battle against the Furies, and the new, perfect human being arises. The idea arises through the spirit, the soul is created by God according to this idea, and the body is created by Natura. This new human being becomes the sovereign of the earth who is to bring back the Golden Age.

That is the story by Alanus ab Insulis in quite shortened form. On the *Portail Royal* we see the Seven Liberal Arts and the Mother of God, enthroned, with the Child on her knee. The question is naturally: Is that Child with the seven handmaidens around Him the new human being who will become sovereign?

Thomas Aquinas and Averroës: The Battle for the Individual Ego and the Mission of the Dominicans

Manfred Schmidt-Brabant

We have described the fire and the enthusiasm with which Bernard of Clairvaux preached the Second Crusade. The question now arises: How did these Crusades come about? We must look at something that took place over centuries—the decay and decadence of the Church beginning in the year 1000 and reaching a culmination at the time of the Reformation. This is not a modern anticlerical statement; on the contrary, it was a situation widely deplored down through the centuries. I will cite here a somewhat longer passage which represents thousands of other, similar expressions throughout the centuries. This one is from a very noble man, Pierre Cardinal, who frequented the courts of Tours and Toulouse. We are assured that he was no heretic; he was actually someone who loved his Church. He writes a detailed description:

> I see how the pope neglects all his responsibilities. He tries to get rich, but shows no concern for the poor, who have no access to him. His goal is to collect treasures, to allow himself to be served, and to sit upon gold-trimmed cloth. As an efficient businessman, he thus dedicates himself to commerce. For a goodly amount of cash, he hands out bishoprics to people in his purview; but sends to us people with begging-letters to collect our alms and sell us indulgences for grain and money.
>
> The cardinals are doubtless no better. It is said of them that from dawn to dusk they conduct unworthy business. Do you want a diocese? Do you want an abbey? Then quickly bring them a lot of money and they will give you a red hat or a bishop's staff in return. What difference does it make if you don't know anything about the things a priest must know? Learned or not, you will receive a fat living. Avoid economy in your gifts as it would hinder your success. As for the bishops, they continually steal their well-paid priests blind and sell them letters that carry the bishop's seal. God knows, it's high time to bring these customs to an end. And the worst of it is that, for a price, they award the

tonsure to anyone who comes along and they thereby do harm to everyone—not only to us who become the sacrifice of such a man, but also to the secular courts of law ... I swear to you that soon there will be more clerics and priests than ox drivers. All of them are degenerate; all of them offer a bad example. These people compete with one another in sales of the sacraments and the mass. When they hear the confession of honest laymen who have done nothing wrong, they impose heavy penalties; but they avoid doing the same with the priests' concubines. Of course, they appear to impose these strict rules for themselves. But when you look closer, they live as well as before ... under the roof of their father ... They do the same thing as the ... monks who deceive the world in the guise of their cowls and nourish themselves at its cost. It is for this reason that so many rogues and good-for-nothings enter the cloisters. Yesterday they had no bread, and today the vestment of the order affords them income, and permits them to cheat in a thousand ways.[1]

This is the opinion held by thousands. Complaints about the depravity of the Church were continually increasing. Even someone as loyal to the Church as Bernard of Clairvaux writes an entire book, *De Consideratione ad Papam Eugenium,* in which he admonishes the pope in every way finally to become humble, to take up poverty and, above all, not to conduct himself as a secular ruler, but to concern himself solely with religious matters.

The Antichrist

Many of Rudolf Steiner's presentations make note of this situation in regard to the Church—a situation that can be discussed at length. Earlier I quoted a single page from a large, three-volume work on the Inquisition by Lea, a nineteenth-century American historian. He takes an entire chapter to show why heresy had to occur and, after citing the above letter at the end of this chapter, he writes, 'Such a religion had to call forth heresy; such a priesthood had to awaken indignation.'[2]

If we read Protestant Church historians, we naturally find this situation highlighted; Catholic historians minimize the matter somewhat when they say it was not really all that bad. But it creates the background for many events of this time—the Crusades, for example.

There was an image, an imagination, that played a large role throughout the centuries, and that was the imagination of the Antichrist.

Again and again, people described the pope and the Church as the Antichrist, and referred to a passage in Thessalonians. I cite it here in an early translation by Emil Bock that is particularly striking and powerful, and makes clear what people at that time experienced. Paul writes:

> Do not permit yourselves to be led astray by anyone, even when he cleverly sets to work at it. First the great separation from the spiritual world must take place. Then will come the person through whom the powers of chaos are active, the son of the Abyss. He sows hostility and contempt against all knowledge and veneration of the world of God. He seizes possession of what should be a temple of God, and presents himself as a god . . .
>
> The Mysteries of Chaos are already taking place. Were a force of resistance not holding back the adversary, he would already be active in the central development of all things. Then, however, the magical destroyer of things will appear revealed
>
> . . . The adversary's spiritual arrival occurs through satanic powers and cosmic forces that announce themselves in the signs and wonders of erring illusion and in many ways that misuse the lofty world of forces.[3]

This image of the Antichrist was often taken up throughout the Middle Ages. There were plays—similar to the Oberufer plays—about the Antichrist; there were theoretical, theological treatises. Today we look at this whole matter of the Antichrist in a way that allows us to identify three main perspectives that play into it.

The first was the chronological-historical view. Immediately after the Mystery of Golgotha, after the Epistles of Paul became known, people compared the Antichrist with personalities of their time. A familiar example is Nero who was felt to be the Antichrist.

Then comes what now concerns us here, the second way of applying the image of the Antichrist, namely, to the people and institutions of the Church, even to the papacy, as Luther later did openly when he publicly referred to the pope as the Antichrist.

Then there is something like an imperial and chiliastic perspective, which is especially interesting to anthroposophists. It was said: The Antichrist is a principle that from time to time—we would say—incarnates in institutions or people, then withdraws somewhat, then reappears somewhat more strongly. And people thought—chiliastically—that this will continue to the Day of Judgment as foretold, to the time when the Antichrist will appear with full power and authority. All of this lived in the inner soul lives of human beings. If we assume an enormous power of faith, an intensity of faith, we can understand that people at that time dealt with such an image quite differently than we do in the present time when we say we take a stand against Hitler or Stalin or some other dictator.

The Crusades

There was an apocalyptic mood from which the Crusades actually arose. The Crusades had no other purpose than to found a Christianity free of Rome or, as Rudolf Steiner says, 'to found an anti-Rome in Jerusalem'.[4] Pope Urban II called for these Crusades in 1095; he had also been an abbot at Cluny.

During his lifetime, Bernard of Clairvaux had lived in uninterrupted conflict with Cluny. A longstanding feud existed because Bernard reproached the Cluniasts for their secularization—their exaggerated display of pomp; solemn, cultic, religious masses the whole day long, without work. At the same time, Cluny was wrapped up in every kind of political intrigue, using the king and princes for all sorts of purposes. In turn, the king and princes used Cluny. This pope—Urban II, a successor of Gregory VII—also showed an odd lust for worldly power. It was he who organized the Crusade in order to increase his sphere of influence. But, according to Rudolf Steiner, those who instigated this Crusade were, in fact, 'for the most part heretics who set out'[5] for Jerusalem in order to create there a new centre of Christianity, unspoiled and unencumbered by everything I have mentioned. In particular, Rudolf Steiner discussed the great leader of this Crusade, Gottfried of Bouillon, who took the side of the imperial party and even murdered the pretender to the throne proposed by the pope. It was as though Gottfried were filled with an esoteric mission to found a state in Jerusalem from which this decayed Church could be renewed. According to Rudolf Steiner, however, behind this was hidden something else entirely.

Rudolf Steiner speaks about the fact that throughout history each of the seven archangels holds a leading role for a particular period lasting approximately 350 years. In the present time—since 1879—Michael has been the archangel in this leadership role; Michael is the time spirit. During the Middle Ages, the time spirit from around 850 until 1190 was Raphael—the physician-angel, as Rudolf Steiner often calls him, 'the physician among the archangels'. He is the one who acts so that the Crusades take place. Rudolf Steiner explains: He (Raphael) inspires the Crusades in order to 'heal humanity of the materialism that was a threat from Mohammedanism as well as from Roman Catholicism. And

Raphael, the physician among the archangels, is the inspirer'[6] of the Crusades.

This was known in various ways to all those who, like Bernard of Clairvaux, preached the Crusades. There was a somewhat different nuance with Bernard. He saw that western Christianity had lost much of its substance, its spirituality, and he hoped that by turning to the East, to the Holy Land, Europe would bring back this spirituality. Rudolf Steiner thus says about the preaching of Bernard of Clairvaux that esotericism was actually the driving force behind finding in the East what had become lost in the West.[7]

Let us look for a moment at the eleventh century in this light. The Crusade is taking place then and Jerusalem is conquered in 1099. Of course, the whole affair has a terribly bloody side to it but behind the scenes all sorts of things are taking place. Rudolf Steiner says that the Templar Order, the Order of the Templars, came about as a result of the Crusades.[8] Let us turn now very briefly to the twelfth century. What parallels can we find to all of this? The true blossoming of the School of Chartres; the founding of the Cistercian Order which flourished around the figure of Bernard of Clairvaux; the founding of the Templar Order as well, with its first great blossoming.

In the first half of the twelfth century, a connection is even forged between the two religious streams. In 1128, a synod takes place in Troyes largely attended by all of the Church dignitaries in France. During this synod, the Templar Order is solemnly installed and receives its rule from Bernard of Clairvaux. The twelfth century has an extraordinarily high concentration of events related to the Mysteries. Something occurs then that once again colours the situation in Europe; a new and deeper meeting with Islam takes place as a result of the Crusades, deeper than what had come about until then through Spain.

Islam

Here I would like to mention briefly the singular figure of Mohammed, the founder of Islam, who lived from 570 until 632. His life was spent in commerce, as a merchant, until around his fortieth year when he was taken hold of by a great revelation. It was from this inspiration that the Koran, the proclamation of his teaching, eventually emerged. Mohammed lived in Mecca, but the population there did not accept his teaching and drove him out. Thus he escapes to Medina in 622; this is the so-called *hijra* or hegira, and it becomes the point from which Islam calculates its calendar. He gains recognition and followers, and returns in triumph to Mecca. What does he do then? He purifies the Kaaba—the holiest place in Mecca, an enormous cube with a large black meteorite set in one corner. He purifies it of polytheism and places in its stead the monotheistic god, Allah. Rudolf Steiner says Mohammed perceived the polytheism of this whole ancient world. We may understand from what was said earlier about Martianus Capella being a heathen that this is a comprehensive designation for all who did not turn to Christ and who were still polytheistic—which was common at the time. It was quite common for someone to make offerings to Isis as well as to an Arabic and Phoenician divinity. It was considered advisable to get along well with all the gods. Polytheism was a carry-over from antiquity. Rudolf Steiner says that Mohammed feared that this polytheism would lead to degeneration, eventually to decadence, and ultimately to the ruination of humanity. We should not undervalue Mohammed. Anyone who reads the Koran knows what a treasure trove of wisdom from the ancient world it contains. Thus the inspiration awoke in him: There is but *one* god, Allah is Allah, and there is no other god. What is, in a certain sense, understandable in regard to this decadent polytheistic world was also something he felt in regard to Christianity—he regarded the Trinity as polytheism and was unable to find access to it.

I told a story that touches on this during the conference on the esotericism of world religions held at the Goetheanum recently. I will retell it here because it made a deep impression on me.

We were with some friends in Durban, South Africa, and had to travel from the hotel to the airport, which as usual was on the outskirts of town. In the taxi, it turned out that the driver was a very devout Moslem who always went to the mosque where he heard readings from the Koran and interpretations of it. We listened cordially to this, and then he enquired whether he might ask us a question. Of course. He said: You Europeans are so clever. You have quite some technology; quite some culture. Everything you make is so great. How is it possible that you can believe that nonsense about God having a son? God cannot have a son!—I no longer recall which theological argument we used at the time, but this point made a deep impression on him. At the conclusion of my conference lecture in which I related this story, an anthroposophical friend who was also connected with Islam approached me and said: You know, I could have asked the same question. Then we tried to put ourselves in the position of someone who holds the conviction that there is one all-encompassing god—a God who can have no son!

This, says Rudolf Steiner, is the great problem with Islam—the fact that it only recognizes the Father God, even if in a somewhat different form. Therefore, it only recognizes the effects of nature and the spirit that derive from the Creator Himself. It is not possible for followers of Islam to understand that only when the Son principle is added to the Father principle can the human being comprehend himself and find freedom. Thus, says Rudolf Steiner, from this perspective Islam is the strongest polarity to Christianity because it only seeks a determinism which is the elimination of all freedom for the future. This is the core of the conflict that began to define itself at the time of the Crusades.

Following the death of Mohammed there is at first a swift and powerful spread of Islam. Eight hundred years after Christ, the Arabic realm had already advanced to the border of India, and across Spain towards France. A powerful Arabic empire arises and surrounds the sun of Europe like a half-moon, embracing many peoples and cultures. The requisite foundations for all these cultures are the Koran and the Arabic language. At the time, translation of the Koran was not permitted. Today it is translated, but that remains a sacrilege for a devout Mohammedan. The Koran may only truly exist in Arabic. Out of this, a vast Arabic empire arises from India across to Spain, unified despite its widespread diversity because of the need to speak Arabic in order to follow the teachings of the Koran.

We know that the push towards Europe, towards France, fails. The great Arabic armies that had already flooded across Spain were driven back at Tours and Poitiers by Charles Martel in 732. Charles Martel, the seneschal of the king at that time, was powerful only because the Merovingians were already in decline. Because of this great victory that prevented Europe from becoming Arabic like the majority of Spain, the power is created by means of which Charlemagne can work in the aftermath of Charles Martel and Pippin.

Islam, however, did take hold, especially in Spain. For almost five hundred years, the whole of Spain would be Islamic, suffused with Islamic culture. Rudolf Steiner made the sketch shown here[9] which shows, on the one hand, Islam pushing forward through Spain, penetrating Spain, and working its way across Spain to Europe. On the other side, the stream of Christianity comes across Greece and Rome on this path to Europe and enters there as well. And Rudolf Steiner says that we understand absolutely nothing about European culture if we do not see how Islam and Christianity intersected with and interpenetrated one another.

Everything we would today call science came through Islam. In one of the conferences for Waldorf teachers, Rudolf Steiner even said that the children should be told about how many words in our language come from the Arabic—like *Al Zukar* and *Al Kohol* and so forth; and they

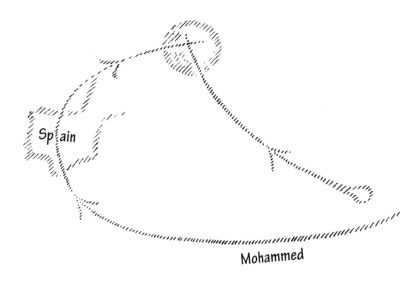

Mohammed

should be told that we use Arabic numbers. Everyone uses Arabic numbers, not the Roman-Christian ones. There are endless descriptions of this influence. Because I always like to mention books, I would call your attention to a well-known one by Sigrid Hunke. She does not hold much to Christianity but wrote a book that glorifies Islam entitled *Allahs Sonne über dem Abendland* [Allah's sun over the West]. I will cite a quite characteristic passage from it because it makes clear that during the time when devout people across Europe were actually still wading through the swamps barefoot and moving around with great difficulty, Cordoba—based on the size of its developed area—was already

> the largest city in the West, including all of Europe. In addition to the residences of the viziers and officials, Cordoba had 113,000 dwellings, 600 mosques, 300 baths, 50 hospitals, 80 public schools, 17 institutions of higher learning and colleges (which alone brought together, on average, 4000 theological students during the ninth century), and 20 public libraries containing hundreds of thousands of books ... 80,000 shops, and paved streets with lighting.[10]

These were only outer indications of what was an infinitely educated, knowledgeable, splendid culture. There were many, many learned individuals who spoke numerous languages, who mastered the ancient and modern languages during a time when Charlemagne laboriously practised the ABCs in bed at night, trying to learn to write—he never really learned to read.

During this time, the mosque in Cordoba was like a paradise of beauty and intelligence. Beyond the Pyrenees lay Europe—dark, vague, and yet bearing the future. You may notice that I speak of Europe and Spain, or Spain and Europe. Because of these experiences, Spain has always thought of itself as a kind of continent unto itself. When speaking with Spanish friends who intend to travel to the Goetheanum, they say: We are going to Europe.

This world cultivated the broadest tolerance imaginable. Christians could, of course, pursue their religion; there were always bishops in Toledo and other Spanish cities. Of course, the Jews had their synagogues and could pursue their faith; however, in contrast to the Arabs, they had to pay somewhat higher taxes. This characteristic of universal tolerance endured for a long time. As late as 1251/52, Alfonso of Castile commissioned astronomical charts, the Alfonsine Tables, and assembled 50 Jewish, Christian and Islamic scholars who peacefully worked with one another in Toledo over a period of several months to create them. People who made the pilgrimage to Compostela and travelled along the perimeter of this miraculous world were, of course, influenced by it—like Gerbert of Aurillac in Ripoll, a crossroads for pilgrims going back and forth. They drank in this miraculous world. For this reason, throughout the Middle Ages we find admiring depictions of what lived in Spain during this period.

All of this arrives at Europe's door. On the one hand, the whole of Islam with its philosophy, its mysticism, comes to Europe. On the other, the whole of the Mystery Gnosis streams towards it, as though bypassing this Islam. Rudolf Steiner portrays this somewhat graphically, saying: What did the Crusaders find when they arrived in the Holy Land? People who were not much concerned about whether someone was a Christian, a Turk, an Arab; rather, they worked with a remarkable devotion to perfect what had existed in ancient paganism as culture, science and religious knowledge. And what the Crusaders take up there, says Rudolf Steiner, now mingles with the existing heretical predisposition. Opposition to the Church encourages reading the Bible anew, interpreting the Bible anew, and finding through this knowledge that the Church does not know everything. Doubts arise about the Church's body of knowledge, and Rudolf Steiner even names Hus as someone affected by this.

Avicenna and Averroes

I now want to speak briefly about what can be described as philosophy and what can be described as mysticism. Two great philosophers deeply influence Europe: Avicenna, who lived from approximately 980 to 1037 (the birth years are always inexact), and, above all, Averroes, who lived somewhat later, from 1126 until 1198, and whose work challenged Thomas Aquinas and his followers. Both were great scholars who also taught medicine; Avicenna wrote over one hundred books. The Europeans learned about medicine from the Arabs. The hospitals in Cordoba had even discovered a penicillin-like substance so that festering wounds could be treated by mould cultures; and a superior surgery existed there while north of the Pyrenees people often did not even know how to help someone with an infected leg—other than by just chopping it off. In Cordoba, wounds were sutured with needles and thread and so forth. Europeans picked up this technical, practical medicine from the Arabs.

There is a nice little story about Avicenna. He had read the metaphysics of Aristotle 40 times—he reports this himself—and had not understood it. Then he came across a commentary by another, earlier philosopher through which he was suddenly able to understand Aristotle's metaphysics. He was now so filled with joy that he hurried out to the streets and distributed alms everywhere. The story is somewhat characteristic; I doubt that today there are many among us who, upon suddenly understanding the *Philosophy of Freedom* or some other work, would run out and at least make a donation to the Red Cross. People at that time had an enormously strong soul disposition that manifested something like this: At last I have understood!—and it immediately brought forth certain deeds.

Mysticism remains to be discussed. In this regard, I would like to point out the large book by Annemarie Schimmel who, because of her strong inclination towards Islam, was attacked some years ago for being anti-Semitic. She is one of the most significant Islamic experts as well as an expert on Islamic mysticism. I understand from her work that there are two great principles here that should interest us.

The first concerns Sufism as the mysticism of Islam, a mysticism of eternity in which everything merges into God. God—as existence beyond all existence—is eternal, timeless, without space; God is absolute existence, the lone reality, a boundless sea into which the individual himself merges like a drop of water into the sea. Whoever pursues this path as a mystic must set aside everything that is not God, must eventually lose his humanity, must shed his humanity completely until what remains is surrendered like drops into the sea that is God. This would be branded as heresy by orthodox Islamic theologians. It is important for us to realize that Islam also founded an inquisition that looked into not only whether all its followers were true to the Koran but whether they followed the orthodox line as well. More than one mystic was beheaded, sentenced to death, because his views were found to be contrary to the Koran. Seen as less heretical is the second sort of mysticism, personal mysticism. This was the relationship between the human being and God, between creation and Creator. The path of personal mysticism was the path of the loving one: to bring oneself ever closer to God through love.

The Ideal of Poverty

All of this flowed over into Europe. Now we see the emergence of the Dominican Order. The founder of the Dominicans, Dominic (1170–1221) begins his spiritual activity at approximately the same time as Francis of Assisi. Rudolf Steiner speaks about the two orders—the Dominicans and the Franciscans—as being the most significant for Europe. Francis did not live as long as Dominic but both begin their activity simultaneously around 1207 or 1208. Dominic was an Augustinian. On his journeys, he sees that those who are opposed to the heretics, who dispute with the heretics—especially with the Cathars—fail and become discouraged. He also understands why this is so—because the Cathars point out the condition of the Church to these opponents who can offer little in way of response. What I have noted here was generally perceived to be the case; the Church is, in fact, venal, decadent, corrupt, and so on. As a result, a decision awakens in Dominic: We must be poor again; and we must be able to preach so that we can come to the most convincing arguments based on our poverty. The 'Order of Preachers'—the Dominicans are actually called the *Ordo Predicatorum*—is confirmed in 1215. Enormous emphasis is placed on study. They immediately move into the cloister of St Jacques on the Rue St Jacques in Paris to establish a centre of learning. Oddly, it is there that Robespierre and his compatriots met; they are called 'Jacobins' because they assembled in the cloister of St Jacques founded by the Dominicans as their first centre of study. A short time later, the order had become so important that a cloister could no longer exist anywhere without the presence of a doctor who had graduated from Paris. It was clear from the beginning that the Dominicans were to be a mendicant order, which means they renounced possessions and income.

We will meet this problem of poverty a few more times and must ask ourselves what it was about poverty that so enthused people. The Fraticelli—Franciscan monks who roamed freely, begging—went almost with a smile to the pyre just to stand up for poverty. Francis of Assisi called her Lady Poverty, the heavenly, blessed one. If someone were to say to us, 'Imagine poverty allegorically,' we would likely paint it with a torn garment, sunken cheeks and a sad gaze. However, for Francis and many others, poverty was a beaming goddess. Why? Poverty represented nothing less than salvation from this world, freedom from every kind of dependence. Rudolf Steiner also says about Thomas Aquinas that he did not produce his powerful writings somewhere in the outside world, but in a simple and quiet monastic cell. This is what they all wanted to have again—even the Cistercians—that their cells, their lives would be free of possessions, except for the most essential things. There would be a sack of straw for sleeping, a footstool to kneel on for prayer and, if the monk wrote, a simple table with a chair or a lectern with a stool, an inkwell—period.

Because all these things are connected, let us—each of us—take a moment to consider everything we have in our home by way of possessions, all the junk we keep in drawers! We take no notice of it until we move. Imagine if we had to make a list of everything we have in our household belongings, no matter how insignificant. It would include hundreds and hundreds and thousands of objects. They saw this coming back then and made a gesture to ward it off. Nothing! No possessions, no income—especially the Dominicans. Francis of Assisi even called it 'apostolic poverty'. A much, much later reflection of this arises in Rainer Maria Rilke when he says: 'For poverty is a vast splendour from within.'[11] The soul element is quite strong, and over and against it is the disappearance of the outer world.

The Dominicans as an Arm of the Inquisition

Why was this Dominican Order founded? In order to convert the heretics, in order to preach. Here again we encounter an archangel; the Raphael period ended and, in 1190, Samael, the archangel of Mars, had taken up his regency. Mars is the planet strongly connected with language—the power of language, the force of language.

Thus it is characteristic that preaching orders and the like arise with the beginning of the regency of Mars, of Samael. Suddenly the word is the weapon—also in a good sense—in the battle for good, for Christianity. Thus the mission of the Dominican Order was in part preaching and teaching against all the existing errors, whether brought by Islam or by resistance to the Church. Next comes the step which is perhaps difficult for many people to understand. Very soon after its founding, the Dominican Order is put in charge of the Inquisition by Gregory IX, who wrote to his Church in a papal bull:

We have thus decided to send out preaching monks against the heretics in France and the neighbouring provinces, and we ask, advise, admonish and command you [bishops, and so forth]—in the name of the reverence you feel for the Holy See—to receive them in a friendly manner, to treat them well and in this, as in everything, to offer them your good will, your advice and your help.

What did he say to the Dominicans?

Thus, wherever your preaching may take you, you or anyone among you are empowered to remove for all time the benefice from those clerics who ignore your admonition to cease such defence of heresy. You are further empowered to proceed against them and all others without further authorization and, if necessary, call upon the help of the secular arm . . .[12]

The Dominicans become an arm of the Inquisition. If we try to get a feel for this with the sensibility that existed at that time, we come across something else connected with it. The Dominicans liked to call themselves *Domini canes*, 'the dogs of the Lord'. There are many medieval paintings in which one, two or three black-and-white spotted dogs are portrayed around the feet of Thomas and others—an intended reference to the Dominicans. What lies behind this?

It was known that humanity was gradually drawing ever closer to the physical body. It is not the case that the intellectual soul simply exists at one 'level' and then suddenly descends into the consciousness soul, which is related to the physical body; instead it is a gradual descent. We could say that the initiates saw that humanity would eventually descend into the physical body and that, as a result, another phenomenon would occur ever more strongly, namely, that a subjective atavism determined by the body would arise out of the physical body. People would have visions, imaginations and experiences—but they would be determined by the body itself, and nothing more than transformed projections of the bodily organs. Again and again, Rudolf Steiner pointed to this problem that is just as present—if not more so—in our time.

There is a well-known lecture about head clairvoyance and stomach clairvoyance where Rudolf Steiner says that genuine, pure clairvoyance is very difficult because it requires tremendous force to pull things together in the head; on the other hand, with stomach clairvoyance the images and visions and so forth arise from the organs. This phenomenon has always been referred to as 'the wolf'. The Dominicans felt themselves to be the *Domini canes*, 'the dogs of the Lord', who protect the flock from the wolf.

This imagination was, at that time, based on a real situation; wolves circled wherever flocks of sheep were kept. We know from the Oberufer Christmas plays that this is a real problem; the shepherds were armed and always had strong dogs to protect them from the wolves. But this real situation was, at the same time, an imagination for the fact that it is in the nature of the human soul quality to be encircled by, attacked by the wolf of atavism. We know this wolf quite well as Fenris in Nordic mythology; Rudolf Steiner speaks seriously about it, saying it is old, ego-hostile clairvoyance.[13] He even says that it would be dreadful if this old clairvoyance were to break through into modern spiritual science. He makes these remarks in the lecture cycle entitled *Die Mission einzelner Volksseelen im Zusammenhang mit der germanisch-nordischen Mythologie* [The mission of individual folk souls in relation to Germanic-Nordic mythology]. The wolf was a primal image; and so, in the face of such atavisim, the Dominicans actually felt themselves to be the defenders of ego-embodied humanity.

We should not confuse all of this with what developed into torture, or with what would be inaugurated much later in the witch trials. This Dominican Inquisition includes much of what we came to know by way of the Maid of Orléans: the mighty will to save the soul, not through fire and death—that was always a secondary matter—but through preaching, through persuasion. The Dominicans were the ones who wielded the truth to correct for other people what had gone astray or had entered into them by way of Islam, and so forth.

Albertus Magnus

Now comes the great change within the Dominican Order that is always discussed in the history of philosophy as the change from Platonism to Aristotelianism, primarily through Albertus Magnus and Thomas Aquinas. This Aristotelianism reaches a high point with these two. We might ask: Isn't it too bad about Platonism, this Sun-Christianity, these intimate esoteric conversations in the garden at Chartres? The answer is that Platonism could not have resisted Islam successfully. In order to resist Islam, the same philosopher had to be brought to bear that Islam used, namely, Aristotle. It is a well-known fact that Aristotle had arrived earlier along with Islam. In Spain, Aristotelian writings were known, often with Islamic additions. Then these writings appeared again somewhat differently; Thomas Aquinas took particular care that they were available in their purest form, in careful translations. Platonism was still too similar to the old wisdom in character; Aristotelianism was necessary in order to take a stand that countered the rigour and severity of these thought forms.

We have before us these two great figures; and there are wonderful pictures of them, like Albertus Magnus holding the hand of Thomas Aquinas—the two friends, teacher and pupil, since Albertus was the older of the two. It is known that Albertus Magnus was born as the Count of Bollstädt in 1193, and that he lived until 1280. Early in his life, he entered the Dominican Order. He taught mostly in Cologne, but in other cities as well; Thomas Aquinas was his pupil around 1244/45 and 1248–52. If we look at both of them, at Albertus Magnus and Thomas Aquinas, we have to say: It is with Albertus Magnus that the power of thought is honed as the instrument of what was then natural science. With Thomas, the power of thought is honed for what was theology, the relationship to God.

Unfortunately, understanding Albertus becomes a problem for us unless we read Latin fluently. His entire body of work—21 large folio volumes—has still not been translated into German or English, only random excerpts here or there; however, there is a whole group of people who have read it and refer to it. According to Rudolf Steiner, Albertus Magnus conceived of nature in a way we can no longer imagine today. Nature had being. Living elemental beings comprised everything about nature. A grasp of this elemental being led the human being into the spiritual world. This is why Rudolf Steiner once said that Albertus Magnus begins with the lowest level of nature and ends with the contemplation of God. But he also said that this was a way of thinking we can barely understand today—the concepts were warm, heartening. A person could, in fact, only approach them by understanding them as beings.

Albertus Magnus' work with nature led to many of his books being understood as books of magic during the later Middle Ages. The 'Little Albert' and the 'Great Albert' were collections of tracts that offered all manner of magic tricks. In fact, there is much in the work of Albertus Magnus that today we would call nature magic or magic remedies gleaned from nature.

Thomas Aquinas

The other great Aristotelian is Thomas. Most noteworthy about Thomas's life is that its actual circumstances are not especially significant. Rudolf Steiner says that all Thomas was and all he wrote was done in the solitude of the monastery cell; what took place in life outside the monastery had no influence on this activity. He lived from 1225 until 1274, a short life. He taught in Paris, lived in Rome for a time at the papal court, then returned to Paris. He spent his last years in Naples and died in the Cistercian cloister at Fassanova while on the way to attend a council. But there are, of course, voluminous biographies of him. They demonstrate that his life unfolded as though he stood on stilts above the physical world while the spiritual cosmos unfolded above him. What he wrote could have just as well as have been composed in Rome as in Cologne, in Paris or in Naples.

Among Thomas's writings are two great works. The first is the *Summa de veritate fidei catholicae contra gentiles* [Treatise on the truth of the Catholic faith, against nonbelievers], against heathens, by which he means, first and foremost, Islam and especially Averroes. The other is the *Summa theologica*, a synthesis of the highest order. It is said that neither before him nor after him had anyone so commanded the art of synthesis and the systemization of the whole of theological knowledge. I cannot say more about this here—the analysis of Thomas's philosophy has created whole libraries. But I want to look at something else. We see Thomas sitting in his cloister cell writing, in conversation, so to speak, with God; and Rudolf Steiner says: This did not happen in the same way that a philosopher creates thoughts today. Thomas received his concepts and ideas from his angel. He would not have written anything in this great work that his angel had not told him or dictated to him, so to speak.[14]

Every person has his angel; every person can ask his angel questions and come into relationship with him. What is astounding is that people discover time and time again that the angel also answers. The angel is really not so distant from the human being. But now we imagine a spirit like Thomas who experiences the angel, we might say, as though behind him, around him, as his higher ego. He writes out of this angel consciousness. This meant something quite particular to Thomas.

We have discussed what is referred to as 'spiritual economy'—when a particular personality has died, the ether body and astral body do not simply disappear or dissolve away. Instead, it is as though these bodies are duplicated in the spiritual world and are available to others who will be born later. This is true, above all, for the figure of Christ Jesus. Just as Francis of Assisi received the astral body of Christ Jesus with the nuance of devotional feelings towards the world, Thomas Aquinas received the astral body of Christ Jesus with the nuance of a leaning towards the ego-organism. When Rudolf Steiner describes that the angel dictates, as it were or, to say it more precisely, that Thomas creates his thoughts and ideas out of the consciousness of his angel, it is an angel that simultaneously protects and surrounds the astral body of Christ Jesus in which the secrets of the life of Christ were contained. It contained everything that entered into it during the time when Zarathustra prepared the bodily nature in the Jesus figure.

It is possible, of course, in these observations to draw additional and extraordinary conclusions at any point because it is also well known that the being of Aristotle himself was reincarnated there. He had accompanied the Mystery of Golgotha from the spiritual world. Standing before us is not merely a human being who writes clever, correct and pious thoughts, but a cosmic being through whom all of the hierarchies speak.

Albertus Magnus and Thomas Aquinas stand in the midst of the great debate about the question of universals: What are concepts? What value does it have that I think? I form a thought; but isn't it just a name, a pale illusion? Until the year 1000, people knew that concepts are actually spiritual beings; concepts are themselves alive, come from the divine world, and work into the physical world. The concept 'wolf' would exist there even if there were no wolves. This was a view that was called *Universalia ante rem*. *Universalia* means 'concepts'. The 'universal' that is present before the thing—*ante rem*—a view especially close to Platonism. Then there was an opposite view that said, No, *Universalia post rem*. This means: things exist, I look at them; and now I create the concept of—let us say—'eyeglasses'. Over there I see a lot of chairs and then I create for myself the concept 'chair'. Concepts are nothing more than the names, *nomina*; and so the representatives of this view are called nominalists. The others say, No—concepts are true realities; and they are called realists.

Abelard

The two figures who introduced nominalism were Abelard, the renowned philosopher, and his predecessor Roscelin, whom Rudolf Steiner also mentions. Roscelin said that *Universalia* are *vox*, the voice. Abelard formulated it in a somewhat softer way and said, No—*Universalia* are *sermo*, speech. There is a modern philosopher by whom many swear, Wittgenstein. We suddenly find the same thing again in his idea that the thought is the formed sentence. When we read about realism and nominalism in histories of philosophy, they always explain that the battle died down towards the time of the Reformation; but the problem has not yet been solved.

Bernard of Clairvaux is described as the greatest theologian and mystical spirit of the twelfth century; likewise, this philosopher Abelard—a contemporary of Bernard—is said to have been the most brilliant philosopher of the twelfth century. He lived in Paris and in Saint-Denis, and is known above all else for his terrible destiny. As a young and fiery lecturer, he had a student Héloise with whom he began a love affair. This angered her uncle, a canon by the name of Fulbert, to such a degree that he had Abelard attacked and castrated. It was horrible. Abelard could now no longer become a priest because an undamaged body was a requirement for the priesthood. He became a monk instead; Héloise entered the cloister. The correspondence between Abelard and Héloise is well known. But his philosophical activity continued. First he was a monk in Saint-Denis, and then he became a lecturer on philosophy in various places.

Abelard was the great representative of dialecticism, of intellectualism, of analysis: A person should not believe what he cannot comprehend and know. His great opponent was Bernard of Clairvaux, for a new way appears with Abelard. He was the first to value Aristotle, to seek the resolution of contradictions, while the faithful merely denied them. At the instigation of Bernard—who, in this respect, was justifiably quite strict because he saw the doubt that would arise concerning revelation— Abelard was declared a heretic and his books were burned. He found refuge in Cluny, and died in St Marcel-sûr-Saône. For centuries the Church had burned books, the mildest form of punishment since the Church also burned people. But the burning of books was for them a matter of course. When someone was declared a heretic, all his books were burned. Thus all of Abelard's books were burned. Of course copies survived.

Concepts in Things

What position do Thomas and Albertus take on the question of universals? This becomes quite important now. They say that concepts do not exist beforehand and do not exist afterwards as *nomen*; rather, concepts are contained *in rebus*, *Universalia in rebus*, 'in the things themselves', in God's creation. Now we come to the most decisive factor. The human being lifts the concepts, the *Universalia,* out of the things through his epistemological activity and, as a result, he creates his individuality. He creates in himself, so to speak, the capacity for conceptualization that is hidden everywhere like a seed of creation; he lifts it out and unites it with himself. This now becomes the great weapon to put an end to the battle with Averroes. Averroes had adherents in professorial chairs throughout

Europe who pursued a view that can be expressed something like this. Every human being has his own physical body, but there is only one, unified human reason which is reflected in these individual physical bodies. When the physical body dissolves, this reflection ceases. What is reflected in the human being as reason does not have an individual existence; it is a commonly held, shared reason. Thus the human being also has no individual ego. An individuality, in this sense, does not exist. There are some who hold the view that Dante was a clandestine follower of Averroes.

Rudolf Steiner says that the Dominicans argued differently than Averroes. What they said could be summarized as follows. That was correct at one time, in the era preceding the Mystery of Golgotha. It is no longer correct. When the human being grasps the *Universalia in rebus* through his epistemological activity, he creates an independent spirit that remains with him even after death. This view is widely disseminated by Thomas Aquinas, above all in his *Summa . . . contra gentiles*. The human being can create his individuality through his epistemological activity. The thought existed at the time that Thomas had not only refuted Averroes, but had defeated him. Thomas is often depicted in paintings with a small turbaned figure below him—Averroes under the feet of Thomas.

What does this mean? At that time, people understood that convictions of this kind are not merely one-dimensional theories, but living beings. The view held by Averroes was that a being had to be defeated, not just refuted. Thus a force lived in Thomas Aquinas to create a being of truth based on the background we have described, a being strong enough to defeat Averroes and this part of Islamic philosophy—to push this being out of the world or to dissolve it, so to speak.

This is what occultists have always known about that time, about that battle, and about the two beings, because Averroes, too, was not a minor being; earlier he had been a significant member of the old Mysteries. In this way a Thomism enters our time that is powerful enough to serve as a foundation for a new science of the spirit. At the beginning of these remarks, I said that observations about the Middle Ages would have no purpose if they were merely historical. We would have to show how it relates to our own individual destiny—to the destiny of every individual, if he really has a relationship with anthroposophy—and with the destiny of the Anthroposophical Society at the most immediate and intimate level.

Rudolf Steiner spoke about 'The Nature of Thomism' and 'The Meaning of Thomism in the Present Time'.[15] This being of truth that was actually shaped by the astrality and ego organization of Thomas lives on. Regardless of whether it is presumptuous to make such a claim, we can say that this being nevertheless lives on in anthroposophy. Anthroposophy is Thomas's being of truth in modern form.

Medieval Imaginations of Hell, the Devil and Resurrection—Capitals and Manuscript Illuminations

Virginia Sease

Our theme concerns imaginations of hell, the devil and resurrection during the Middle Ages. From the beginning of the Middle Ages and into the seventeenth century, into the Enlightenment era, the great question about life was: Will the grace of God have an effect on the salvation of the human soul?

Origen

If we follow this question further back in time, we come across Origen soon after the Mystery of Golgotha—he died in AD 254—and his conviction about what is called apocatastasis. Apocatastasis is a theological concept meaning there will someday be a restoration of the original state of things in which everything will be good again, in which all things will be made whole. According to Origen, this would occur not only for human beings and the angels, but for the devil and evil beings as well. The people who took this into their practice at that time always phrased it more or less catechistically as question, answer; question, answer. How will this be possible? It will be possible by the grace of God which has been present from the very beginning. God created the world and saw that it was good. It is the re-establishment of the state of good that existed at the primal beginning. Even if it takes aeons, God will persevere until all beings are returned to this state of goodness.

Apocatastasis is a very optimistic attitude towards humanity and creation. Then Augustine appeared in the fourth century; this was not at all his view. The view of the restoration of good remained in the background throughout the following centuries until Bernard of Clairvaux. Bernard of Clairvaux brought yet another approach into his philosophy of life, his religious thought—it was not apocatastasis, but it was optimistic nevertheless. It was a small next step in the direction of the restoration of primal good.

Augustine

Augustine (AD 354–430) had a quite marked effect on the Church with his thought that every being would face the eternal fires if he did not act well and properly. If he sinned, there was only one outcome and that was eternal punishment. On the other hand, if a person lived a good and moral life, he received a proper reward in the life beyond.

Augustine created a phrase that has been handed down through all the centuries—'God leaves no sin unpunished'— although we must note that there have always been streams, underground streams, which brought back small moments of hope, in spite of this phrase.

Along with this pessimistic view, something else could be found in Augustine's work that was new and also quite formative for all of Christianity—that every person would face the judgment of God. Before God, all people are the same. It makes no difference whether a person is a king, a prince, a count, a beggar or poor; every person is the same before God. If we think back to the prevailing class consciousness in the fourth century and throughout many later centuries, we can understand the importance of Augustine's view. Everyone will be judged; everyone will be punished, but everyone will be punished equally.

Augustine then brings yet another important theme into the matter of God's judgment. If a person truly recalls the story of the life and passion of Christ, really lives into it, then he is already on the path of salvation. We have already mentioned that Augustine carried in his ether body a copy, a replica of the ether body of Christ Jesus that had been preserved. There was a living memory in him that the human being forms his life so that—if we express it in our terminology—he always experiences himself in the stream of the life and passion of Christ.

As a result of Augustine's view that everyone would be judged equally, the story of the rich man and the poor Lazarus was told for many centuries. This is not the same Lazarus who was awakened by Christ; his name was simply Lazarus. The story goes like this. The rich man passes by the poor Lazarus, giving him nothing to drink or eat. Poor Lazarus is sick, hungry and thirsty. The rich man does not notice him at all, and passes right by him. Then death comes—Lazarus dies; the rich man dies. Only then does the real drama begin and it would be illustrated in innumerable ways over time. We find it in illuminated manuscripts, on capitals, on architraves—down through the centuries this theme has been depicted everywhere. Lazarus enters the realm of the angels; the devil takes the rich man.

The Chiliastic Mood

Centuries later—close to the period around the turn of the millennium—we arrive at a next step. Rudolf Steiner offered a very interesting portrayal of the circumstances surrounding the turn of the millennium to the then young Karl Stockmeyer. He said that during the first post-Christian change of millennium all of humanity in Europe lived in great fear. This is called the chiliastic mood, the fear that the world would come to an end, that everything would disappear, and that the Last Judgment would then occur in this moment.

Rudolf Steiner mentions that when there are major numbers in the decimal system, like centuries, millennia, it brings a greater possibility of exerting an influence through the ahrimanic, more hardening forces and the luciferic, more dissolving forces. These fearful anticipations were especially in evidence around the year 1000. Furthermore, Rudolf Steiner also predicted that at the turn of the millennium in 2000 humanity would find itself in a situation where it thinks that everything will be all right. It could perhaps be said: Humanity may not think this way today because of the quite terrible things that happened during the last century. Nevertheless, I believe that Rudolf Steiner's statement is still understandable, that we can still feel a certain sympathy with it, because the modern scientific view shared by virtually everyone today is that science will master everything. It does not really matter whether we have so much air pollution, whether we will run out of oil or whatever it is—science will find an answer. With this, we live in a kind of luciferic blindness based on an ahrimanic conviction. Rudolf Steiner believed that by the third millennium, around the year 3000, circumstances will become so bad that many, many people will wish never again to incarnate.

If we go back to the year 1000, around the year 900, we find that—although anticipatory fear became stronger and stronger—there was still hope. The idea of the imminent Last Judgment was so shattering that people helped themselves a bit by saying: It simply has to be that God will have mercy; it has to be that not everything will come to an end. God will bring to bear a righteous anger against humanity for a while, but then, in time, if a person does penance, the Father God will somehow be satisfied. From this, the attitude arose that Christian life is primarily about doing penance.

This idea then continues far into the Protestant Reformation with all kinds of things that were taken up by the Church, and it leads to quite unhealthy circumstances. The idea of penance was taken quite seriously and led to the selling of indulgences. It was Pope Urban II who, when the

Crusades began in 1095, forgave all the past sins of knights and others leaving on the Crusade and, through indulgences—in a future-oriented act—also forgave them all the sins they might commit in the time before they died. It is precisely this system that had such a disastrous effect over time until, on 31 October 1517, Martin Luther nailed his 95 theses opposing this and other abuses on the door of the church in Wittenberg. This then was the next step in what Pope Urban II had begun as a help for people who could not have had the last rites administered; a practise that became increasingly decadent during these five hundred years.

The question arose: Where was the best place to carry out this penance? It was close by and at hand: in the monastery. The cloister is just the place for it. Benedict—in the sixth century—took it upon himself to prepare every monk in his cloister community for the Day of Judgment. This preparation was comprised of what we might refer to as three ways to do penance: fasting, so that a person did not remain too bound to his physical body; alms, which is more in the realm of the etheric since the person gives up everything, keeps nothing for himself; and prayer—the individual is engaged at the soul level. Thus, the ways of doing penance are fasting for the physical body; alms for the etheric body; and prayer for the astral body, for the life of soul.

God is Love

All this notwithstanding, the view of a merciless God continued to have an effect for centuries. Then came the point in time that I have mentioned; it came with Bernard of Clairvaux who effected an enormous change. This may be difficult to grasp because we stand firmly in the mentality of our time. And yet most of us probably also had an incarnation at that time and were able to experience these events in some way or another. Even if someone lived more in Judaism or in Islam during the Middle Ages, there were still similar tendencies. Bernard of Clairvaux said: 'God is love'.[1] That was the change—a very simple one—that appeared in the first Epistle of John: *Deus caritas est.* That was his Bible passage; nothing carried a greater weight for Bernard of Clairvaux than this passage and he led his life in accord with it. Nevertheless, the view remained that God leaves no sin unpunished. God is love, and He also punishes out of love.

Bernard of Clairvaux's view remained mainly within his community during that time. Only later—a century to a century and a half later—did the view that 'God is love' begin to spread with a group of people whom we refer to as the great mystics. They possessed an organ of understanding for this view precisely because they were well grounded in theology, but also because the beginning of the consciousness soul age was approaching, in their souls. This was especially true of Meister Eckhart.

Meister Eckhart

Meister Eckhart was born in 1260 and studied with the Dominicans in Paris and Cologne. It is said that he was the most significant theologian of European mysticism at the time. Meister Eckhart approached this whole question much as Bernard of Clairvaux had earlier described it in his own way: from the standpoint of the consciousness soul, which was, however, born in him before its time. How was this possible? Meister Eckhart is another personality who carried a replica from Christ Jesus—specifically, His astral body with the imprint of the consciousness soul. This meant that he was able to work out of the ego force by means of this consciousness soul imprint in the astral body. When we hear what Meister Eckhart thought, we experience the reality of this. He believed that the human being can actually restore a unity with God, that the human being can himself—by his own efforts—restore this unity. This is always described as the *Unio mystica*, that every human being has within himself a spark of God, and he is in a position to create this bridge between himself and the Creator by means of this spark.

If we read the writings of Meister Eckhart where he describes this—and there are many—we might recall the first sentence of *Knowledge of Higher Worlds*: There slumber in every human being capacities through which he can acquire knowledge of higher worlds.[2] Meister Eckhart: 'If the human being raises himself fully above sins and completely turns away from them, the true God acts as though the human being had never fallen into sin, and not even for a moment will He allow him to pay for all of his sins. Even if they were as many as all the sins of man combined, God will never allow him to pay.' The most remarkable thing is that Meister Eckhart took a further step beyond Bernard of Clairvaux. He understood sin based on the paradox of love, and says: 'And the greater and weightier the sins, the more is God's immeasurable will to forgive them; and all the more quickly they affront Him.'[3] This is a completely new and revolutionary thought for that time—and perhaps for today as well.

The Fall of Man

In spite of all this, the great theme was and is the Fall of Man. This idea has remained in human consciousness down through the centuries and lives on: God made everything good and also called it good. What occurred afterwards was brought about by Adam and Eve through their expulsion from the Garden of Eden. This is difficult to understand. Rudolf Steiner spoke about it and explained it more than once. If we try to summarize what Rudolf Steiner said about it, we might express it something like this: The human being, as he goes from incarnation to incarnation, is actually not himself responsible for the Fall of Man. This represents a large next step in how humanity is viewed, but what does Rudolf Steiner mean by this? On the one hand, understanding the Fall of Man itself means understanding that the human being is pushed deeper into matter—not because of his own nature, but by a luciferic temptation. However, the luciferic temptation is somewhat differently understood here; it was more a deed of the gods that the human being entered into matter too quickly. What originally existed as the physical body was invisible, without matter, and would have and should have been able to stay that way. But because of this descent into matter, the invisible physical body drew matter into it and, as a result, we are able to see it. Lucifer's role as a cosmic being really has two sides to it that we can also come to understand. When the earth was still united with the moon and was becoming increasingly hard, humanity—in order to assure its continued existence—had to depart from the earth. Those not familiar with this can read about it, for example, in *Occult Science, An Outline.*[4] Humanity then divided itself among the various planets. Lucifer was the leader of the human souls who departed the earth at the time of its hardening. It might be said that Lucifer performed a great service then but it was accompanied by the implantation of the luciferic principle into the human astral body. That was the other side of these events. Since that time, the human being—who had been led prematurely to try to understand good and evil—is also in a position to be able to err. Rudolf Steiner mentions in this respect that original sin continues to have an effect. It accompanies humanity, so to speak, on its continuing path when a person attempts to take action without sufficient wisdom, without knowing enough about the consequences. If we consider how we live today with genomes and such things, we experience the presence of a thirst for knowledge where people are taking action without being fully in possession of the wisdom required to consider all the consequences.

The temptation of Adam and Eve is often portrayed in art. For example, there are wonderful capitals throughout Europe—like the ones in Vézelay—where the Fall of Man is depicted. The altarpiece by Meister Bertram in Hamburg has a beautiful image of this luciferic temptation. It depicts Adam and Eve—as well as Lucifer with the body of a snake and a human face, as he speaks to them. Rudolf Steiner spoke about this Bertram Lucifer, saying that the situation in which mankind found itself then can be seen in these images. He spoke as well about how Lucifer acted during the hardening of the earth and the lifting out of humanity.

Angels

Let us now turn our attention to angels and devils. The life of the angels played a very important role in monastic life, especially for the Cistercians. They often viewed their cloisters as places of the angels. Angels were important for the early Christian population down through the centuries because they hoped that after they died the angels would chase the devils away from them. This was their great hope. They also thought that when the Day of Judgment dawned the angels would blow their trumpets to herald the resurrection. The angels attending to the Day of Judgment would also be the ones who would hold the great book in which the good and bad deeds of men are written. The angels represented hope for people.

Imaginations of the Devil

Many people were still in a position to see the angels. Rudolf Steiner mentioned that this was also the case in regard to demons—even for Martin Luther himself. According to Rudolf Steiner, there is truth to the story about Martin Luther throwing an inkwell at the wall to drive off the devil. First, he actually did throw it; second, he did it because he saw the devil. With Martin Luther, this is actually connected to a pre-Christian initiation.

Humanity at that time perceived itself to be completely at the mercy of the devil. People lived in this perception—which is difficult for us to imagine. They always thought that they had to be constantly on guard against the devil, that they had to protect themselves from attacks, had to protect themselves against the devil's wiles. If we leap ahead to the period of the Enlightenment, we find the phrase: The greatest trick of the devil is that he isn't. He does not exist. But that came much later. At the time we are discussing, the world of the devil was a reality. The Christian population thus lived in a constant state of anxiety. People saw themselves— and this is frequently depicted—as a tower continually besieged by demonic beings. We see also temptations by the devil. For example, St

Anthony is often depicted with temptations coming towards him. All saints were attacked, even St Benedict. Demons were depicted with incredibly horrible heads.

An interesting thing about the world of demons—and the eighteenth-century German author and essayist Gotthold Ephraim Lessing understood this very well—is that demons do not remain in solidarity with one another for long. This is a difference between good and evil—evil soon falls into disagreement with itself.

There were many kinds of devils: beautiful devils, devils of lasciviousness, even devils who played music. For centuries, all the wind instruments, flutes and so forth—with the exception of the trumpets of the angels—were thought of as unworthy. It could be said that they were actually considered demonic. This might have been handed down through the idea of Dionysian music connected with Dionysius, the god of wine. In any case, decent people were not depicted in early times with flutes or other wind instruments.

We see, therefore, that these ideas were quite vivid. For example, Hildegard von Bingen—today, she has quite a devoted following—once described a vision she had had in which she saw the devil as a horrible serpent. I will cite only the first few sentences:

> The serpent was black and bristly, full of abscesses and pustules. Its body bore stripes of five different colours, and they went from its head over its stomach to its feet ... filled with deadly poison. Its head was so shattered that its left cheek seemed to collapse in on itself. Its eyes, outwardly bloodshot, glowed with an inner fire; its ears were round and bristly. But its nose and mouth resembled a viper's. It had hands like a human, but feet like a viper; and his tail appeared short and terrifying.[5]

This is not something you would like to see! The devil is often seen as a serpent, even in Rudolf Steiner's Mystery Dramas.[6]

During the entire Middle Ages there was an enormous group of images about the Christ. The cathedral at Chartres has by far the largest group of these images as well as images of the Virgin Mary; however, there are also an unbelievable number of demons depicted. The most important thing to note here is that, throughout the Middle Ages, the demonic had a principal role as an antagonist of God. Demonic figures are often openly visible on the altars and the capitals. Many capitals are always in shadow and, since our eyes are much weaker today than they were back then, we see them only with the aid of additional lighting—otherwise, these capitals with their wonderful depictions would never be illuminated enough to see. But it is also often the case that the best natural lighting falls on these demons on these uppermost capitals, which means they can easily be seen.

From a theological point of view, devils were considered to be fallen angels. This view lived quite strongly at the time. For example, Augustine described this precisely; he also added his own view of the world of fallen angels. What shines through this view is an incredible and—for us—complicated theological explanation. He said that devils should be able to better their circumstances on their own because they are fallen angels. If the devils are not willing to better their circumstances—which is within their power—then they should be condemned. Augustine brings the argument in a logic peculiar to him.

We have mentioned how a genuine renewal arose in the twelfth century through the School of Chartres, especially in regard to God as love. With the School of Chartres, and then most especially in the Scholasticism that immediately followed, it was possible to speak speculatively about the devil and about the demonic world. Until then, people were very cautious, not ever daring to speak about such things if it could be avoided. But with the School of Chartres coming more from the side of Platonism, and then with Scholasticism more from the side of Aristotelianism, it was now possible to speak speculatively about evil and the devil himself. But that in no way contributed to minimizing the fear of the devil. These two points never came together. Speaking about the demonic was one thing; that everyone lived in fear of the demonic world was another thing entirely. In time, this demonization lessened, but it shifted in a different direction—in the direction of the witch-hunts.

Before dying, people often experienced an enormous fear for their souls. The hope was that the world of the angels would offer its assistance when the soul leaves the physical body. We often see depicted in art the battle between angels and devils for the human soul. Goethe also portrayed this quite faithfully at the end of *Faust*. There was a prayer in Christendom at this time that was actually called *commendatio animæ*—people prayed with their last breath that the Father would receive the soul, in accord with the words of Christ: 'Father, into thy hands I commend my spirit.'[7] This *commendatio animæ* had a powerful presence.

If we pursue this imagination further, we find that it not only involves the soul's vulnerability to angels or devils but also a quite dangerous journey that begins immediately after the soul has left the body. The journey includes the departure from the body and the battle among angels and devils until we finally arrive in the kingdom of heaven. We will hear more about this in connection with Dante. It is significant that this is

actually not grounded in the Gospels, but in other texts, especially II
Corinthians. We hear a quite specific description, for example, in *Muspilli*,
one of only two surviving old high German epic poems from the ninth
century. The author speaks about the dangers of the demonic world at the
moment of death. It is said that an element of heathenism enters through
it that we can hear in the following passage:

> Then straightaway, when the soul rises along its street
> And it leaves behind its lifeless corpse,
> A host comes from heavenly lights,
> Another from pitch, they pluck it at once.
> Distress is carried by the soul, until sins are atoned,
> About the host which will have it.
> Then, if Satan's servants have won the soul,
> They will lead it straight to where it languishes
> In fire and in full darkness,
> A judgment free of peace.
> If those who have the soul come down from heaven on high
> And it becomes the angels' own,
> They take the soul straight to heaven's realm.
> That is life without death, Light without dark,
> Sweet bliss without distress, where no one is sick.[8]

The description is very clear.

In addition, there is the imagination of the ladder of virtue that was
widespread during the Middle Ages. The person can practise the virtues
on this ladder, but he can also slip on any rung; even if he has ascended
quite high in the virtues, he can still fall.

People at that time saw not only the devil and angels, they also saw
many elemental beings. These elemental beings were often seen in plants
as a face peering out; in the English tradition, this is called the 'Green
Man'. It is a concept in the history of English art—they are elemental
beings.

There was also an entire culture of gargoyles during the Middle Ages.
Of course, these creatures also had a practical application diverting water
away from the eaves trough through the gargoyle's spout. Why do they
have such ugly faces or often very funny faces? First of all, so that people
always have before them the existence of a second layer of life, the level of
the elemental world, the demonic world, that is always present. This is the
one aspect. The other aspect in regard to these gargoyles is that some of
them are quite ugly figures that seem to be peeping out at the world.
People often have the feeling while looking at them that they are looking

back. Try it sometime. They are often made to be quite demonic or repulsive, but also quite humorous—some stick their tongues out and so on. The thought was that if they are ugly enough, they will frighten away other demons who perhaps want to enter the church. This was another view.

Now let us turn to a somewhat difficult theme closely connected with a Christian concept from the earliest period. After the burial, following the crucifixion, Christ descended into the underworld, into hell—*descensus ad inferos*, descent into hell—where He saved all the souls who were worthy of salvation, whether they had lived in the pre-Christian era or during His time. There are wonderful pictures of this descent; it was a quite beloved theme. We find a description of this by the two sons of Simeon the Elder, the Simeon who said: I have seen the Saviour and now I can die. This Simeon was the same personality as Asita at the time of the Gautama Buddha's birth. Simeon's two sons told the apostles Nicodemus and Joseph of Arimathaea, and others, that they had been in hell and what they had experienced there. According to this report—which appears in the Gospel of Nicodemus, a book of the Apocrypha—they both say they visited Hades. It must be mentioned here that Hades was always viewed as a being, not as abstraction. This Hades had a huge maw, quite horrible. They describe it this way:

> We were thus in Hades together with all those who, from the beginning of time, had passed away. However, in the midnight hour a light like the sun's shone into the darkness and illuminated it; and it shone on all of us and we saw one another. And immediately our father, Abraham, together with the patriarchs and the prophets, filled with joy among themselves, said one to the other: That is the light from the great illumination that was promised us! The prophet, Isaiah, who was present there, said: That is the light of the Father and of the Son and of the Holy Spirit! While I was still alive, I prophesied this . . .[9]

According to tradition, the relationship between Hades and Satan was that Hades actually ruled the underworld. In this role—also reported in these Apocrypha—Hades entered into a big argument with Satan. They speak about the odd fact that something had changed in the realm of Hades. It is a bit long, but since it is rather humorous, I will cite it here nevertheless. It comes from the Gospel of Nicodemus. Satan, the 'Heir of Darkness', says to Hades:

> You, devourer of all and insatiable one, hear my words! One from the race of the Jews named Jesus calls Himself the Son of God, but is only a

man. Thanks to our help, the Jews crucified Him. And now that He has died, be prepared that we will take Him into our care here! Because I know He is only a man, and I even heard Him say: 'My soul is saddened deeply unto death.' He caused me great harm in the upper world as He walked with mortals. Where He met my servants, He persecuted them, and however many people I crippled, made blind, lame, leprous, and the like, He made them well again by the Word alone. And I prepared many to be buried and He brought them back to life through the Word alone . . .

Hades answers: Heir of Darkness, Son of Ruination, Devil! You claimed that He brought many of those you prepared for the grave back to life through the Word alone. But if He has freed others from the grave, how and by what power are we supposed to contain Him? Recently, I devoured a dead one by the name of Lazarus; soon after, one of the living ones sucked him forcefully from inside me by the Word alone. I think it was the One about whom you speak. If we receive Him here, I fear we will come into danger with the others. You see, I notice that all those I have swallowed since the beginning of time have suddenly become restless, and I have pains in my stomach. It seems to me that Lazarus—who was snatched from me then—is not a good omen, because he departed me not as one who is dead, but as an eagle, so quickly did the earth fling him forth. For this reason, I swear to you on your well-being and my own: Do not bring to me the One about whom you speak. Because I believe that He will only appear here in order to resurrect all the dead. I say that to you—by the darkness that we have in common—if you bring Him here, not one of the dead will remain here for me.[10]

We experience that as humorous; but people at that time did not find it in the least bit funny. Instead, it was a very deep confirmation that it would be possible one day to hope for salvation through the Christ.

It is often the case that we see the fully manifested resurrection in manuscripts, naturally with wonderfully illuminated pictures along with beautifully illustrated letters. But the Day of Judgment is also frequently depicted. There are various images from the Book of Revelation in the art of this period, especially in the manuscripts.

One characteristic of the Day of Judgment is that there will be a division of souls. One group of souls would go down into the realm of the devil while the other group would be saved on the Last Day, at the Last Judgment—all this based on the notion: No deed will go unpunished. We see in these images that the archangel Michael is present, weighing the souls. This is an important concept, this weighing of souls by Michael. It means that there is a quantifying of the intensity and extent of evil that a soul might have experienced and from which it could be saved.

There were also streams during the ninth century and beyond that begin to demonstrate a new conceptualization of Christ—Christ (rather than Moses) as the judge after death. There is a report by Ansgar, the so-called 'Apostle of the North' and Archbishop of Hamburg and Bremen, that tells of a vision. He confesses before Christ and is consoled by Him, saying: 'Fear not; I am the One who takes away your sins.'[11] If we ask ourselves how that is possible, we can become conscious of the following thoughts from Rudolf Steiner's Christology:

> If we think about the body of Christ that rose from the grave, we can imagine: Just as the bodies of human beings on the earth are descended from the body of Adam in so far as they are bodies that decay, so are the spiritual bodies, the phantoms of all human beings, descended from what was resurrected from the grave. And it is possible to establish that relationship to the Christ through which the earthly human being adds into his decaying physical body this Phantom that rose from the grave at Golgotha. It is possible for the human being to receive in his organization those forces which were resurrected at that time just as he received the Adam-organization by means of his physical organization at the beginning of Earth evolution and as the result of luciferic forces... And you can think of each of these bodies received by the human being as having the same relation to what rose from the grave that human cells in the physical body have to the original human ovum. This means we must think of what arose from the grave as multiplying, as increasing in the same way that the ovum—the foundation of the physical body—grows. In this way, in fact, as a result of the development that follows on the event at Golgotha, every human being can acquire something that is already in him and is descended spiritually from what arose from the grave, just as—in the words of Paul—the ordinary body that decays is descended from Adam.[12]

From the World of Imagery in the Middle Ages

There are many examples from the medieval world of images through which we can gain insight into the imaginative wealth of people at that time. Please refer as well to the list of illustrations and credits on pages 209–10.

Illustration 1. This is the poor Lazarus. His soul is being received by the angels. We note here how the soul is as though placed in a cocoon and how softly the angel receives him with the left hand. It is quite amazing that such tenderness can be expressed in stone

Illustration 2. Here we see the miserly rich man who never gave even a crumb to the poor Lazurus during his lifetime. The devil is fetching his soul. Interesting here is the serpent at the bottom of the carving

Illustration 3. The famous altarpiece in Hamburg by Meister Bertram. Between Adam and Eve we see the serpent with a beautiful human head

Illustration 4. The same altar. The Father God scolding Adam and Eve. Below we see the head of Lucifer, the slithering serpent body

Illustration 5. This is the temptation of Adam and Eve on a capital in Vézelay

Illustration 6. This head of a demon can be frightening even today. We can well imagine how it was in the Middle Ages. (Vézelay)

Illustrations 7 and 8. In medieval imagination, the demons also fought among themselves. (Vézelay)

Illustration 9. Here the temptation of St Benedict by the demons is depicted. (Vézelay)

Illustration 10. This figure of a bird is called a basilisk; it is also connected with the devil. (Vézelay)

Illustration 11. This is the devil of sensual pleasure. The whistle he carries is characteristic. With it, he lures a devil out, although this devil looks somewhat frightened because his hair is standing on end. (Vézelay)

Illustration 12. Elemental beings, as they can be seen in Saulieu

Illustration 13. Gargoyles at Notre Dame de Paris. The one in front looks out over the city; the other is shouting

Illustration 14. Christ's descent into hell was a popular theme. This image is taken from the so-called Stuttgart Psalter. Here He enters into hell. We can see the door and the archangel Michael who accompanies Him. Michael stands behind the Christ and to the side of the souls behind the grating

Illustration 15. Here the maw of Hades opens; the angel is closing the door. The jaws are visible and within them all of the souls tumbling around together. The devils with their instruments of torture

Illustration 16. This picture shows something quite remarkable. This capital is in Autun (Burgundy, France). Christ carries the yoke from which six bells are hanging. It might be said that Christ represents the yoke for all of humanity, and also represents the fourth tone, the 'F' in our musical scale. When bells are shown like this, and Christ is presented or thought of as the fourth tone, the esotericist understands it as a reference to the Mystery of Golgotha. What we have here is a very special interpretation, with the third tone on the one side struck by one figure, the figure of the Christ in the middle, and then the fifth tone is visible. It is also being struck. What we see here in stone is actually a very mystical image

Illustration 17. Here we see the conversion—or the vision—of Paul. It is an unusual image, not because of the figure of Paul but because of the figure above, the Christ figure surrounded by seraphim. Compare this with the description of Francis of Assisi and his vision—Christ as seraph, or Christ gazing through the face of a seraph. This is from the Urbino or Urbinate Bible from the fifteenth century

Illustration 18. This is the Last Judgment from the Book of Revelation. Below, the 24 elders in their full glory and holding up their crowns. Then four apocalyptic figures are below the oval around the Father God, two on either side of the seven stars; the Father God is surrounded by the heavenly hierarchies. Just above the apocalyptic figures are the angels, three by three, with their instruments. This is an especially beautiful image, also from the Urbino Bible

Illustration 19. In time, images of the resurrection became quite popular. This picture shows the resurrection of the dead with trumpets sounding. Below we see the angels holding trumpets; on the Day of Judgment, the dead rise and experience the Christ figure with His wounds. This is in the Ingeborg Psalter from northern France, *c.* 1195

Illustration 20. The famous 'Mystical Mill' in Vézelay. Gottfried Richter asks, 'Is this image of the mill really . . . as we find it explained, an image of the Christ through which the corn poured into it by Moses is milled to flour . . . that every person is corn that first needs to be milled?'[13]

1

2

3

4

5   *6*

7   *8*

9

10

11

12

13

15

14

16

17

18

19   *20*

Cabbala and Jewish Mysticism in the Middle Ages—'Heretical Streams' as a Transition from Antiquity to the Modern Age

Manfred Schmidt-Brabant

Judaism naturally played a completely different role than Islam in the confluence of these many spiritual components during the Middle Ages. It was, of course, known that Jesus, His apostles and the early circle around Him had been Jews. And naturally the Old Testament was a holy text as much for the Jews as for the Christians. Thus the connections between Jewish mysticism and Christianity are different from what they ever were between Islam and Christianity.

The Jews in the Roman Empire

Let us look briefly at this situation. Throughout the Roman occupation and the rebellion of the Jews against Rome, efforts were made again and again to destroy the Jews in Palestine. Yet another great effort at destruction began in AD 135; 985 villages were destroyed and 580,000 Jews murdered. The seriousness of this is not usually understood. These rebellions—about which we know little, at best—gradually led to the destruction of the Jewish kingdom as the centre of Judaism at that time. Nevertheless, at the end of the second century a body of 71 rabbis came together in Jerusalem to seek to summarize the existing esotericism that had arisen over a period of a thousand years, and to pass it on to the generations to come.

In the beginning, Judaism was on an equal footing with all the other religions in Rome. I have already noted that any religion could be practised in Rome as long as its people showed Caesar divine respect. But then Constantine came to power in the fourth century bringing Christianity with him, and punishments were meted out to the Jews. All the rabbis had to leave Rome; if a Jewish man married a Christian woman, his punishment was death. There was also an interlude under Julian the Apostate who attempted to re-enliven the old Mysteries. He asked the

Jews: Why don't you sacrifice animals any longer? They said: We can only sacrifice animals in the temple and we no longer have a temple; it was destroyed. Thus Julian gave the order to rebuild the Temple in Jerusalem, but soon after he was murdered and so the reconstruction work came to a halt.

Then—in 614, at the latest—Palestine's role as a centre for the leadership of Judaism came to a definite end. The great migration, the exodus of the Jews in all directions, began—to Persia, into the Orient; to North Africa, France, Germany. The entire region of the Rhine was settled—Mainz, Worms, Speyer, Frankfurt, Cologne. Large Jewish settlements arise everywhere, particularly in Spain. In their dealings and their confrontations with the community around them, the Jews bring with them the Pentateuch and the Old Testament wherever they go, but also the Haggadah, the collection of legends, and the Halakhah, the collection of Jewish laws; taken together, all these comprise the Talmud. Above all, they bring with them something that has formed the unshakeable foundation of every Jew's life from the time of the exile until today. Following the destruction of the Temple, the family becomes the sacred core of life. The holy Sabbath is celebrated in the family circle which is actually the place of religious experience. The synagogue is the place of teaching or a communal building; the Torah is read there, and the men meet there. But the actual centre of Jewish life is the household, the home, the Sabbath table. It must be said over and again that the Jewish housewife is actually the one who—since the earliest times—acted as a priestess and managed everything connected with the family's religious life.

The Jews in Spain

Thus Jewish communities develop everywhere, alternately tolerated and persecuted. Not until the nineteenth century were these persecutions the result of racism; racism did not exist before then. Earlier persecution was either focused on religion or, frequently, a Jewish city was plundered out of rapaciousness or avarice. In Spain, Judaism simply became a second culture. I have already spoken about how difficult it is to understand the degree of tolerance that existed during those centuries of Moorish rule. Of course, just as the Christians had their churches and bishops, the Jews could pursue their own religion, had their synagogues, occupied highly respected positions, were often personal physicians to the caliphs. I have often thought the great Spanish culture that flourished then was the result of this quite liberal and broadminded tolerance. The caliphs had Christians had Christians as viziers and leaders of armies; Jewish scholars and Jewish physicians were to be found everywhere. It was a mutually beneficial milieu.

Thus it is no wonder that the single greatest philosopher to come from Judaism, Maimonides, was born and grew up in Cordoba, Spain, during the twelfth century. He was a doctor and philosopher, and wrote a large textbook entitled *The Guide of the Perplexed* which very quickly became known in Europe. It is already clear from the title that the human being who is perplexed in the world, who no longer knows which way to turn, finds guidance here that will show him step by step the way to knowledge and clarity.

Above all, however—and this is the main idea of our discussion—what spread across Europe had developed out of Jewish mysticism. Since I always relish recommending primary sources, I must cite Gershom Scholem whose great standard work *Major Trends in Jewish Mysticism*[1] is widely read, especially in the English-speaking world. Gershom Scholem was born in Berlin and emigrated to Israel. At the University of Jerusalem he assembled what may well be the largest extant library of books on mysticism and the cabbala. He was once asked if he would, at long last, catalogue this library; his response was that such a catalogue would not be worth the effort. He would rather write a small catalogue of the books that he did not have. With a Hebrew play on words, this book would be called 'Go ask Gershom'.

He portrays in detail how early mysticism was once influenced by everything that arose out of the old Mysteries—Zarathustrianism, the light and darkness; Neoplatonism with its teachings about the aeons, teachings about the emanations; Pythagoras; Gnosis from Syria and Egypt. Above all, this early mysticism—which was pre-Christian and then flowed into the post-Christian era—was influenced by something to which Rudolf Steiner also repeatedly drew attention, namely, by a kind of secret interpretation of Genesis. He said that none of the initiated Jewish rabbis read Genesis literally; instead, they knew the secret meanings connected with certain things. Rudolf Steiner says that this tradition was entering Europe as late as the seventeenth and eighteenth centuries.

The Ten Sefiroth

In approximately the third century after Christ—or so it is supposed—the book appears that formed the basis for all Jewish mysticism, the *Sefer Yezira*. It is a very small, slender volume and it is concerned with how

God called forth all of creation through the ten numbers and 22 letters. As a young man, I even copied it by hand once—just after the war when it was still impossible to get books. It really is not that long. Nevertheless, this little book contains the central secret of all Jewish mysticism—the teaching about the ten Sefiroth. Throughout the centuries, and even into modern times, endless commentaries have been written about it.

I will summarize it here. But first, to offer a more visual impression of them, I have made a drawing based on one by Rudolf Steiner. It shows how these ten Sefiroth meet one another, how they are depicted in various engravings in the books of the cabbala, and so forth. It is most often shown in this form, and the lines indicating the relationships may vary some. There are three Sefiroth at the top, Kether, Hokmah and Binah; three in the middle, Hesed, Gevurah, or Din, and Tifereth; and three more below, Netsah, Hod and Jesod. At the very bottom is Malkut, the realm.

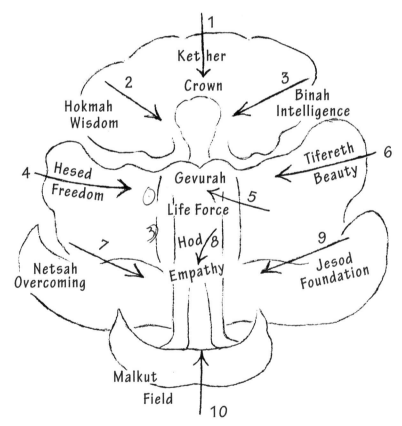

Drawing according to Rudolf Steiner, from a lecture on 10 May 1924

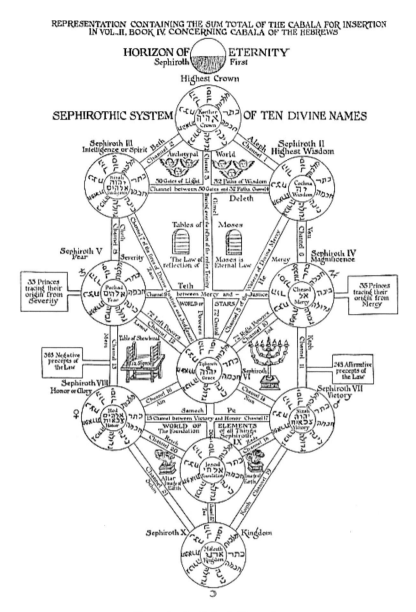

Example of a Sefiroth illustration

These were the attributes of God, the principles according to which the creation was formed. Above all, they were the principles through which the human being finds the path into the spiritual world if he takes them up in the right way. I want to repeat here something Rudolf Steiner said in connection with this: In all esoteric content, there are images of the Guardian of the Threshold. We only have to look for them.[2]

In this regard, there is a wonderful image from Jewish esotericism. Through the arch of a gate we look inside at an old Jewish man—a wise rabbi, perhaps—sitting on a stool. The floor around him is set in tiles, but there is a break in them that creates a yawning hole, an abyss, one might say. He sits there and points with one hand to this hole, to this abyss, as if to say: 'Take care that you don't fall in the abyss.' With the other hand, he holds the framework of the ten Sefiroth aloft. Past him, through the arch of the gate, we gaze, so to speak, into a paradisaical landscape as if he wants to say: Enter only when you have found your way through these ancient principles of creation.

We look at that now and cannot do much with it unless we immerse ourselves in reading cabbalistic literature. Rudolf Steiner picks this up during a lecture in 1924 and immediately proceeds to a discussion of the ten Sefiroth based on a practical knowledge of the human being.[3] Here is an illustration of the human being after one by Rudolf Steiner. At the top, in shading, is a red sphere; then, in the middle, a yellow sphere; then further down, a blue sphere; and, here at the bottom, is violet.

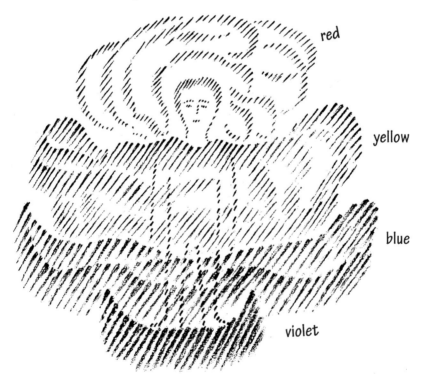

Rudolf Steiner speaks about these ten Sefiroth and what they actually mean. There is the upper trinity—Kether, Hokmah, Binah; crown, wisdom, and intelligence. He says: This is actually what distinguishes human beings at their loftiest, their higher, pure spirituality. Then he explains this in detail. Kether, crown, is what comes to people from heaven as the loftiest spirituality. He even makes a small addendum, saying: Later, people put actual crowns on their heads, whether or not they deserved them. But these crowns originally meant what came from the spiritual world to people and for people in the way of spirituality. At that time, he says, the old Jewish esotericists made a clear distinction between Hokmah and Binah, wisdom and intelligence. And they knew—he says that all of these words are only rough translations, of course—that wisdom from the spiritual world is really what carries human beings, that intelligence is a human capacity, and that there are many who may be quite intelligent but not at all wise. Thus these three upper Sefiroth form what constitutes the human being as a spiritual being.

Then we come to the three Sefiroth in the middle. One impulse, Hesed, belongs on the right-hand side and means freedom because we claim freedom for ourselves, so to speak, with the right hand. On the other side is Tifereth, beauty. He says that it comes on the left hand, which is always gentler and milder. In the middle lies what the ancient Jewish esotericists always called Gevurah, the life force, concentrated in the heart and heartbeat. All this is the region of the sun; sun forces are active there, periphery forces.

It then moves more into what makes up the human being as metabolic-limb system in the moon region; this is Hod. He calls it empathy, Hod. He says, at the same time, that it is everything connected with repro-duction, with sexuality. Then he says on one side is Netsah, overcoming. This offers the possibility that we can walk, that we are not held in one place like a tree, and that we are also not limited by having adapted to a specific environment like the animals. Instead, we are able to overcome the earth's gravity and determine for ourselves where we want to go. Jesod, the foundation, is what makes us capable of standing up on our legs, of supporting ourselves with strength.

As help from the earthly depths comes Malkuth, the field or realm. In general, it is translated as realm, but Rudolf Steiner says, for example, that the physical field radiates Malkuth, its earth forces, upwards into the human being.

Rudolf Steiner said that pupils of esoteric Judaism did not merely memorize this; these Sefiroth were only letters on a page—just as we have the alphabet with A, B and C, which are of absolutely no use if we know only the alphabet. We must begin to read by means of learning this alphabet in its changing combinations; and this is how the students of esoteric Judaism learned to read as they viewed these Sefiroth together. What is it when Hesed, Hod and Binah work together, or Hokmah, Hesed and Netsah? These were letters and through their connections to one another the pupil learned to look into the spiritual world, to look into their lawfulness, into the relationship of the spiritual world and the physical world.

This great work, the *Sefer Yetsirah*, was circulated in the outer world beginning in the third century—although, of course, it had existed prior to this. We must always take into consideration that, even then, there was a mutual awareness about these books. After the book came out, it was not only read by Jewish esotericists but Islamic ones as well. It was known in the Christian world as well.

There are two great phases in Jewish mysticism. The first is called Throne Mysticism, *Merkabah*, concerned entirely with losing oneself in a view of God—God on His throne, the Mysteries of the heavenly throne world. Gershom Scholem states that this was nothing other than what the Gnostics called 'Pleroma', 'Fullness', the view up into the world of the aeons.

The Zohar

There follows the origin of the cabbala itself. The cabbala first arose quite late, in the thirteenth century; often the whole of Jewish mysticism is designated as cabbala. As the cabbala came into being, it also reached back into elements of earlier mysticism. In 1295, the so-called Zohar, the 'Book of Splendour', is authored by León Moses ben Shem Tov de León in the beautiful Spanish city of León. What did he create? A work that was very soon given equal standing with the Talmud by the Jews. It is a comprehensive work in which the innermost esoteric secrets of Jewish mysticism are revealed. They are described in such a way that the Zohar requires study; the Jews have a rule that no one should study the cabbala before the age of 40.

Here there is a change from the old Merkabah mysticism. They no longer gaze upon God's throne, but instead the following happens. There is the loftiest divinity, En-Sof. The ten Sefiroth radiate forth from this En-Sof, but they belong to the divinity itself. The whole is God in His dynamic unity. When we look at the ten Sefiroth, we see what occurs, as it were, within the divinity as a universally powerful, cosmically dynamic element. What is in the cabbala moves out into Europe. And then comes the catastrophe.

The Spread of Jewish Mysticism after 1492

It is striking to read the history of Judaism written from a completely modern point of view, because what comes to expression in it again and again is the phrase 'the catastrophe of 1492'. It is a strange year. In 1492, the Spanish Christian army conquers what remains of the area occupied by the Moors, the kingdom of Granada; and they conquer the wonderful Alhambra that had been restored. In 1492, America is discovered. In that year, too, the Spanish monarchs, Ferdinand of Aragon and Isabella I of Castile—known as the 'Catholic monarchs'—gave an order that meant catastrophe for Judaism: All Jews have to leave Spain immediately. A horrible and cruel exodus begins. We think of how many centuries they had lived there—of course, they had property, homes, professions, and so on. They could take only very few of their possessions with them, just what could be brought along on a wagon, a cart. When we read the descriptions today, what comes through above all is the infinite despair that comes from being driven out of the cultural homeland where they thought themselves to be firmly rooted. There is also an interpretation that claims Columbus and his family were Jews who sought out another country where Jews could live without hindrances. It is only a theory that Columbus was Jewish, but the theory is directly connected to this catastrophe, to this forced exodus.

Once again there is a great wave of emigration to Europe. What is important for our observations is that a completely new cabbala appears; it deals with the way esoteric secrets are to be handled. The previous cabbala had been intimate, an intimate esoteric teaching, theosophy, theogony and cosmosophy. Now, because of this cruel exodus, so-called Messianism—the anticipation of a messiah who comes to right injustices or, at least, to bring the Jews back to their homeland—suddenly enters into the Cabbala. It is a chiliastic anticipation. From the quiet study of the esotericists arises an active movement based in religious piety, with Hasidism as one of its offshoots. Hasidism had already begun in cities on the Rhine during this time, and later flourished in Poland and in the East. More recently, the legends of Baal-Shem and so forth were collected by Martin Buber and read by many.

Before the catastrophe of 1492, an assimilation of the cabbala into the Christian realm had already begun. A Christian cabbala began to arise. The first to take it up was someone we have already mentioned, Pico della Mirandola—this young Renaissance hero who only lived to the age of 31. He presented his nine hundred theses and invited the scholars of Europe to discuss with him the idea that all things shared a single root, that everything was a unified whole. Contained in these nine hundred theses are, if you will, many, many pieces of cabbalistic wisdom. He brings them into connection with Christianity; and he feels himself to be the founder of a Christian cabbala. Thus he is cited by all those who now write about Christian cabbala. Cabbalistic views—particularly the ten Sefiroth—begin to spread throughout the Christian world; we find them in the works of Paracelsus, Jakob Böhme, Fludd, and, somewhat later, in Reuchlin and Oetinger. A scholar, Knorr of Rosenroth, translates the cabbala into Latin—calling it *Kabbala denudata,* the Cabbala available to everyone.[4] Someone we will consider later, Agrippa von Nettesheim, assimilates the cabbala into his books of magic so that the cabbala rays outwards to England through these magical works of Agrippa von Nettesheim, and finally even to America.

Here an enormously fruitful world reveals itself and, despite all the persecutions, it is a world of mutual understanding among the esotericists that transcends religious confessions. This was what distinguished these centuries—to the consternation of orthodox circles on all sides, the esotericists often understand one another. Without hesitation, the esoteric Christian actually understood the esoteric Sufi; understood the cabbalist. They knew what each was talking about. In this sense, we can understand Rudolf Steiner when he says: If Pico della Mirandola had succeeded, we would have had a completely free, Platonic Christianity in Europe. But what he intended was covered up again. I have already explained that he only narrowly escaped being declared a heretic.

In this way we look into the confluence of powerful spiritual steams that must constantly defend themselves, must even hide themselves from the accusations of heresy coming from all sides. It is odd that all three great, monotheistic religions—Islam, Judaism and Christianity—know the concept of heresy; I spoke earlier about the fact that Islam even instituted an inquisition. Orthodoxy in all three monotheistic religions persecuted, declared as heresy, did not tolerate the appearance of the divergent views that often arose from esotericism.

What then takes place? Why this marginalization, this persecution and even death that was brought down upon the heretics? It had already begun in early Christian times when a person could only be a real human being if he subscribed to the opinion of the group, if a person believed, spoke and thought what lived in the group as opinion. In anthroposophy, we speak about it as a time when, in fact, the quality of the group soul still had a very strong meaning and justification; and only gradually was the I wrested from this quality of the group soul—in fact, it took a thousand or even fifteen hundred years.

Rejection of the Gnosis

We must also understand how difficulties arose then. In the beginning, it was a matter of coming to terms with the Gnosis as a method of knowledge. True Gnosis was differentiated from false Gnosis. Genuine Gnosis, genuine knowledge, was tolerated if it dealt with the New Testament or the Old Testament, as we see in Origen, Clement or others whom we always cite today as Gnostics. False Gnosis was everything into which elements of the pre-Christian Mysteries flowed—Egyptian elements, elements from Mesopotamia, the remains of Greek or Roman Mysteries. This was false Gnosis.

Coming to terms with this false Gnosis was, of course, also connected with coming to terms with the old Mystery religions. They all lived on into the early period of Christianity. The Caesars were not yet Christian and the Christians could not simply fight against the Isis cults, Astarte cults, and so on. Instead, they had to defend themselves within their own communities against these religions. Rome was filled with the most varied Mystery religions; it is known that Christians could have set up their altars—like the Egyptians and Greeks, North Africans and Teutonic tribes—in peace and freedom if they too had paid divine homage to Caesar. That was the condition. There was tolerance, freedom for all religions, provided that people venerated Caesar as god. The Christians could not do that and did not do it. Thus, very early on, the persecution of the Christians began, and in the course of this dispute all Gnosis was rejected. Very quickly, a fundamental anti-Gnosis arose; it can be said that people wanted absolutely no knowledge, only faith. Clement and Origen still differentiate 'Pistis', the communal faith that a person holds in common with the group, and 'Gnosis', the knowledge of those who know. There were actually certain steps of Gnosis, and it was said: When I pursue the path of Gnosis, I first read the text literally; then I read it at a second level, morally; then I read it at a third level, allegorically-mystically. Now I actually come to the content of the work.

Arius and Athanasius

The great conflict between Arius and Athanasius is another element that played into this period and then enters into the Middle Ages. It concerned the great question of the relationship of the Son to the Father. Arius and his followers, the Arians, said: The Son is the highest of all creations, but

He is not the same as God. Athanasius and his followers said: The Son is equal to the Father.

Whole councils were held; there were exchanges of views. Rudolf Steiner once said that every human being was occupied with that question during this period. There is a rather humorous story from a contemporary during these centuries:

> It's terrible. If I go to my barber, he says to me: The Son is not equal to the Father. If I go to the tavern for a bite to eat, the barkeeper says to me: The Son is equal to the Father.

This is a like a small confirmation of what Rudolf Steiner said. It lived in people on the street; one person would approach the other and say: What do you think—is the Son equal to the Father or not?

This had a deep effect on souls and on spiritual development, and then, from the year 1000 on, a new resurgence of heresy begins. It arose, according to Rudolf Steiner, through the search for the inner light and through the discovery of the principle of the individual, and also the assertion of the principle of the individual—of individual opinion. First there was opposition to the decadence and corruption of the Church. What people wanted was the re-establishment of the Church; they wanted a truly Christian Church, one of poverty and humility. Increasingly, opposition arose against the political power of the Church—above all, the power of the pope—particularly because of the awakening and growing feeling of national identity.

Emperors and Popes

The first half of the second millennium is—as I have explained earlier—also characterized by the great polarity between the emperor and the pope. The question was: Should there be a hierarchical structure? Is Gregory VII correct when he says that the pope is the overlord of the whole world? Or are there two realms of power, a secular one and an ecclesiastical one? Is this latter view perhaps what leads to a true picture of the human being—that the human being is a secular being and must contend with everything subject to the emperor; that the human being is, moreover, a spiritual being subject to the pope—so that it is precisely in this duality that his true humanity arises? Just as Christ Jesus was both God and man, the human being should cultivate his divinity as his religious life which the pope governs, and lead his secular, physical life for which the emperor is responsible.

The Conflict about the Last Supper

But then other things came along as well. The growth of individual intellect was accompanied by doubt about merely faith-based sacraments. People no longer wanted to believe what they did not grasp through insight, or even contradicted what they saw. Here we again meet Berengarius of Tours, the pupil of Fulbert to whom Adelmann had sent a letter containing the following sentence. We remember the secret evening colloquia in the cloister gardens. This is only a passing remark. Adelmann wrote the letter to argue with Berengarius' views, addressing him figuratively as 'My dear milk brother'—by which can be meant someone who, though unrelated, suckled with him at the breast of a wet-nurse; here it is used in a more metaphorical sense. Both of us, Adelmann wants to say, you and I, have lain at the breast of the wisdom of our revered teacher Fulbert. The correspondence focused on the fact that, in the debate about the inner reality of the Last Supper, the so-called transubstantiation, Berengarius of Tours had become increasingly radical in his criticism. We know from reports that he had always been one to raise questions; in Fulbertus' school, he was already making remarks to refute all of the Seven Liberal Arts, and saw merit only in the dialectic. He was a very peculiar fellow. But he was already something of a modern spirit, because he asked: Are we to understand that bread and wine transform into the body and blood of Christ? But after the consecration, it is still bread and wine. I do not see body or blood. This was one phase in the great conflict concerning the Last Supper, a conflict that had already begun two centuries earlier when the radical point of view said: It is the flesh of Christ—when you take it into your mouth, you crush the Christ with your teeth; and this is real blood. Berengarius of Tours, actually a quite modern spirit, said: I do not see it that way. I will not allow my eyes to be deceived. The host remains the host; and the wine remains the wine. Then came the turning point. He says: I can only understand the whole thing symbolically. The Last Supper is a symbolic event. It is, after all, the eleventh century, a very early period, so that Berengarius of Tours is named in Church history as the 'arch-heretic', as the first great heretic who thrust himself into the centre of the Christian Mystery with something so outrageous, saying: I do not believe this—this is symbolic; it is not at all reality.

Countless disputes arose from this. Heyer, who presents the matter in detail in his book, says: It is a sign that 'a spiritual understanding'[5] for the context of the Last Supper had already vanished.

Now something else quite extraordinary takes place that I must mention here. Berengarius of Tours defends his interpretation and is ordered to Rome. He has to recant all of it. Fearing the pyre, he recants. He has hardly returned home, when he says: No, I was correct. It is only to be understood symbolically; it is not reality, and so on. He is summoned back to Rome where he is forced to recant. He returns and once again asserts the same thing. This is worth noting. A heretic who repudiates his recantation is immediately put to death at the stake. That was an iron rule. They were prepared to let Joan of Orléans go free, but she said: No, I was correct. And she was sent to the stake. The Grand Master of the Templars was tortured for a long time until he recanted. But when he was released from torture, he said: No, I really am correct; we did not sin. And he was sent straightaway to the pyre. It was obligatory: a heretic who reversed his recantation, who refuted his recantation, was immediately burned. Why was this not the case with Berengarius of Tours?

Berengarius had a great protector, Abbot Hildebrandt of Cluny—none other than the man who would later become Gregory VII, but meanwhile was the legate in Rome. This protector visited Berengarius on behalf of the pope in order to converse with him, and then later became pope. I can only tell it the way it is portrayed in history. It is a puzzle. Why did Gregory VII—who was so ruthless—protect him? We have heard some of Gregory VII's 27 theses—the ones about everyone kissing his feet, and so forth—and suddenly he is protecting this arch-heretic, so that Berengarius of Tours is not burned but dies in peace.

Thus there is a riddle within history. A question about the meaning of the sacraments was, of course, always present within the ecclesiastical view. But then groups appear with deep-seated doubts about and objections to the fundamental views and structures of the Church.

Old and Young Souls

I would like to insert a little something here in order to provide a certain understanding. When we look at the people who were active during the Middle Ages, we can ask ourselves: Where do they come from? What kind of souls are they? Which earlier era did they come from, and what do they bring with them from that earlier time? Rudolf Steiner draws attention to the fact that there was a vast difference among human beings during this era after the Mystery of Golgotha, and even slightly before. There were people who already had quite a few incarnations behind them; he refers to them as the 'old souls'. And there were people who had only very few incarnations behind them; these he refers to as the 'young souls'.

Much earlier, there was a time when the whole of humanity departed the earth in a kind of cosmic emigration. It was the time up until the last third of the Lemurian epoch when relationships were so hardened on earth that scarcely any more bodies could be created; humanity departed the earth and lived in the planetary spheres. Then the souls return. Some return very quickly and thus have quite a few incarnations before the Mystery of Golgotha. Other souls remain longer in the spiritual world, returning only much later and, accordingly, have fewer incarnations. Each group distinguishes itself through a certain character.

The souls with many incarnations behind them had something like a longing for the spiritual world, for the sun, for the homeland of the sun. In a certain way, they grew tired of always being on the earth. The others, the young souls, fell to earth with great gusto; like a dachshund puppy with a slipper, everything interested them—the sanctuary, the Mysteries, and knowledge. Thus the young souls were inclined towards Aristotelianism, creating concepts and working with concepts. The old souls were inclined towards Platonism, towards a vision, a vision of ideas.

As a result, the following took place. During the period after the Mystery of Golgotha, the old souls fell into a kind of confusion and said to themselves: But we always experienced the Christ in the Sun. Now we no longer find Him there. Where is the Christ now? What does it mean that the Sun-Christ is now on the earth? They fell into confusion, they came to doubt what they had experienced previously. Therefore, Rudolf Steiner says, it was precisely the old souls who often connected themselves with sects and heretical streams.[6] This was not the case with the Aristotelians; they were quite clear. Later, when they were active in the Dominican Order, clarity of thought was what concerned them.

With the Platonic souls—and this had already begun a bit in the School of Chartres—there was always a kind of ambivalence about their view. This view into which these doubting, uncertain Platonists—the old souls—fell had an old, even ancient origin that goes back to the great religious founder Zarathustra and his doctrine about the twofold nature of the world, about light and darkness, about a god of light, Ormudz, and a god of darkness, Ahriman. Ahriman ruled the world where it is dark because it is made of matter. And it was a god of light, Ormudz, who governed the spirit where it was light.

Manichaeism

This view continued; the doctrine of light and darkness passed through many cultures and, in the third century after the Mystery of Golgotha, finally led to a Persian, Mani, who now attempted to bring all of this together with Christianity—a view commonly referred to as Manichaeism. It is actually quite difficult to penetrate to its sources because both sides, Catholicism and Protestantism, loathe Manichaeism and perceive it to be heresy. In the West, it led to well-known and clearly heretical statements. Next came the Patarines, then the Bogomils, and finally the view that the world was comprised of light and darkness—also called dualism—arrives in Europe, in the south of France, in northern Italy, and gives rise to the Cathar movement.

The Cathars

The word Cathars is a collective concept; the Cathars were not a unified group in that sense. There was the Cathar spiritual content and then the Cathar interpretations. The Cathars said: Everything visible here on earth is of the devil—the church, the altars, the sacraments, the veneration of images and saints. All of it is of the devil, and we reject it. There was only one path for human beings to follow—lifting themselves out of this world through asceticism, becoming free of sin and, whenever possible, strengthening freedom from sin in the world around them. This movement was situated primarily in the south of France—from Provence all the way to Toulouse—and was protected by the nobility there. Many of the nobility were Cathars and protected other Cathars; for this reason, Cathar castles were built everywhere. If you visit the eastern Pyrenees today, you will find this fact reinforced by the tourist industry through signs announcing everywhere: Cathar country; Cathar castles and so on; Cathar literature. In fact, all of this can be found there—you can see the great Cathar castles, and can even get a feeling for what had once lived in these valleys. It is an enormously charming area where it is still possible to get a whiff of what this singular movement was at that time.

The popes—especially Innocent III—moved ruthlessly against the Cathars. Soldiers were recruited for the campaign launched against them; the French from the north took part, primarily in hopes of acquiring land confiscated from the defeated nobility who had protected the Cathars. Thus a horrifying slaughter began, carried out by an army led by one of the most evil creatures of that period, Simon de Montfort, who famously said: Strike them all dead, Cathar or not; God will seek out His own among them. Thus they proceeded. Castles fell until the last great Cathar castle, Montségur, was taken in 1244 and hundreds of Cathars went willingly to their deaths.

The Inquisition arises during this time. We have seen that it is not so easy to understand what was at work there—especially when we hear that the Dominicans were put in charge, and then other orders. On the one hand, I have already spoken about the attempt to repress everything to do with atavism, and to compel people to clear thinking in regard to ecclesiastical matters. On the other hand, the Inquisition called forth some peculiar things we can read about in its records. To inquire means to interview, to question; the Inquisition thus had the strict task of sniffing out everywhere whether or not someone might be a heretic—not merely waiting until a heretic was pointed out.

Thus the horrible fear arose among people more or less connected to the Cathars that an Inquisitor would appear at their house, at a farmhouse or the like, and would subject them to a hearing: Do you believe this or that? People were required to arrive at self-knowledge through a kind of self-interrogation: What do I actually believe? I know the Cathars; I take them to be good people, ascetic and pious. I, myself, am not one of them. But I don't dare say any of this or I, too, might end up on the pyre.

At that time, there was a wave of reflection concerning what could and could not be said aloud, and there were whole handbooks for the Inquisitors which they had to follow exactly: 'Do you believe in the Church?' The person being questioned answers: 'I believe what you believe.'—'No, I asked you if you believe in the Church.'—'Yes, I believe in the Church and in everything the good people say.'—'Ah, the good people (they are the Cathar teachers)!' This was the way that the person was pressured, sentence by sentence, until he no longer knew which way to turn; and then, in fear, he pointed the finger at others.

This is, of course, a dark chapter in the history of mankind, but one that makes extraordinarily clear how a shift occurred away from the old naivety. The old heretics were still naive and simply said what they believed; they were not immediately burned. Now a turn inwards occurred that sought the inner light as well as this inner thought: I am now something inwardly that I dare not reveal outwardly. For many secretly thought: 'I actually believe that in the end it remains a wafer and wine and is in no way flesh and blood. But I am careful about not saying so.' A very strong inner space of self-observation, of self-control, began to develop.

Black Magic

Something also existed that must be mentioned whenever we talk about this period. There was another, quite hidden stream, a very evil stream that was, at the very least, extraordinarily problematic in human history. Here we must go far back in time to what is referred to as old Atlantis. There were Mystery centres then, arranged according to the planets—thus Sun Mysteries, Venus Mysteries, Mercury Mysteries, and so forth—as well as a kind of Mystery that was called with good reason the Vulcan Mysteries. A fateful event took place during the middle of the Atlantean period. The situation can hardly be described here; how and why lead to very complicated considerations. In all the Mysteries, Mystery knowledge—and magical powers are always a part of this Mystery knowledge—would only be given to people who, through self-development, through a path of schooling, offered a guarantee that they would only use these powers selflessly, for the general good. The trouble began when Mystery secrets, magic secrets, were given out to people who had not practised this self-cultivation, who were still completely consumed by egoism, and who then misused these magical powers for egotistical purposes. Even initiates fell victim to this tendency, and a number of Mysteries were contaminated by it, but not the Sun Mysteries. This whole series of events marks the birth of black magic.

Black magic is the misuse of spiritual forces for the benefit of lower egoism. This is how we find it portrayed in *Occult Science, An Outline*.[7] As Atlantis was coming to an end, there were good Mysteries that remained connected with the Sun Mysteries; and there were corrupt Mysteries of various kinds—satanic, black magic, demonic, devilish Mysteries—that also continued. And, like the other Mysteries, these, too, streamed across the turning point in time into post-Christian lands, into Europe. Here we find a whole different history—for good reason, it is always handled with care lest it become sensationalized and thus, for the most part, wrong. We find a whole series of streams. The old conjuring of demons continues. Heathen practices of all kinds are found at every possible level—including genuine magic, including the genuine conjuring of demons. That was the least harmful. There is a large ten-volume set by the Swiss author Stäubli called the *Handwörterbuch des deutschen Aberglaubens* [Concise dictionary of German superstition].[8] What you find in its pages is about nothing but magic. If it is said that a person should not do something on the thirteenth of the month, or that someone should not walk under a ladder, or this or that, these are all small kinds of magic, small magic elements that persisted.

A second level was more serious, the level of genuine black magicians, the real witches—both men and women. We will look again at witches towards the end of our considerations, because the witch trials, the witch laws, only begin during the time of Faust and Luther, not in the early Middle Ages or in the High Middle Ages we are discussing here. But everywhere there were people who practised magic with an intent to do harm, in the Islamic world, the Jewish world; the so-called Christian world—it surfaced everywhere in this cultural sphere.

Then there was the worst form, the genuine satanic and devil-worshipping cults. These also existed during this time. In a lecture about black magic and white magic, Rudolf Steiner cites as an example the famous Gilles de Rais, the so-called Bluebeard. There is plenty known about him from trial documents. Rudolf Steiner explains that Gilles de Rais murdered more than eight hundred children in order to acquire powerful occult forces. He had a castle in the region around Nantes, west of Paris, at the mouth of the Loire. At the time, France had been devastated by the war between the English and French. There were many children, beggar children, poor children, wandering throughout the region; he lured them to his castle and slaughtered them by utterly indescribable, bestial means. Rudolf Steiner says that the black magician has to learn to cut into living flesh in order to gain occult forces.

This was finally uncovered, and he was arrested and executed. Most of the trial documents are published. I do not want to develop a history of black magic here, but I cite him as an example. Parallel to reasonable, justified heresy there were streams to which not only the Church but, in all likelihood, all sensible people took exception.

Precursors of the Reformation

A final step leads us to the stream of the Tertiaries. By Tertiaries we understand the following. The great orders—the Franciscans, the Dominicans—had their male communities which make up the first order; then there is a second order comprised of women, the Franciscan and Dominican nuns; then there is a third order, hence the designation Tertiaries. These were lay societies connected with the order. They participate in the ascetic life as much as possible but remain active in the outside world through their professions. Among them are many women, the so-called Béguines. It is interesting that they were not received into the crowded sisterhoods in the cloisters, but this is also a part of their signature. The cloisters were full to overflowing with women; and there were always lines of women waiting outside their doors as well. So these women join with one another in the so-called Béguinages, live communally, more or less taken care of by a local priest. Gradually, heresy creeps into this movement. It was a quite specific heresy that arises during the last period under consideration here, a heresy connected to the fourteenth-century Englishman John Wycliff. For the first time in a cogent, consistent way, this John Wycliff calls for a national reform movement against the pope. That was the first thing. The second is that John Wycliff asserts that Holy Scripture is the sole measure for all ecclesiastical doctrine and institutions—here we stand at the eve of the Reformation. He attempted to reform the Church and was declared a heretic for this, but he was not persecuted and died in peace. However, even in England his followers were persecuted by the still-powerful bishops, and many executions took place.

Why was there such a poisonous atmosphere, such fierceness? This whole stream of the Béguines and the Lollards—the followers of John Wycliff—was carried by a stream that comes from an older time, a stream that Virginia Sease has discussed, the Irish-Celtic Mysteries. Those Mysteries were, of course, carried over into Christianity, and during the early centuries there was a quite spiritual Irish-Scottish-Celtic Christianity completely independent of Rome—not at all opposed to Rome, but completely sovereign and spiritual.

There was a monk by the name of Winfried in these monasteries of Irish–Celtic Christianity who learned everything there was to know about the spiritual Mystery secrets of the Culdean Church, as it was also called. He then went to Rome and betrayed everything to the pope. He received a new name—Boniface—and the pope showered him with titles. He was named the General Vicar of all Germania; he then founded the cloister at Fulda, the monastery that has been, as a result, the seat of the conference of Catholic bishops since the nineteenth century. Rudolf Steiner says that it was through this betrayal that the Catholic Church acquired power over the old, spiritual Christianity.

There were, of course, other streams throughout the centuries that now flowed into what lived around John Wycliff, flowed into the Lollards, and continued in a figure I have already named, Jan Hus. He was a Bohemian preacher, rector of a university, a recognized scholar; he actually continued what Wycliff intended. Once again, the discussion concerned scripture; that was the substance of the quotation at the very beginning of our discussions where he speaks about the truth and nothing but the truth as found in Holy Scripture. I showed how he was lured by a false promise to Rome where he was subjected to weeks-long hearings. He did not recant and was burned at the stake; the founding of the Hussite movement came as a consequence. The Hussite movement in Bohemia has been decried because it fought against everything. At the

time, people did not have such tender feelings; when a Catholic monastery was stormed, it was also burned to the ground. This continued in
the somewhat milder stream of fraternal communities, the Bohemian
Brothers. And with this we find ourselves on the eve of the Reformation,
that turning point around 1500 that closed the Middle Ages and began a
new era. We will look at this period in our final discussions. But first we
will look at the wonderful phenomena connected with the names of
Joachim of Fiore and Dante.

Joachim of Fiore, the Realm of the Holy Spirit, and the Cathar Question

Virginia Sease

I would like to begin by referring once again to the goddess Natura. During my earlier comments about Francis of Assisi, and later about the Seven Liberal Arts and the goddess Natura, I made a parenthetical remark I would like to return to now. Joachim of Fiore lived at approximately the same time as Alanus ab Insulis. He died in 1202; Alanus died in 1203. For us, what is most interesting about Joachim of Fiore is that Rudolf Steiner often speaks about him. It cannot be said that he actually taught in the School of Chartres because, geographically speaking, he lived in Italy. And yet Rudolf Steiner included him in the School of Chartres. This, as well as the fact that he entered into the spiritual world around the same time as Alanus ab Insulis, is significant. We will recall that the School of Chartres in that configuration came to an end with the departure of Alanus ab Insulis.

Rudolf Steiner makes a quite significant observation about Joachim and the others—Bernardus Silvestris, Alanus, and so forth—when he says they had to draw attention to the other, night side of the goddess Natura. Rudolf Steiner leads us back to the relationship of the goddess Natura to the goddess Proserpina which, in turn, leads us to the Greek Mysteries. Through these remarks we can see how Rudolf Steiner viewed these individualities and why we must turn back to them in relation to this other side of the goddess Natura. For example, Bernardus Silvestris, Bernardus of Chartres, Alanus ab Insulis who, in this medieval '. . . period still . . . went among other people with the character of an initiate, with the character of a person who knows much about the secrets of existence, like that great Joachim de Fiore who was also initiated in the medieval sense.'[1] Through the life of Joachim of Fiore , we will see what it means to be initiated in the medieval sense.

The Karmic Background

Rudolf Steiner goes on to describe how these people might have been able to speak with one another; as a result, the karmic backgrounds begin to come to light. We have heard about young and old souls—about old souls with many incarnations, and young souls with fewer incarnations. The individualities we are considering here offer us insight into what it means that a person can have many incarnations and that someone had undergone various initiation processes in the past. Rudolf Steiner places us in that atmosphere so that we are really able to understand the source of Joachim of Fiore's creative activity.

It should probably be mentioned here that Rudolf Steiner is speaking to an audience in England; it lends a slight nuance to his tone. He describes a conversation about the goddess Natura that might have taken place at the time of the School of Chartres.

> Then Alanus ab Insulis, once he had warmed to the soul conversation, would have clapped someone on the shoulder and said: Oh, if only we still had the sleep state of the ancients, then we could come to know the other side, the hidden side of the goddess Natura. But we sleep unconsciously precisely where the ancients revealed the other side of nature. If we were able to sleep in they way they did, to sleep clair-voyantly like the ancients, then we would know the goddess Natura.— Speaking this way, Alanus ab Insulis would have clapped someone on the shoulder.

Sleeping was already experienced as unconscious during the Middle Ages. But, based on an earlier state of initiation, people like Alanus and Joachim could at least understand that something was missing from their time. And then Rudolf Steiner depicts how Joachim of Fiore would have spoken:

> Yes, given our sleep, which is poor in content and completely dims consciousness, it is difficult for us to come to know the other side of Natura, the great goddess, who creates and weaves in all that creates and weaves. The ancients knew both sides of her ... They used another word [for the goddess Natura]. They used the word 'Proserpina'. That is the truth.[2]

Another image was also in their consciousness—that the goddess Natura spends half her time in the upper world, in the world of waking consciousness, and the other half in the underworld. In the Greek tradition, there is an upper world—day-summer consciousness—and the underworld—for the other half of the year corresponding to the state of unconsciousness.

What we find described here was like a retrospective, a looking backwards, for Alanus, for Joachim, for Bernardus Silvestris, for Bernardus of Chartres, and for others—back to a Greek initiation, back to other initiations that took place in that period.

The Mysteries of Ephesus

This leads us to the Mysteries at Ephesus. Rudolf Steiner describes an image, an imagination, from the Akashic Record, an image from the cosmic memory that he himself had found. Through this Akasha imagination we come closer to the connections, the relationships, the circumstances that had a decisive effect on these people in the Middle Ages. It is a substantive image if we also take into consideration that these people had other experiences in the early Mysteries. Rudolf Steiner describes this image as follows. There is a twilight mood and the teacher speaks to the pupil—it is a Mystery conversation between teacher and pupil:

> Observe the majesty, the greatness, but also the burgeoning, the budding of life above and below. And then observe yourself. Consider how a complete cosmos lives and weaves in you ... Feel how you yourself are a complete world more mysterious, greater than the universe, even if the space is smaller than the universe you survey from the earth up to the stars ... Then you will have gone out of yourself with your soul-spiritual part ... Then you will live in the radiance of the stars, the exhaling of the earth ... Then you will live in your outer world and will look back at what you are as a world unto yourself.[3]

This, in brief, is the requisite circumstance for these people around the Mysteries of Ephesus when they had these nature experiences—that what they experienced as small and limited within themselves was actually only a reflection of what lives outside in the cosmos. This was the training, the education, they received in these old Mysteries: to experience themselves, but also to experience the concordance between their own soul, their own essence, and the great world of nature that lived outside.

When we immerse ourselves in the deeper background of the period in which Joachim of Fiore lived, we see the foundations of his experiences in the Middle Ages. We can say the same about Alanus and his *Complaint of Nature* and *Anticlaudianus* in connection with a new image of the human being. Both men are great spirits—Alanus ab Insulis with the School of Chartres, and Joachim of Fiore in Italy.

Joachim of Fiore

Let us turn now to the biography of Joachim of Fiore. He was born in 1135 in Calabria, Italy. For the first 30 or 32 years of his life, he lived what was a normal, secular life for that time. Then he made a pilgrimage to the Holy Land. It is quite significant how many people from all walks of life took it upon themselves to make such pilgrimages. There were troubadours among them who also made pilgrimages, as did Joachim of Fiore. I am referring here to the period of the troubadours, especially in the south of France.

There is a tradition that Joachim of Fiore had a vision on Mount Tabor. Later he had two other important visions. This vision on Mount Tabor—where, according to tradition, he apparently had an experience of the greatness of the Father God—is not confirmed by him. I mention it only so that we have an accurate picture. What is confirmed is that he returned and began a life as a wandering preacher. We have also heard about other wandering preachers, how they simply went around the countryside and began speaking to people, and how people streamed towards them. This was also the case with Joachim of Fiore. I want to emphasize this because we mostly speak about his written work. But based on this work as a wandering preacher, we see that he could also orate—a wandering preacher without an audience was no preacher.

Then he entered the Cistercian Order and lived for some time south of Rome. He received permission from the pope to write three texts, but not all at once. This demonstrates something quite important—even if a person was truly faithful to the Church and the pope, he was still required to seek permission and have it granted in order just to write thoughts down on paper. Joachim was granted this permission without any difficulty because he was already known and the pope trusted him. The body of this work is comprised of three main volumes: the *Expositio in Apocalypsim*, about the Book of Revelation, the *Psalterium decem chordarum*, and *Liber Concordia Novi ac veteri Testamenti*. The last is a book about the concordances between the Old and New Testaments. I will speak about all three of these.

Joachim's Visions

While working on his volume about the Book of Revelation, Joachim had a genuine vision. He wrote about it himself:

After a year, the festival of Easter approached. Around midnight, awakened from my sleep, something happened to me as I was considering this book [the Book of Revelation] ... as I pondered, [I] suddenly saw something of the abundant wealth of this book and the whole harmony of the Old and New Testaments with a clarity of understanding before my spiritual eye.[4]

It is quite significant how he expresses this. He says he saw it 'before my spiritual eye'. He later describes this as his *Intellectus spiritualis*. *Intellectus spiritualis*: he perceived something as a vision through the inner eye of his own capacity for thought, his thinking, his intellect. This is the first time it is expressed in this form.

It was not a vision with great images in fantastic colours that appear to him outwardly; we recall descriptions of such visions—for example, those from Alanus as he described Natura, her clothing, and so forth. This was not the case with Joachim of Fiore; his was a vision in his innermost being and for his spiritual eye. In German we would say *das Geistesauge* [literally 'eye of the spirit']. In English this would be called 'the mind's eye'. Then he continued work on his writing. About a year later, around Whitsun, he had the sense he could go no further. As he describes it, he goes into the church in order to pray before the holy altar:

And then a doubt about my faith in the triune God came over me. As this happened, I prayed fervently. I was very fearful and called to the Holy Spirit, whose festival day it was, to descend and show me the most holy secret of the Trinity ... I repeated it and began to sing psalms in order to fulfil the number that had been my intention. In this moment, the image of the ten-stringed psaltery appeared before my spirit. The secret of the Trinity appeared so brilliantly and clearly in it that I was immediately carried away to cry out, Where is a god as great as our God?[5]

What he experienced there in this ten-stringed psaltery was not a vision in the sense of a great, detailed picture, but a vision in the form of a symbol. That this vision was a symbol is quite peculiar to him—he later had other visions of symbols in which numbers also played a big part.

The symbol in his vision was a psaltery, an instrument something like a small lyre. It was in the form of a triangle—this one had ten strings—and it was played upright on the musician's lap with a point of the triangle at the top. Joachim leaves out this upper part of the triangle, which does not at all bother him. During the Middle Ages, the psaltery was often played with a plectrum, a small device used to pluck the strings. It was possible for the musician to play it with his fingers, but most of the time it was not played that way. In our book on Compostela there is an illustration of such a psaltery, depicted on the Pórtico de la Gloria.[6]

The point at the top of a properly drawn triangle would disappear in Joachim's imagination of it. It has to be thought away in Joachim's image; it is not in his symbol. Nevertheless, he saw at each corner an image of the Trinity. On top was the Father God, on the left was the Son of God and on the right side was the Holy Spirit. He also describes all three elements of the Trinity together in each corner—three with the Father, three with the Son and three with the Holy Spirit. This was how he imagined it. He was not pedantic in his vision. This was the Trinity. Thus we see the three elements at the top, plus three more makes six, plus three more is nine— and the unity of them all in the middle makes ten. This is my explanation; I have not been able to discover another explanation for why a ten-stringed psaltery would be so significant for him in this vision related to the Trinity. All ten strings together make up this musical instrument.

For Joachim, what he described as the *Intellectus spiritualis* was something derived from the Christ. His spiritual eye, his *Intellectus spiritualis*, had as its source the Christ Himself. This is a fundamental thought for Joachim, and very significant in understanding his other thoughts. It should perhaps be said that he was highly regarded during his lifetime. He was truly seen as a leading, well-known individual. He knew the popes, and had even had a conversation with Richard the Lionheart in which he allegedly told Richard when the Antichrist would appear. This is part of a legend about Richard the Lionheart.

Because Joachim of Fiore was known and so highly regarded, after his death many texts appeared that were attributed to him, but they cannot be authenticated. There were a number of people who wrote their own works based on Joachim's ideas, thus assuring that their work would enjoy wider circulation. What we have in the way of verified writings from Joachim of Fiore are the three cited here as well as several smaller works that are quite important although they are not among his three principal texts.

Joachim's Signs and Symbols

We find that there are two pillars on which Joachim's writings rest. We began with the visions he had—not a pillar in themselves, but the background for a pillar. He never allowed himself to be called a prophet. He said: No, that is not correct. I am no prophet, also no visionary.

Instead, he said God had given him a gift in the form of signs and symbols which he then had to decipher. Here I would like to recommend a new work by Delno West and Sandra Zimdars-Swartz about Joachim's system of philosophical thought. It is an interesting volume based on an extensive study of these symbols.[7]

If we look at such a symbol, it is, of course, much more complicated than what I have described here. On every page of Joachim's work we find categories of virtues, of the realms and sub-realms of nature, of the hierarchies. These pages are teeming with names and categories; they are quite lively.

The first pillar of Joachim's activity is the ongoing study of history. That a study of history can form a path of knowledge to God is completely new with him. This first pillar takes on an additional meaning if we consider that several hundred years later and continuing into our own time, the first level of the Rosicrucian path begins with study—the thorough study of history is a path of knowledge leading to God. The second pillar is the following. Joachim of Fiore believed that his intellect, his own *Intellectus spiritualis*, could lift the veil to reveal the Holy Scripture. Study, Joachim asserted, is objective; his own intellect as a tool for understanding the Bible is more subjective. It was from both these perspectives—objective, study; subjective, his own intellect—that he wrote his great works.

Here we also experience what might be an echo of the Ephesian Mysteries in relation to the two sides of nature. If a person has experienced something of the Mysteries in one incarnation—for example, the Ephesian Mysteries in pre-Christian times—it has a continuing effect. There follows a long journey through the spiritual world in which all the person's experience is deepened during his passage through the planetary spheres—we have already spoken about the Mars sphere. It is in the spiritual world where, one might say, something is extracted that is especially valuable; it then presents itself in the next incarnation as the result of experiences in the Mysteries, in the schooling. A next incarnation occurs for these people about whom we have spoken and about whom Rudolf Steiner says that they were initiates in the Middle Ages. It is a different kind Mystery now. In Ephesus, perhaps, they had met one another at dusk in the forest and so on; there had also been a temple. But what they had been able to research as the two sides of nature returns during the Middle Ages in another form. It returns now, especially for Joachim of Fiore, in the form of thoughts. He is such an important figure for us because his visions take the form of thoughts. We find understanding his thoughts to be difficult; they are very complicated. But we can experience how he groped his way towards a formulation of all of this for the intellect, for the power of thought. Only later does the great leap to Thomas Aquinas occur, a leap in which the world of thinking really makes its mark.

Joachim's Picture of History

Joachim divides history into three epochs, into three realms; each epoch is associated with a part of the Trinity. In these three epochs are many sub-epochs, many sub-chapters. Not only is the number three important but also the numbers five, seven and twelve. The symbolism of number plays an important role in the early Christian period, not just with Joachim of Fiore but with others as well. People had the impression they had access to a deeper meaning through numbers; on the one hand, numbers are objective and, on the other hand, they can also be subjective. Both elements are evident in the symbolism of numbers. Three was very important to Joachim; it was the most important number—the number of perfection—because unity was experienced through the triangle. It was a decisive number for Joachim because this unity was experienced through his vision of the triangular psaltery. Also of interest here is the triad, the Trinity. People then did not allow themselves to be put off in any way by the fact that the triune had been declared an illegitimate belief in 869. The trichotomy was no longer valid; the spirit was only an aspect of the soul, but this did not disturb them in the least.

We know from his *City of God* that Augustine also spoke of three epochs, but he divided them differently. Here we again find a leap—we have described others—from Augustine to the medieval world of thought. Joachim describes his first epoch as the period from Adam to Moses, and refers to it as 'before the law'. Then he describes—in what is naturally a very long description—a second epoch from Moses to Christ, 'under the law'. And then there is a third epoch, from Christ to the Judgment Day, 'under the Testament'. This three-part unity is described more fully by Joachim of Fiore and is connected to each personage of the Trinity.

In the first epoch the Father God is active and works in a mysterious way through the prophets and the patriarchs. The Father God is not only creative in the moment of creation, but continues always to be creative. This is quite significant. A thought about evolution begins with Joachim of Fiore which includes the idea that the Creation is not complete—that Adam and Eve, the Fall of Man, the animals and the world come into being, but then God cannot, as it were, rest. With

Joachim there is an on-going process of evolution, of what might be called metamorphosis.

The second epoch bears the signature of the Christ; this is something in process. With Joachim, the Christ is never described as having been revealed, is never in the past; the Christ is continually being revealed until the end of the world. This represents a meaningful idea that is taken up in a completely different form centuries later. If we consider the ideas about history presented by Gotthold Ephraim Lessing, the eighteenth-century German man of letters, we can discover in them a continuing develop-ment of the human race, the education of the human race.

The third epoch is the period of the Holy Spirit, which Joachim says would begin after 1260. Joachim used his numerology to arrive at the year 1260 as the beginning of the period of the Holy Spirit. Because a date is specified, this year takes on enormous importance; people could do something with that. Joachim of Fiore is less specific about what the period of the Holy Spirit entails. He simply said it continues. His idea was that human beings are not able to guess how God will continue to form history. However, what is certain is that it will be an epoch during which the Holy Spirit will act decisively. According to Joachim of Fiore, in time the Holy Spirit will bring about enormous changes, especially in the structure of the Church and everything connected with the Church.

Naturally, the Church was central in Joachim's life. As an abbot, he was part of the Church; it was never his intention not to be a part of the Church. We must be clear about this in regard to Joachim of Fiore and with Francis of Assisi as well. He was part of this Church; it was his life, his biography. It provided the arena for his activity as an initiate in the Middle Ages. But he saw that changes would enter into it during the epoch of the Holy Spirit. Instead of such a formal Church with a pope, a hierarchy, and so forth, it would be a place of love, of joy, of contemplation. Instead of priests, monks would have leading roles. It was, of course, very threatening to the existing structure to say that the monks—called *Viri spirituales*, devout men—would have a leading role instead of the priests. Monks occupied a completely different place within the Church hierarchy.

Joachim of Fiore found a basis for his view in the Epistles of Paul, particularly when Paul writes to the Corinthians: 'As the body is a unity and yet has many members, and as all the members of the body create the one body despite their multitude, so is the Being of Christ.'[8] Joachim of Fiore takes up this idea—that all the members create the body of Christ—and goes one step further. The Church asserted: The Church is indeed the body of Christ, and its parts—the people who are in the Church—contribute to the reality of the body of Christ on the earth, which is the

Church itself. This idea, at least in the eschatological sense, began to wane a bit with Joachim of Fiore. For him, it was no longer the Church, but humanity—as it would then live in the epoch of the Holy Spirit—that would experience the Holy Spirit in a new way, for example, as it had been experienced at Whitsun.

He structured these three epochs according to their qualities and, although they are only presented in his writings as a list of words, he compared them as qualities. When we understand this, we see that they are similar to the Aristotelian categories in that they are not just empty concepts. These rubrics are filled with great substance. People of that time who were able to enter into his writings—they appeared as actual publications only in the sixteenth century, but were in circulation as handwritten copies earlier—saw that these rubrics for the three categories were like living beings. They became a gateway through which a study of history could be undertaken—which is characteristic of Joachim of Fiore. Today he is acknowledged widely as the first person to describe a method of studying history. This is why he is so recognized in scholarship; he was the one who discovered a historiographic method. This method required that these qualities, these attributes in the three epochs, be recognized. I will quote here from his description, and then I will offer several examples of these qualities from the first, second and third epochs. The following comes from his book on the concordance between the Old and the New Testaments.

> The first epoch was the one during which we were under the law; the second was when we lived in grace; the third, when we were able to rest in the expectation of a still fuller grace ... The first epoch was in knowledge; the second, in the authority of wisdom; the third in the perfection of understanding ... The first in the chains of slavery; the second in service to the Son; the third in freedom ... The first in fear; the second in faith; the third in love.[9]

This—the third epoch in the future, love between human beings—is, of course, very much in agreement with spiritual science. There are many detailed descriptions, more than the few I quoted here. As I indicated, Joachim brings a new picture of Christ. This image of Christ is connected with an inclination to view history as an evolutionary process, as a metamorphosis—to see that the Christ as God is always working actively for humanity; that His activity did not stop with His death on Golgotha and His resurrection but, instead, He remains connected with humanity and active. After Joachim's death in 1202, his writings became increasingly known and thus his view in regard to the third epoch and the status of priests in relation to the monks. In 1215, the Church condemned his doctrine of the Trinity. This had no apparent effect.

Bonaventure

We now take one step further to St Bonaventure. We have mentioned how Francis of Assisi's whole Order fell into a state of crisis following his death. The two factions drifted apart. The one group is the Spirituals, the ascetic ones who want to pursue poverty in every aspect of life. The others, the Conventuals, saw: If we want to build something up—centres of learning and so forth—we need to have a little property.

Bonaventure himself believed that the epoch of the spirit—the epoch that had been announced by Joachim as beginning in 1260—had begun with the person of Francis of Assisi. Bonaventure adopted and circulated this idea. Francis of Assisi is the beginning, the leader, the guide of this third epoch. Bonaventure even took this a step further, saying that—spiritually speaking—Francis of Assisi was actually the Christ on earth for the second time. The idea of Christ for a second time is not so wrong when we consider that a copy of the sentient soul of the Christ was at work in Francis of Assisi. Bonaventure and many others sensed something in Francis of Assisi even after he had died.

Petrus Johannis Olivi

Next in our considerations is someone who was active in the Spirituals movement and who, in time, became highly regarded. His name was Petrus Johannis Olivi and he was perhaps the best known of the Spirituals. Petrus Johannis Olivi lived from 1248 until 1298; he came from the Languedoc in southern France. There is a particular language there which gives rise to the name of the region, *Languedoc, Langue d'Oc* [language of Occitania]. He entered the Franciscan Order and studied at the University of Paris where he was taken very seriously as a Franciscan scholastic. He reviewed all of the works of Joachim of Fiore quite thoroughly, and then developed his own teaching based on them. He also saw Francis of Assisi as Christ for the second time—even more so than Bonaventure. He experienced the Church as the 'Whore Babylon' that consumed every-thing there was in way of spirituality—and he actually said that this was the case. The impression was that he was fairly ruthless. In spite of everything he said against the Church, he remained loyal to it—not out of fear, but based instead on conviction. He said: The Church still has many people who live a Christian life. He never split from the Church, but remained completely loyal to it.

After his death, an Olivi cult developed whose members revered him and made pilgrimages to his grave. The Church took note of this and was not particularly happy about it. As a result, 19 years after Olivi's death, Pope John made arrangements to have his body exhumed—taken from his grave—and the grave itself destroyed. No sign was to remain of where the grave had been. His writings were not burned, but if it was discovered that someone had read them, that person immediately became suspect in the eyes of the Church. We see how this was an attempt to eliminate them root and branch.

The Spirituals, however, were in despair about these actions of the Church because they held the conviction that their poverty had its beginnings with Christ. This created a theological problem at the time. The genealogy of the Franciscans did not go back to the beginnings of Christianity; they could not trace the history of the Order back to Paul or to Peter. This remained an ecclesiastical problem for them.

The Languedoc, the area where Olivi lived in the south of France, can be identified as a confluence for many spiritual streams. We find here the followers of Olivi as well as the Béguines and the Cathars. The troubadours also wander through here. They were virtually untouched by all of this; they were true artists, singing at royal courts. They did come into contact with the Cathars; some among them were Cathar sympathizers but did not declare it openly because that was not their task. They traversed the countryside—particularly in the area around Narbonne—so that we see how all of this flows together. There were all classes of people in this area. The followers of Olivi always insisted they were not heretics. They were also not Cathars, and did not want to hear anything about the Cathars. This was not for them; they were Franciscans.

We will see shortly how these streams that began with Joachim of Fiore and Francis of Assisi were formative, active in relation to the New World. It is for this reason that the main ideas of Joachim of Fiore are so important; they have a further effect, a further influence, in much wider circles than just Europe.

Neither Escape from the World nor the Ideal of Poverty are Victorious

To close these remarks, I would like to mention a way we might think about these medicant orders. The *Fraticelli*—the 'little brothers'—also belong to this, although we have hardly discussed them; the Tertiaries we did mention, and many other groups either on the side of poverty in these orders or on the side of the heretics—the Cathars, the Waldensians, and so on. The Church persecuted them, which is of course quite cruel, and we have to ask ourselves: Why? What was that about?

One perceived purpose, as Manfred Schmidt-Brabant explained, was to save their souls: It is better to burn on earth than eternally in hell. The Church, in part, had a clean conscience. Its position was that it had saved these souls from the pain of hell. That is open to interpretation. The other thing—this is only my opinion—is that all this had to have had an effect on the course of history, but one that took place below the level of consciousness. This is not said in order to excuse this cruelty, nor to say that a tyrant like Simon de Monfort who sent many, many Cathars to the pyre, might be innocent. Certainly not. But neither those who revered poverty nor those who wanted nothing to do with the physical world because it was synonymous with evil, the Cathars, the Waldensians, and so on, would have been otherwise able to further a task for Europe—not the only task for Europe, but it was a significant one, namely, to transform nature into beauty, to transform nature in such a way that human souls, human spirits could be further refined through beauty.

I have spoken about King Arthur and how these knights—with their Sun Mystery as a background—came over to Europe from England, Ireland, and fought the wild elemental beings and the unformed, wild astral bodies, the human astrality that prevailed then. That was their task and also Europe's. This is evident from the early Middle Ages. The task is constantly being accomplished through the arts. When visiting Chartres, for example, you can see these wonderful sculptures, the windows, the colours of the windows. Whether in the windows, sculpture or architecture, there was a mastery and transformation of nature by hundreds and thousands of people so that nature came to mean something for human beings. These were alchemical processes. If we think of the colour blue, for example, not only the substance but what was fed into this substance as spiritual power appears in the colour blue.

This could be explored in many, many realms. In recalling the evolution of music that came from Spain with polyphony and was developed in the School of Notre Dame de Paris, we think of two great figures—Leoninus and his colleague Perotinus—and how they further elevated this polyphony. Polyphony is the art of counterpoint where the various voices sound together. Why was this important? It contributed to the development of the consciousness soul; a person had to be able to maintain his own voice in the midst of choral song in order for the whole to be successful. This was a secret connected to the development of polyphony, a great artistic development in the Middle Ages that would not have occurred if the upper hand had been won by poverty or by the denial of the world because of its evil character. This is something to consider when we think of this period and the many cruelties connected with it.

Lecture 10

Templar Secrets in Dante's *Divine Comedy*— Spiritual Alchemy and the Social Formative Power of Gothic Architecture

Manfred Schmidt-Brabant

We now want to look at the continuing effect of the Middle Ages—direct or indirect—in our time. Among other things, there is Dante's powerful poetic work *The Divine Comedy*—a title coined only later by Boccaccio. It is a powerful epic poem comprised of three times 33 cantos, three canticles each with 33 long cantos.

Rudolf Steiner spoke many times about Dante. There are well over 60 places in his works where he spoke in the most appreciative way about Dante himself and about this poetic work. There is one place in particular which I would now like to explore. It is where Rudolf Steiner looks at the figure of Beatrice in the third canticle of the *Divine Comedy* and says that she is none other that the Sophia of the Templars.[1] An understanding of the *Divine Comedy* is impossible without an understanding of this Templar background.

The External History of the Templars

For this reason, we have to look a bit at what is connected historically with this Templar Order. We begin with the First Crusade, which we have considered already. In 1099 Jerusalem is taken, the Christian kingdoms of Palestine and Jerusalem are created, and kings are crowned there. Gottfried of Bouillon refused to be king in the place where Jesus Christ had worked, so another Frankish nobleman, Baldwin, becomes king. Following his sudden death, a relative of his takes the throne, Baldwin II.

In 1118, a good ten years after the conquest, seven Frankish knights arrive. Many historians say that there were nine knights, but this remains an open question. These knights are of noble lineage, from prominent noble families. They explain to the king that they want to establish a knightly order in Jerusalem to protect the pilgrims, and receive from Baldwin II lodgings near what had once been the Temple of Solomon. Very soon they come to call themselves the 'Poor Brothers of Christ and the Temple of Solomon', which is always shortened to the 'Templars'. Their undertaking does not last long at all; ten years later they return to France. In 1128, a national Council of the French Church takes place in Troyes, east of Paris; everyone with a rank or title in France takes part. At this council, the Templar Order is ceremoniously installed and receives its rule from Bernard of Clairvaux who has a leading role in the Council. The Templars continued to revere him as their spiritual leader throughout the almost two hundred years of their existence. The Order spread very quickly, astonishingly so. Castles are built throughout all of Europe and, of course, in Palestine; the Order becomes powerful in possessions and money.

Then comes the great stroke of fate. Almost two hundred years later, in 1307, the French king Philip IV, the so-called Fair, had all the Templars arrested overnight in what amounted to a secret police action—organized in a very efficient and almost modern way. It remains a riddle why they did not defend themselves. Whether it was because their castles were not fortified enough or for whatever reason, it matters little. The Templars in France were arrested. A long trial begins. The Templars stand accused of heresy, and a Council is convened in Vienne to investigate the charges; however, the Council is actually unable to uncover any wrongdoing. But then there is Pope Clement. Even Rudolf Steiner who usually expresses things quite politely calls him a 'creature'.[2] Pope Clement is dependent on Philip the Fair; this was the time of the so-called exile of Avignon, and the popes did not rule in Rome. At the urging of and under pressure from Philip, Clement V dissolves the Order. This was in 1312. The Templars are interrogated further and found guilty of heresy. In 1314, the Grand Master of the Templars, Jacques de Molay, and his friend Gottfried of Normandy are burned on the Île de la Cité in Paris. The biography of the Templars comes to an end, but there are successor organizations up to the time of Goethe. This is as far as we will go into the outer circumstances. Countless descriptions of this Templar history exist.

The Esoteric History

Less known is the internal, esoteric history of the Templar Order. Rudolf Steiner draws attention to the fact that these orders were always prepared and accompanied by great initiates. Here we find ourselves in the period around the turning point in time, shortly after the life of Christ Jesus; we come to Mark the Evangelist who had served for a while as the Bishop of Alexandria. About 15 or 20 years ago, a letter from the second century was found in a monastery on the Sinai in which someone writes: There is, however, actually a second, secret Gospel of Mark. The letter cites passages from it. The American historian who found it allowed it to be examined. For years his colleagues gave expert opinions about it, tested it and, in the end, concluded that it is genuine. Some passages from the secret Gospel of Mark are also cited in this letter. They do not offer any new facts—but they shed a special, deeper light on known ones like the awakening of Lazarus and on other matters. The letter also says that a copy is in the hands of a Gnostic sect, the Carpocratians.

Here we are looking at evidence that a Christian Gnosis develops in Alexandria—a strange place, indeed. This is the famous Alexandrine cathechistic school—we would call it a school of Christian esotericism. Great figures emerge from this school, like Clement of Alexandria, whom we have mentioned, and the even more well-known Origen, whom we have also mentioned. They are both great Christian Gnostics.

What is actually behind this? Based on the Akashic Record, and in agreement with ancient esoteric traditions, Rudolf Steiner describes that Mark, the Evangelist who wrote a cosmic Gospel, worked in Alexandria with a high-ranking priest in the Isis Mysteries, Ormuz. The two of them, Mark and Ormuz, transformed the old Isis cult into a Christian cult. Both, says Rudolf Steiner, were disciples of the risen Christ.[3] The cult created by these two men in Alexandria as the root of the Christian-esoteric school there spread during the next centuries through the West along various paths. Above all, they enter the Templar Order.

The Templar Order had secret esoteric cults—so esoteric that Rudolf Steiner says something very interesting about them: 'Their sacramental rites, based on opposition to Roman secularization, were so hostile to the Church that today it is still not appropriate to speak about them publicly.'[4] Anyone who has concerned himself even a bit with the Templar churches knows that their structure, their architecture, their construction all point to the fact that a quite special cult must have been celebrated there. Templar churches always consist of a round church attached to a long house containing the altar. It was clear that something like two cults must have taken place there, one in the round church, esoterically intimate— and another at the altar, publicly. Little is preserved of this; the Church destroyed practically everything. But in Spain, at the edge of Segovia, there is a Templar church, Vera Cruz that is completely preserved in the ritual sense. I would like to put to you a riddle known to everyone who is concerned with these questions. The usual round church is there, to which has been added a long house. The altar is there. Then, within this round church there is a second round church with a storey above it. Stairs lead to this storey, two sets of steps—on the left and the right—which lead to a second altar. Near this second altar is an opening so that a person standing there can look down at the other altar below. We may see in such a detail that a very complicated, inner, esoteric cult had been celebrated there by these Templars.

What then was the purpose of these Templars. To what end were they prepared and accompanied by initiates? They were to bring about a new European socio-political order in a form through which the individual could be free and independent of both the emperor and the pope. In modern terms, we would say the religious and political autonomy of the individual was to be established by means of the socio-political structure. The emperor or the pope would not be done away with, but the structure of the empire and the structure of the Church would be changed in such a way that each person would be able to develop his autonomy within these structures. This purpose was described and brought to expression in the Templar rituals and esotericism through great imaginative pictures. Rudolf Steiner expresses it this way: They were to raise Europe to another level and carry it forward.

The Templar Order, which of course could not speak openly about such goals, had allies within society, people who stood in life, pursued their profession, but who were initiated into the esoteric purposes and often even the rituals and the esotericism of the Order. These were the so-called Affiliates. We will now turn our attention to two such Affiliates.

Brunetto Latini

The first of these was Brunetto Latini. He was born in Florence in 1220 and died in 1294. During his lifetime, he was thrust into the battles between the so-called feudal factions there. Individual dynasties and families were either followers of the pope, and thus Guelphs, or were followers of the emperor, and thus Ghibellines. This does not mean that one was more pious than the other; the decision to stand with the pope or the emperor was based on political expediency. At the same time, during this whole period and in this whole context, there was general internal agitation against the existing order. Dora Baker writes in her edition of *Il Tesoretto*, to which I will return in a moment: 'Florence was teeming with heretics. In Tuscany, there were numerous secret societies.'[5] Brunetto Latini studied jurisprudence in Bologna, then returned to Florence where he made a career based on his studies and his family background.

In 1260, he was sent to Spain as an envoy to Alphons X of Castile—

whom the pope had intended to be the next Roman-German king—in order to provide Alphons with help against the Ghibellines, the imperial faction. It remains uncertain as to how much he accomplished. He returns from this diplomatic mission by way of the Pyrenees; along the way he meets a travelling scholar, a student. They enter into conversation, and he learns that a battle had taken place which the Ghibellines had won. The result is that all of the leading Guelfs, the papal adherents, were driven out of Florence and Brunetto's name is on a list of those banned from the city.

Something now takes place that has been variously described. The shock of this news sends Brunetto into a state of unconsciousness; evidently, he then suffers a sunstroke as well. Brunetto Latini excarnates. The whole thing plays out in the valley of Roncevalles where centuries before Roland, the famous rearguard to Charlemagne, had stood his ground and then fallen in battle after loudly sounding his well-known horn one last time. In Rudolf Steiner's descriptions, Brunetto excarnated and experienced a spontaneous initiation into the being Natura; Brunetto Latini himself describes this later. Rudolf Steiner says that it was as though he had been taken hold of by the still active aura of the School of Chartres,[6] or one might say as though he had been etherically immersed into this aura. And he experiences in every detail the many-sided perception of the goddess Natura and her retinue so often portrayed in the School of Chartres.

Brunetto cannot return to Florence so he lives in exile in Paris, attends the Sorbonne, comes into contact with Albertus Magnus and Thomas Aquinas. He reads the books by the teachers at Chartres, especially Alanus ab Insulis. He begins his great encyclopedia, the so-called *Il Tresor*, becoming the first encyclopedist. He was the first, but later, in the eighteenth century, in the period of the Enlightenment, there are many who play a role in summarizing all of the knowledge of their time encyclopedically in one book. What is most significant is that during this visit in Paris he becomes an Affiliate of the Templars. Their great temple was in Paris, a huge facility and centre of the esoteric life of the Templars; however this contact was established, he becomes an Affiliate and is initiated into the esotericism of the Templars. Then, in 1266, there is another battle, the famous Battle of Benevento; now the Ghibillines are defeated. Brunetto can return to Florence and resume his prior government career.

Brunetto becomes acquainted with the family of Dante. He enters very quickly into the family circle, befriends the young Dante and guides his studies until Dante's 28th or 29th year. Now begins the great and famous passing of knowledge from Brunetto to Dante. Gradually he conveys to the young Dante the entire content of his own initiation knowledge and, as later noted by Rudolf Steiner, he stimulates in Dante the supersensible capacities he already possessed; Dante had a rich supersensible experience, but it had to be set in motion. Dante himself thanks his fatherly friend with verses; it might be said that he addresses Brunetto Latini in the *Divine Comedy* when he writes: 'Because deep in my heart lives your dear, good, fatherly countenance and moves me; you, who in life, hour upon hour, taught me how the human being unfolds his eternal life.'[7] He was not able to be more explicit about this during the time of the Inquisition; it is clear enough that it is not a matter of external studies and teaching, but rather how the human being unfolded his eternal, his spiritual life.

During this time, Brunetto Latini writes a second small book which he calls *Il Tesoretto*, the Small Treasure. In it he describes the initiation experiences he underwent in the valley of Roncevalles, the initiation though the goddess Natura. It seems likely that he also wrote this *Tesoretto* for his young pupil Dante. Above all, he initiates Dante as an Affiliate in the esoteric of the Templars. Dante, like his great teacher Brunetto Latini, becomes an Affiliate and therefore someone who knows Templar esotericism and the Templar rituals.

I would like to mention here another book—an odd volume that arose under odd circumstances. A Cistercian monk lived in Budapest; he was very knowledgeable about history, the history of the Templar Order and Dante's history, and he writes a book about Dante with numerous footnotes and references. The Second World War comes to an end and the Russians occupy Budapest so that this Cistercian monk has to secrete his manuscript on his person, flee to Vienna, and more or less leave behind his entire set of references. He is Robert John—and is also known in connection with other matters. The book appears in 1946 or 1947 in Vienna. What does it contain, written by a Cistercian? The initiation of Dante into the Templar esotericism and a defence of Templar esotericism. Robert John, as a Catholic and a Cistercian monk, says repeatedly: They were not heretics in any sense; they wanted only the best. The book is an extraordinary rarity; it was never republished for good reason but every Dante scholar cites it. Whoever owns it can count himself fortunate; naturally, you cannot get hold of it any longer. This book by Robert John is a quite exact and detailed exposition of what I have said so far, including what follows—which is also known from other sources.

Fideli d'Amore

The Affiliates of the Templars could never meet openly with one another as such, so they camouflaged themselves in various secret associations.

One of these secret associations was the famous *Fideli d'Amore*, the 'faithful of love'. Under cover of various forms of love and love rituals, they communicated about their esotericism. *Amore* in reality means 'a longing for unity with God'; with *Pietà* they meant the *Ecclesia spiritualis*, the spiritual Church. The Loving Ones said: *Morte e Crudelità*—death and cruelty—prepare me for when you turn away. In reality, they were referring here to the Inquisition. Finally, *Beatrice*, the beautiful woman, was always the heavenly Sophia.

They knew the four levels of initiation. (As an aside, anyone who has ever studied the troubadours notices that they bring us into a broad and related field.) The first step of initiation was: The *Adept* shyly approaches the lady, the Sophia; this is called 'study'. The second step, *Postulante*: The lady Sophia greets the Adept; this was an imaginative image. The third step, *Auditor*: The Adept receives from the lady a belt or glove. He hears her words; inspiration is meant. And finally, *Servant*: The Adept is kissed by the lady and unites with her; intuition or unity with God. Thus these forms nurtured in small associations contain everything that Brunetto Latini personally passed on to Dante, as well as all that Dante experienced about the esotericism of the Templars from other sources.

Dante

Dante was born in 1265, attended a Dominican school and then studied in Bologna. Afterwards he held political offices just as Brunetto Latini had. However, yet another battle took place between the two great parties, the so-called black Guelfs and the white Ghibellines. The Guelfs, the papal party, win again, and the Ghibellines, the leading figures in the city, are expelled or are forced to do significant penance. Dante refuses to bend so he was sentenced to death and all of his assets confiscated. He flees and never again sees Florence.

From this time on, he lived as an expatriate in various places. Of course, again and again he finds benefactors, noblemen, with whom he lives in castles and palaces. He is in France where he witnesses the arrest of the Templars in 1307, the burning of Jacques de Molay and his friends on the Île de la Cité. The *Divine Comedy* originates during this period of exile. All of his knowledge about philosophy, theological problems, mythology, flow together. He was a quite highly educated man, and everything he knew about the esotericism and the Mystery knowledge of the Templars flows into it as well. It was not just a matter of his worldly knowledge about these things but, according to Rudolf Steiner, Dante had also seen clairvoyantly what he describes.[8]

The *Divine Comedy* was permeated by Dante's view of how the problems of the time, the opposition of the pope and the emperor, could be solved. This was, of course, the Templar view. It is also completely understandable that he adds the appropriate descriptions when he meets Clement V in hell. Nonetheless, the book is, on the whole, not partisan.

It is for me a happy obligation to a friend to point out the work of one of our anthroposophical members in Hamburg, Dr Georg Hees. He is a lifelong student of Dante who speaks fluent Italian and translated the *Divine Comedy* anew, with a thorough commentary also based on anthroposophical knowledge. There are three volumes with the German text on each page opposite the Italian. It is very well done. There is always a short introduction, then a longer, more extensive introduction, then the whole canto itself, and, in the appendix, a thorough commentary on everything discussed in each canto. These three comprehensive volumes are not inexpensive but I can recommend the edition to anyone who wants to work with the *Divine Comedy*. I own them as well and have found them to be infinitely more useful than many translations. Of course, it is possible to purchase inexpensive paperback editions for less. But those three volumes are truly a work that could occupy an entire vacation's reading.

The Divine Comedy

Now to the external plot of the *Divine Comedy*. The first-person narrator is Dante himself. He reports how, in the middle of his life, he comes to a place about which he must say, 'In the middle of our life, lost in a dark wood, I strayed from the right path.'[9] This formulation appears again and again at the beginning of books of instruction. In Maimonides' *Guide of the Perplexed*, it says: The human being awakens to the path of schooling for the first time in the moment when he notices that he has strayed. People who continue to live in a state of happy ignorance get nowhere; but we then suddenly have to stop short, begin to wonder, and say: Where have I gotten to actually? What is the meaning of my life? Where am I? Am I on the right path? He wants to continue, but three beasts obstruct the path, a lynx, a wolf and a panther. As he does not know what to do, help comes to him from a spirit figure who turns out to be the ancient poet Virgil. Virgil says, 'I will now lead you along the right path.' Virgil leads him through three great cosmic realms in which initiation is reflected in three steps.

The first step is the *Inferno*, hell. Virgil leads him into hell, down through seven levels of hell, ever deeper and deeper until they reach the very bottom of hell. Now it is interesting that all sorts of devils emerge here, howl at Virgil, baring their teeth; he only says, '. . . above where will and power are one.'[10] This is repeated, and we suddenly notice a whole path of initiation steps along which the Dante individuality is being led—which he describes—is something that is directed from the spiritual world. Virgil says: I am sent for this purpose.

Next there is the second great section, the *Purgatorio*, a mountain of purification on which they climb ever higher and higher. While the first step characterizes the manifold steps of self-knowledge pursued in all paths of knowledge, the *Purgatorio* is a reflection of what is always called the catharsis, the purification. The human being now overcomes what he has recognized as sin within himself, lays it aside, purifies himself.

Then comes the third step, *Paradiso*, paradise, which is actually what the human being can experience in the spiritual world; in initiation, it is always called illumination. Now Virgil withdraws, and Beatrice, the divine Sophia, becomes Dante's guide. On the last steps, Bernard of Clairvaux becomes his guide.

As I have said, there are three times 33 cantos. Everyone has discovered—and Rudolf Steiner also mentions this—that the last word in each canticle is always 'stars'. Each of these three great parts ends with the word 'stars'. Again, it is as though something is partially revealed because we speak of the star service of the Templars who had participated in the old Isis cults in an earlier incarnation. Later, in the circles around Pythagoras, many of them had experienced the harmony of the spheres and the relationship of music and mathematics; and even later they experience in their Templar esotericism a star wisdom, a star Mystery appropriate to their time.

When we say that an initiation process is described, we have to add: one that was valid at that time. As Rudolf Steiner says, the *Divine Comedy* is a work that wanted to preserve what was known throughout the millennia about the relationship of the human being to the macrocosmos. It is a testament of a time past.[11]

When we look in detail at what takes place, we must of course be a bit discerning. There is a basic tenor through all three stages: How are the heavenly world and the earthly world related? This is a familiar theme for us. How are the empire and the Church related? What is the relationship between the pope and the emperor?—always expressed as the eagle and the cross, a concept that appears here more than 30 times. Dante himself carries the eagle and the cross on his coat of arms. As an aside, there is a lovely bust of Dante in Vienne on which a row of letters is inscribed, and historians are convinced that the last ones mean 'A Brother of the Templars'.

The *Inferno* is divided into seven levels of sin. Dante moves through them, led by his guide from level to level of self-knowledge, so to speak, ever deeper; and he illustrates these seven levels of sin with every possible historical figure. This is what makes hell and the inferno so vivid. After limbo come the sins of frailty: the first is the level of carnal sin; the second, gluttony; the third, miserliness and waste. Oftentimes, it is really not for the faint of heart to read about how people there revel and are plucked to pieces on glowing iron grills, and so forth. There is nothing that does not exist in this hell.

Then one of the greatest puzzles in Dante scholarship surfaces, one that drives Dante scholars and pupils to want to pull their hair out. In hell—not completely at the bottom, but also not at the very top—he meets Brunetto Latini. The words, '... the ... fatherly countenance ...' and '... you who ... taught me how the human being unfolds his eternal life...'[12] are addressed by Dante to Brunetto Latini. How is it that this beloved teacher—about whom, based on his biography and the external facts, nothing bad is known—is in hell? How does Dante come to place him in hell? There are countless theories about this. One that always surfaces goes as follows. The way Brunetto Latini presents himself and says 'my vice that is shared with many priests and many scholars' suggests that the vice was homosexuality, and that Dante knew Brunetto Latini was a homosexual. Through a kind of esoteric objectivity, he places him in this imaginative world where what was still seen during the Middle Ages as a very serious failing will be atoned.

Then they leave behind the sins of frailty and arrive at indifference towards goodness, which leads to godlessness. These are all those people who could have done good deeds during life, could have helped and so forth, and who did nothing, were too indolent to turn to religion, to spiritual things, to the divine.

Now things become more serious with the appearance of the sins of evil. The fifth level is acts of violence based on anger. Every single canto could be described at length because even the nuances of these acts of violence—or miserliness and waste on the third level—are described. The sixth level is deceit, not yet based on a breach of trust but rather on envy; and then, at the seventh level, deceit, fraud and so forth with a breach of trust, out of arrogance.

As we read this, we can understand how people experienced it as a mirror for self-examination: How does this apply to me? Do I succumb often to carnal lust? To gluttony? To miserliness or waste? Am I too indifferent towards what is good? Am I perhaps hot-tempered and thus inclined towards doing violence? Or something even worse? In the deepest abyss, we find Lucifer, half-frozen in ice. He has three faces and three maws. In each maw a sinner is continually being crushed. One of the sinners is Judas, which is understandable. For the medieval sensibility, Judas is in the deepest level of hell and the devil chews him constantly. But who are the other two? Brutus and Cassius. Brutus murdered Caesar, but he is not considered to be in the same league as Judas. There he is however! Here we can take note of what is at work in this for Dante. There is betrayal at the level of the divine, and there is betrayal at the level of the state, betrayal of Caesar. We will see that this motif surfaces again and again. The one betrayed what is spiritual; the other two betrayed what is worldly. Because this betrayal of God and of the emperor, of Caesar, weighs so heavily for Dante, these three are in the deepest level of hell.

Then comes the *Purgatorio*. Hell is often portrayed as if it were a giant funnel down which they pass. Many artists have also painted it like this; there are medieval images and sketches of all kinds. Lucifer is down below. Then they exit through a kind of corridor and the *Inferno* ends with: 'And from their distant heavens, I am again encircled by the light of the stars.' Thus the stars are visible from hell. In the *Purgatorio*, they begin to climb a mountain, which is again described level by level in detail and quite pictorially. Here we find all those who cast off their sins in a catharsis, in a purification. This is naturally something every path of schooling must contain: the faults that have been uncovered must now be overcome; they must be diminished by efforts of various kinds and then brought to a point of vanishing.

Those who get through this *Purgatorio* arrive at a certain point—and it is at this point that Virgil takes his leave of Dante, saying: My task here is now fulfilled. Then come the famous words that have always been perceived as the central message of the whole *Divine Comedy*. Virgil says: 'You are now free and lord of your world. Be now your own emperor and your own pope.'[13] Here we have the great Templar goal: to free the human being from being told what to think in the political sphere, in the *Vita activa*; to free him from the imperium and the state; and to free him in his religious life, in his *Vita contemplativa*, from the pope and from the Church.

It is peculiar how this phrase has come down through the centuries. We can discover, for example, that the Swiss like to hear the phrase put this way: Indeed, let the human being be his own emperor and his own pope. Englert-Faye writes about this in his large volume about Switzerland.[14] Thus, either in a more public or more hidden way, the Templar goal expressed in these words has made its way down through the centuries and into the present time: autonomy in social self-determination; autonomy in religious, spiritual, soul life.

Dante calls the last cantos of the *Purgatorio* one of 'the most charming parts'. The one who has ascended there, Dante's soul, enters the earthly paradise, the Garden of Eden. A magical female figure, adorned and colourful, by the name of Mathilde, approaches him. But he notices right away who she is and addresses her as Proserpina. The goddess Natura stands in the Garden of Eden, receiving him, and she says something quite strange to him: 'You stand here at the cradle of humanity.'[15]

It is painful to try to summarize what is going on here—and yet it is necessary. What does it mean that we ascend into the spiritual? It means that, at the same time, we are also going back in time. If I want to seek out my angel, where do I have to go? To the day of my birth; he is there in the Akasha. If I want to seek out my archangel, where must I go? Where he was active as a folk spirit when that folk group began. I find the archai where the cultures of the past began. If I want to go to the exusiai, I have to go back in time to the period of Lemuria.

Many people know there is a secret of human existence—that the human being actually treads this path every night. Every night, when outside his physical body during sleep, the human being goes through all his incarnations until the moment he was created as an individuality out of the elohim, the exusiai. This means that at the point where he meets Natura in the Garden of Eden, Dante has really arrived at the cradle of humanity. The path of catharsis, of purification, has led him to the point where the earthly path of all humanity began. For this reason, he also says: 'Prepared was I for the world of the stars.'[16] Mathilde-Natura-Proserpina steps back, and now Beatrice, the heavenly Sophia, arrives. She leads him through the *Paradiso*—which means out through the planets into the world of the fixed stars.

This is where the neophyte finds the saints whose powers conquer sin all over the world. After Dante has gone through the planetary spheres—where he meets Thomas Aquinas and all the greats—he comes to the heavenly rose, a powerful vessel that fills the cosmos; in the middle of it is a sea of light, a reflection of divine light. All the saints and blessed ones from the Old and New Testaments sit in this heavenly rose, become visible there. Then Bernard of Clairvaux leads him a bit further on high and he has a view of the Trinity; he sees the Trinity, the three circles, and he describes them wonderfully. Led by Bernard of Clairvaux, he recognizes what holds the world together at its innermost: 'That my soul circles with the seraphim from whom daily I learn love anew. This moves the sun and the other stars.' It is the end of the *Divine Comedy*, and the third time the stars are mentioned.

Why have we placed the *Divine Comedy*—to which hundreds of hours could be devoted—alongside Gothic architecture and alchemy as our theme?

Gothic Architecture Begins

A very unusual phenomenon has often been noted in regard to the Council of Troyes. All the abbots, bishops, archbishops, and so forth were present along with the Templars, and important discussions took place. Bernard of Clairvaux wrote the Templar rule; we do not know everything they did—although there are several documents from the Council. Then they return home. And what happens? When they return home, the participants inaugurate Gothic architecture, the Gothic style, everywhere.

The first to do so was the well-known Abbot Suger—in Latin his name would be Suga—from Saint-Denis. Saint-Denis was the royal abbey, the most important, the most beautiful abbey in France. Consequently its abbot held a high rank in the Church. The construction took some time; then the abbot circulated a letter of invitation throughout France in the form of a booklet. Of course he expresses it differently, but the intent of what he writes is the following: We want to present you with a new style of architecture by means of which we come another step closer to the Temple of Solomon. He extends this invitation to the local people of rank and title, asking them to come to Saint-Denis in order to admire the first ever Gothic choir. For that time—when there was still a spiritual sense for form—this is completely shocking. Today we would say that the Gothic choir in the church of Saint-Denis is extremely beautiful, but not as significant compared to the cathedral in Reims, to Note Dame de Paris, to Chartres Cathedral, and so on. Nevertheless, at that time, it must have been breathtaking—suddenly this other form.

Shortly thereafter, another participant, Henry of Sens, the Archbishop of Sens—which is south of Paris—creates the first Gothic façade. A third comrade in the circle, Gottfried of Chartres, creates in Chartres the first Gothic westwork. It is impossible to overlook the connection between these participants and the creation of Gothic architecture in France. There is such ample evidence of this.

They were all together at the Council in Troyes so there was naturally a lot of speculation: What did the Templars contribute? Or: What did the Templars set in motion? There are, of course, romantic notions that we have all heard about: The Templars contributed the Ark of the Covenant which had once been in the Temple of Solomon, was lost, and had never surfaced as archaeological booty. It is sometimes said that the Ark of the Covenant contained the secret measurements of humanity. Others say we should not think so romantically about the Ark; the Templars had contact with the Islamic world, they brought with them knowledge of temple measurements. We have heard from Rudolf Steiner that the Templars had direct contacts with people who passed along the ancient body of Mystery knowledge.

Rudolf Steiner also says—and this is demonstrable—that all temples of the past were built according to great cosmic measurements, but the sequence of these temple constructions—from the Mastaba to the ziggurat, to the pyramids, to Greek temples and Roman sacramental buildings—was directed by the wisdom of the guidance of humanity in such a way that the human being would always be helped to take a further step in his ego development.[17] And now, from the circles of those who were true initiates[18]—often referred to as the White Lodge, a romantic concept—it became known that an architectural style had to arise in Europe that would lead the ego development of European humanity a bit further.

Thus we can reasonably gather from indications by Rudolf Steiner that the inner, spiritual system of measurement in Gothic architecture is connected to the Temple of Solomon, even to the Ark of the Covenant, although we do not need to imagine that in a strictly physical way. Naturally, experiences of all these past constructions play a role in the emerging Gothic architecture and the cathedrals as they gradually arose. If we were to travel through Europe, we would see the beauty of the Romanesque style with its capitals, its small alabaster windows, its often impressive spaces like those in Vézelay. In contrast, the aesthetic force of uprightness that suddenly emerges from Gothic architecture is unmistakable. Rudolf Steiner repeats often that all these architectural styles were inaugurated by initiates. Above all, this Gothic style of architecture was inaugurated because it could have a quite specific social effect.

There is an oft-repeated saying: The Gothic cathedral is finished only when people are praying within it. We have to understand that during the Middle Ages cathedrals did not have the horrible wooden pews churches have today; we must, instead, imagine hundreds of people standing—or kneeling on the floor—with hands folded in prayer. Only then is the

Gothic cathedral finished, not before. The Greek temple, says Rudolf
Steiner, is complete even when there are no people in it; it was made for a
god. And this is again different in a Romanesque church where people
often have the sense that the church has been erected over a crypt or a
grave. The Romanesque cathedral exists more for the spiritual world, for
the dead. Gothic architecture exists for human beings,[19] which can be
understood in a double sense. It has an effect through its formative force,
and it was a socially determining factor in a medieval city.

Every architectural form genuinely founded on what is spiritual draws
spiritual beings to it, beings who snuggle up to it and live in it, and who,
one might say, experience the exterior as well as the interior as a welcome
resistance to their own spiritual nature. Naturally, it can be said that
modern forms of architecture also attract spiritual beings; and we would
do well to imagine what kinds of spiritual beings find square blocks
attractive. Back then, great and powerful angel beings were drawn to
these buildings. This had an effect on the social life; they were socially
formative forces. When such a cathedral stood in the centre of a medieval
city, these forces rayed out from it—even, according to Rudolf Steiner,
forming people right into their next incarnation. This effect continues. If
we consider what this means, we can conclude: The Romanesque style
always has a sense of relationship to the group soul; the congregation in a
Romanesque cathedral is communal. The crowd praying in a Gothic
cathedral is made up of individuals; it is as though every single ego surrounded by these flying buttresses realizes that he is on his own path to the
spirit.

The Tabula Smaragdina

This also relates to what the title of his chapter calls spiritual alchemy. It is
unfortunate that today's understanding of alchemy is becoming increasingly banal, even materialistic. Images of some sort of smoky kitchen
where people are attempting to make gold, supposedly discovering
porcelain, are common—along with other such nonsense. That is all
recent rubbish. Behind alchemy, however, are hidden great and ancient
Mysteries in which attention has always been paid to the original father of
alchemy, the great Egyptian initiate Hermes—or Thoth. Both he and
Moses were pupils of the even greater Zarathustra. Spiritual science
reports that the Zarathustra-being endowed its pupils with its own substance in which an infinite number of cosmic secrets were contained—
Moses with the ether body, Hermes with the astral body.

Thus alchemy always looked to this great initiate, Hermes—who is thought to have a continuing effect down through the ages—and to the ancient primal formula of all alchemy that originated with him. Let me interject here that by alchemy I do not mean the transformation of matter alone; this transformation of matter was, in fact, used to achieve an initiation. What is attributed to Hermes is the fundamental document of all alchemy up to the present time, the well-known *Tabula Smaragdina*—also called the Emerald Tablet—on which are written twelve short phrases. There are those who try to explain this away, saying that emeralds of that size do not exist and so it probably had to be another kind of green stone or something else entirely from who knows when.

That is all nonsense. The *Tabula Smaragdina* is a tablet in the spiritual world. Rudolf Steiner often speaks of such tablets existing in the spiritual world. This is, of course, an image for a certain situation: the existence of spiritual tablets which people could approach and which could be read. In a meditation that Rudolf Steiner gives, a Michael meditation, meteoric iron is a tablet in the spiritual world. Rudolf Steiner is not the only person to have experienced this. Around the turn of the last century, there was a woman from England, Mabel Collins, who wrote one of the best-known volumes about a path of schooling, the famous *Light on the Path*. It has been reprinted hundreds of times. She describes how, in an excarnated state, she is led into the spiritual world and reads what she saw, so to speak, as though on a wall; it is something she retains and then writes down once she is back in her body. In the early days of spiritual science, Rudolf Steiner translated parts of *Light on the Path*—short pithy phrases—from English into German.

Thus we see that the *Tabula Smaragdina* is a place in the spiritual world where this tablet can be read and has always been read by initiates who have then brought it back in their own languages. I will quote its twelve phrases here.

The famous beginning reads: *In truth, certain and without doubt: What is below is as it is above, and what is above is as it is below, to effect the wonder of one thing.*

Second: *Just as all things are derived from and through the contemplation of one single thing, so will all things be born out of this one through variation.*

The third is a famous phrase: *Its father is the son and its mother is the moon. The wind carried it in its belly and its nursemaid is the earth.*

Fourth: *It is the father of all the wonders of the world.*

Fifth: *Its power is perfect when it is transformed into the earth.*

Sixth: *Separate the earth from the fire and the fine from the coarse, gently and with great care.*

Seventh: *It ascends from earth to heaven and returns from there to earth in order to receive the power of what is above and what is below. Thus will you possess the light of the whole world and all darkness will flee from you.*

Eighth: *It is the power of all powers because it overcomes everything subtle and penetrates what is solid.*

Ninth: *Thus will the small world be created according to the model of the great world.*

Tenth: *Thus and in this way will wonderful applications be produced.*

Eleventh: *And therefore am I called Hermes Trismegistos because I possess the three parts of the wisdom of the entire world.*

Twelfth: *Complete is what I have said about the activity of the sun.*[20]

Of course, this seems at first to be quite a cryptic text, and certainly the translation may be inadequate. Nevertheless, this text has passed down through the millennia, and there have been many commentaries written about it, right up to our own time. There is a thick volume in which someone has collected everything said throughout the centuries about this *Tabula Smaragdina*, the instruction in what alchemy actually should be, namely, work with substances that produces an inner, spiritual transformation.

Salt—Mercury—Sulphur

It is said that salt, mercury and sulphur were the great elements of alchemy. As Rudolf Steiner describes it, when the alchemist experienced how salt precipitated from something, when salt was formed, he then experienced the thoughts of the gods. Mercury involved everything connected with the processes of dissolving through which the alchemist experienced the love of the gods. Sulphur was everything that burned. Where burning processes took place, he experienced the sacrifice of the gods.[21] This is, of course, expressed quite aphoristically. These were life processes in which alchemists underwent a real path of schooling, in which they experienced how effects in the spiritual world were produced by means of their work with material substances, but not only in the spiritual world. There were effects in the social sphere as well. When an alchemist then carried out the processes with great piety—salt processes, mercury processes, sulphur processes—the elemental beings were pleased, which was something that had an enlivening effect. He always accompanied it with a meditation; for this reason, every alchemist had an *oratorium* near his *laboratorium*.

It is claimed that this is a Rosicrucian matter. There is certainly truth in that, but not exclusively—the Templars were connected with the alchemists too. A Christianized alchemy begins with the first initiation of Christian Rosenkreutz in the middle of the thirteenth century. Rudolf Steiner describes how the young man who later becomes Christian Rosenkreutz is surrounded by twelve initiates who educate him; how he dies. But before his death, he once again proclaims a new initiation knowledge. Rudolf Steiner further indicates that these initiation teachers live on[22] and have pupils. All this has a role during the centuries when the Templars were active. The Templars always had a close connection to the spiritual-esoteric alchemists. They lived with the feeling that the alchemist could actually bring about the Christ-presence by means of the very special way he handled the material substance and the three powers of salt, mercury and sulphur.

Between the two towers of Chartres Cathedral there is a statue of Christ. One way to see it is to stand far away from the west side with a good pair of binoculars. Another is by climbing one of the towers and looking down at an angle; it can be photographed from there as well. The Christ is depicted in a quite definite gesture called *solve et coagula*, dissolving and binding. The Christ is the Lord of what dissolves and binds, the Lord of the processes of mercury and salt, of what Lucifer can effect in way of dissolving and what Ahriman can effect in way of firming. And the Christ Himself stands in the middle as the sacrifice of the gods, as the flame.

When we look at the figure of the *Representative of Humanity* at the Goetheanum, we also stand before an ancient Mystery that comes from the Middle Ages: the gesture towards Ahriman, towards all the salt processes; the gesture towards Lucifer, to all the processes of dissolving. The striding Being of Christ in this threefold depiction, understood as the divine sacrifice, sulphur, is then also the divine sacrifice of Christ Himself.

Now that we have arrived at the end of the Middle Ages and will begin considering the changeover to the modern age and the effects of the Middle Ages, we can ask ourselves again: What is the meaning of the Middle Ages for us? Let us once more allow to pass before our imagination what people thought, believed, suffered; how they sacrificed themselves, went to their deaths, what they experienced as longings and fears. These are, spiritually speaking, our ancestors, our forefathers. If we take all this up with warm hearts—the destinies that were not always horrible, those that also led to triumphs, to knowledge, to insights, to initiations, to meetings with the Christ—then I think we can never again look at the Middle Ages with a cold eye. Every time we look at a cathedral or a work of art the potential is there for something to be reawakened in us. We can look upon the period of the Middle Ages with love only if we do not take it up abstractly and say that it is merely a historical period. It is not just a period of time past; it has being. The ancients were correct when they spoke of the aeons, the great and lesser aeons. Time—and space as well—is only an abstraction for the abstract consciousness of this world. For the spiritual world, everything has the quality of being. If we come lovingly to terms with this thought, we can create an imagination of a being that gazes at us just as the being of the Middle Ages gazes at us. Then we immediately see that 'the Middle Ages' is not just a phrase; it is a piece of human history, human joy, human tragedy, human progress, human regression, a piece of human destiny. It has been our intent to awaken a bit of love for the Middle Ages.

The Emergence of a New World—Columbus and the Mysteries of America

Virginia Sease

We will now turn our attention to the beginning of the modern age, which means we will be considering certain discoveries. It can be said that a period of discovery had begun—not with Columbus, but during the middle of the thirteenth century when the mendicant orders and the merchants made their way to central and eastern Asia. The land routes to Asia, to the Far East, were first established after 1245 or 1247 when the roads made it possible for people to undertake these journeys. Today, these beginnings can be traced to the first adventurous undertakings of a Franciscan monk, Giovanni da Pian del Carpini. He is not very well known in history because research about him was not really undertaken until the twentieth century, but it was this Franciscan who undertook this journey.

These land routes were closed again in the middle of the fourteenth century because the Tartars had converted to Islam, making the border regions too dangerous to cross. Quite a few people made the journey when the routes were open, among them, of course, the famous Marco Polo. They were always greeted in a more or less friendly way. From the stories that have been handed down, we know this to be true even of Genghis Khan.

The Sea Route to India

As the land route was closed, other ideas surfaced: How can we get there? How are we going to cross over to Asia? The hope was reawakened—of course, it was not the first time—that a sea route to India could be found. The Portuguese were particularly adventurous. They sailed down along the coast of Africa, and in 1415 they took the region of Ceuta in North Africa. Then Columbus sailed westward in 1492—although, as we know, he did not plan his route that way; and in 1499 Vasco de Gama made an expedition around the Cape of Good Hope, thus quite far to the south. Today these two journeys are referred to as the twin voyages of discovery.

Both expeditions had an enormous effect on the self-awareness of Christianity in Europe. Christianity had worked in a more or less confined area up to then. Now the idea surfaced: The Gospels can reach all the peoples of world, and in all languages. Of course, these languages first had to be learned, although learning languages was not such a problem at that time. When we think about this stream of human beings—about the royal courts, the Spanish courts for example, this mixture of Arabs, Jews and Christians—there is no indication, even among the troubadours, that they needed help with translations. They were able to make themselves understood.

Those in Europe who were inclined to mystic Christianity saw these discoveries as a sign from heaven and interpreted them to mean that this was the beginning of the end of time during which the Holy Word was to reach all people. That was their interpretation.

Joachimism

This lent even more force to the views of Joachim of Fiore. After his death in 1202, Joachim of Fiore actually lived more strongly than he had during his lifetime. It was then that Joachimism—as it known today—began and grew stronger and stronger. Joachim's own writings were read, but there were many other texts written in the manner of Joachim of Fiore, especially ones expounding his view concerning the third epoch, the epoch of the Holy Spirit. These authors understood the events of their time to be the opening of the third epoch.

John of Rupescissa lived in the area of Catalonia at that time and was especially well known as a Joachimite; he developed Joachim's ideas much further, not only through his own writings but also by going out among the people. The cloister at Ripoll is situated in Catalonia, and he lived in this region. He died around the middle of the fourteenth century, but during his lifetime he made people strongly aware of Joachim of Fiore's views and he was the first to prophecy the imminent conversion of the Tartars and the Jews. He said the converted Tartars and Jews would join the Christians to conquer the Arabs—it was a chiliastic prophecy—and then the time would be fulfilled. Since around the middle of the twentieth century, this special man, John of Rupescissa, has been viewed as a direct forerunner of Christopher Columbus.

Columbus

Thus, at the time of Christopher Columbus the idea was going around
that the entire population of the world could be converted, and Christopher Columbus carried with him this mighty apocalyptic and mystic
vision. This is precisely the side of Columbus I want to consider. I will not
go into detail about his four ocean voyages—we know about that from
our studies in school. Instead, we will look at this other side of Columbus,
this messianic, mystic, apocalyptic side.

Christopher Columbus was closely connected with the Franciscans;
they stood by him and offered him assistance. After his second journey, he
was seen in Seville wearing the vestments of a lay order, an indication he
was performing a kind of penance in gratitude for his safe return. Then—
and this is confirmed by his son, Diego—when he had died he lay in his
coffin dressed in the vestments he had requested—the vestments of the lay
order of the Franciscans, the Tertiaries. Thus this connection is clearly
confirmed. During the last years of his life—between approximately 1515
and 1523—the language and style of his letters change. He wrote many
letters and they are worth reading, very interesting; there are translations
from the Spanish with the German on the facing pages. It is apparent—
even in how he expresses himself—that he is becoming more and more
Franciscan, especially in his use of the style and language of the Spirituals.
He wrote a book entitled *The Book of Prophecies* that was never finished.
This book deserves particular attention here. In it, Columbus provides his
commentaries on the Psalms; it is also, in part, a report of his fourth ocean
voyage (1502–4). Here we see that Columbus evokes the mood of
Joachim of Fiore and represents his views. It contains a letter intended as
an introduction and addressed to the royal couple Ferdinand and Isabella,
although it never reached their hands because an old monk, Gaspar
Gorritio, was supposed to have delivered it but failed to do so. Fortunately
the letter was not lost entirely. In it, Columbus writes somewhat auto-
biographically that from the time of his youth he had many friends—Jews,
Christians, Muslims, clever men, simple men, priests, monks, and so on.
In addition, he had studied many works about Christianity, Judaism,
astrology, arithmetic, geometry—that is, portions of the Seven Liberal
Arts; moreover, as he thought about it, he had come to the conclusion
that none of these people or writings had a decisive influence on him.
Instead, he had undertaken his journeys of discovery through the direct
inspiration of the Holy Spirit. Thus Columbus calls upon the Holy Spirit
as a source of inspiration. Columbus was convinced that the world would
soon come to an end; he thought that this would happen in about 155

years, around the beginning of the sixteenth century. Thus it was urgent that all people receive the Holy Word. He referred to the Revelation of John where John says that people from all nations, tribes, peoples and languages will stand before the throne of God. Therefore Jerusalem must be liberated as quickly as possible from the heathens, the 'infidels', as he called them. He saw his own sea voyages as the opening of the door to the western seas, a gateway that missionaries should hurry through so they would lose no time getting to the people who were not yet Christians. He regarded opening this door as his great achievement because it was then possible for people to reach Asia where, he concluded, most of the population had not converted.

Columbus felt himself to be an instrument of the divine guidance of the world. This was not arrogance on his part, but an intuition. Rudolf Steiner actually uses the example of Christopher Columbus in describing such a configuration. He says that certain people have their own law of destiny—like everyone else—but their individual, personal law of destiny also converges with the laws of destiny of the whole of humanity.[1] Just such a convergence occurred with Columbus. That he sensed this is not wrong. Columbus then went on to say that he understands himself to be the fulfilment, and he cites Joachim of Fiore in his *Book of Prophecies*. Earlier the *Divine Comedy* had offered a beautiful portrayal of Joachim; in the *Paradiso*, three personalities are placed by Dante in the circle of the sun—St Bonaventure, St Francis of Assisi and Joachim of Fiore. This is significant, because these three—Bonaventure, Francis and Joachim—are all leading Franciscans. According to Dante's conceptualization, they are all in the region of the sun.

It is often said that the discovery of America was actually the last Crusade, a view about discoveries that became especially prominent during the twentieth century, and one that is consistent with the view held by Christopher Columbus. He thought that he would find islands and so forth laden with gold, and he believed that when these places were found, the gold there could be used to free the Holy Lands, the Holy Sepulchre, thus sanctifying the gold. This is a Templar ideal by which Columbus lived. We know that he also took part in the sailing school of Henry the Navigator. Of course, Henry (1394–1460) had already died, but the school still existed and Henry's connections with the Templars are known. When the Templars were destroyed by Philip the Fair and Pope Clement V, a few Templars were able to flee to the west; some fled to England where they were able to live, and some fled to Portugal where, in part, they were able to live under the protection of the royal house. It was in Portugal that Henry the Navigator made his connection with the

Templars. Columbus also learned about these ideas through what was later handed down. Thus, on the one hand, we see the Franciscans—especially Joachim of Fiore—and, on the other, the Templars. In Dante, we see both streams flowing together at a very lofty level simply through his portrayals and his relation to the Templar Order, to the Templar view.

In looking at Columbus, we also sense in him a high level of self-awareness. He took Joachim of Fiore's idea quite seriously that development is possible, that a metamorphosis can occur, even in one's own biography. The human being himself begins in the first epoch, in the time of the Father. If he makes Christianity his own, he will be able to develop into the second epoch, the epoch of the Son. Then, if he grasps genuine apocalyptic intentions, he can also personally enter a third epoch, the epoch of the Holy Spirit. While Joachim of Fiore presented these three epochs more in the context of human history, three hundred years later we see that Joachimism in Europe has developed to a point that a spirit like Columbus could personalize it even more, could draw the consequences for his own biography. This can also be understood in the following way. We can see the fourth post-Atlantean cultural epoch reflected in Joachim and note how it differs from the beginning of the fifth cultural epoch in a spirit like Christopher Columbus who brought with him the consequences of ego-development.

Columbus also had an apocalyptic vision in which he himself was a messiah who had to accomplish a certain act of salvation; he refers again to Joachim who said that such a leader of humanity, liberator of humanity, would come from Spain. Columbus adopted this thought quite decisively and believed he had to bring this task to fulfilment. He saw before him three great goals. First, according to his view, he had already discovered the New World; this was already accomplished. Secondly, all heathens had to be converted—not such a big problem, for if the Jews and the Tartars were brought together with the people of the New World, Islam could easily be conquered. Then, thirdly, the Holy Sepulchre could be rescued. Of course, for Columbus, the Holy Sepulchre was not only a geographical place connected with tradition; the Holy Sepulchre epitomized for him—as well as the Spirituals, the Joachimites and the Franciscans—the beginning of the third epoch. That the Christ had lain in the grave and had been resurrected from death was for them like a symbol for the whole of humanity; the whole of humanity can find the way to the Holy Spirit, to the Paraclete, if humanity itself is resurrected from its own grave. For this reason, the Holy Sepulchre was even more important in his view, and everything he did was to serve the recovery of the Holy Sepulchre.

A strong Joachimite stream was active at the court of Friedrich III of Sicily, around 1295 to 1337, a century before Christopher Columbus. At this court we find a very interesting, somewhat hidden thread which became quite important to Columbus. A certain doctor, also a Joachimite mystic, lived there; he was an alchemist and also well versed theologically, a real light of his time. Arnold of Villanova—alchemist, doctor, theologian, mystic, prolific writer—was also friends with people in the Templar stream, and a Templar sympathizer. It is said that he discovered or developed a fine wine for the Templars by means of his alchemy. His writings were especially valued by Columbus, and, in them, Columbus also found an emphasis on the thought that someone from the Spanish-speaking world would come to rescue the Holy Sepulchre; it was also from Arnold of Villanova that he took up this thought.

We have heard the view—it actually dates back to the 1940s—that Columbus came from a Jewish background and that he undertook his voyage in 1492 because the Jews were banished from Spain that year. This idea was argued by Salvador de Madariaga. He maintained that Columbus was of Jewish descent and wanted, therefore, to conquer Jerusalem because conquest could equalize or overcome the differences between the Christians and the Jews, and help to unify them. As proof he offers evidence of a unification of Christians and Jews that resulted from the conquest. This view has, in the meantime, fallen into doubt. The weakness in this interpretation is that he does not at all see how connected Columbus was to the writings of Arnold of Villanova, or how connected he was to those of Joachim of Fiore or, moreover, how connected he was with the Franciscans. There is much in the newer research that speaks to the fact that Columbus was not of Jewish descent.

The Indians

We see, then, that Columbus arrived in this New World where he discovered a new kind of human being he called 'Indians'; he had landed in the islands of the West Indies, and called them Indians—some say because he thought he had landed in India. In a relatively short time he came to the conclusion that these Indians were human beings, and he makes note of this in a letter to the monarchs written during this first voyage, as well as in his diary. He describes how these Indians have a head, two arms, two legs, and walk upright like a human being. They speak with distinctive sounds—naturally, he could not understand the language—that were different from the unique sounds made by animals. He indicates various other features; for example, they bow attentively. That was also interesting. We might laugh to think that at the end of the fifteenth century he wrote of his conviction that the Indians were human beings. It is shameful, however, to admit that it was not until the middle of the nineteenth century in America that African Americans were finally determined by law to be human beings. Imagine—not until the middle of the nineteenth century! Abraham Lincoln was quite instrumental in seeing the necessity for this declaration.

The question, however, was: Who were these Indians? Various theories arose during the fifteenth, sixteenth centuries, and these theories continued to live into the eighteenth century among the various people who settled in America. The principal view was that the Indians belonged to the ten lost tribes of Israel from the Old Testament and that these tribes had emigrated from the Holy Land. A Spanish Franciscan, Gerónimo de Mendieta (1525–1604), had a particular reason for believing that the Indians were descended from the Hebrews. He described his view this way:

> Who knows whether we are so close to the end of the world that the conversion of the Indians fulfils the prophecy—for which we pray— that the Jews may be converted in our time. Because, if the Indians are descended from the Jews, the prophecy is certainly fulfilled.[2]

This means that if the Indians are actually Jews and the Indians are converted, then the Jews are converted because the Indians are descendants of the Jews. One last sentence from Gerónimo de Mendieta:

> I have, however, little trust that the Jews of the Old World will be converted unless God Himself performs it as a miracle.[3]

Although Gerónimo de Mendieta was a highly educated Franciscan, this is still a bit of a short cut. The logic is a bit linear—A equals B; B equals C; therefore, A equals C.

Cortéz

Mendieta actually shed light on a particular aspect of Hernando Cortéz, the conqueror of the Aztecs, whose conquests had been made only about 50 years earlier. Mendieta, himself a Franciscan, reports how twelve Franciscan missionaries went to Mexico City in 1524. When Cortéz heard that these twelve Franciscans had come as missionaries, he called together all the Spaniards in his retinue and all the Indians. They went out to greet the twelve Franciscans and Cortéz bowed, fell to his knees, and kissed the hands of the Franciscans. Because he presented himself in this fashion, the Spaniards and Indians followed suit. A man from Sahagún, Bernardo de Sahagún, was present and described this in his great history.

Understand it as you will; the modern view of Cortéz and his conquest is rather negative, to say the least. There are descriptions of the methods used to enslave the Indians, as well as those used in the conversions. Mendieta's assessment of Cortéz's greeting of the Franciscans was that Cortéz had been inspired in the moment by the Holy Spirit, and that he had not acted as a mortal human being but as a divine angelic being. The gesture demonstrated how he had conquered his lower self.

Cortéz would never be described as an angelic being in the current view of history! I say this only because I am coming to other aspects of the tasks of the Franciscans in the New World. During the last third of the twentieth century, the Franciscans were subjected to a vast campaign that cast aspersions on them and their activity in the New World—in Mexico and California. To put it differently, history has been rewritten. What I have described here are two views. Both are very strongly held, especially in the western world, as an explanation of the role the Franciscans actually played in the New World.

Gerónimo de Mendieta

These twelve Franciscans arrived first. Gerónimo de Mendieta, who arrived somewhat later, was quite interested in the Indians. He learned their language in Mexico; then he learned Nahautl. What he undertook was done in service. He also described that the Indians were much more like God than Europeans; he cited their humility, love, compassion and patience—all characteristics we would perhaps not use to describe Indians based on the traditional view. They are the qualities that Christ preached in the Sermon on the Mount, qualities by which people could achieve the Kingdom of Heaven. Mendieta thought that these Indians were not only like 'children of God'; he also referred to them as *Genus angelicum*, 'angel beings'. We must recall that this was a view held right at the time of the first encounters, and not after the Indians came into conflict with the Europeans. Mendieta refers to Joachim of Fiore, saying that in these Indians we see a model of human beings as they will be in the third epoch, the epoch of the Holy Spirit. Only one small deed was still required in order to take these natural children of God to the next step, namely, that they accept Christianity. That would be the final step.

Black Magic Mysteries in Mexico

Now we will look at what we can describe as the condition of the etheric aura of Mexico in what is now the Baja peninsula and the west coast of California. What has happened in history impresses itself into the etheric where it remains; however, it can be transformed. There are people today who understand this and take up the task of changing the etheric aura in places where something terrible has happened in order to improve that aura through their own spiritual activity. When we look back at this period around the fifteenth, sixteenth, seventeenth centuries, we find an etheric aura that was much the same as it had been for a thousand years. What lived there—somewhat mitigated by a certain act of salvation, but as a tendency nevertheless?

We discover pre-Christian Mysteries in this part of the world. There were Mystery sites throughout the world—good Mysteries as well as completely evil, horrific Mysteries in various places. During the pre-Christian era and also around the time of the Mystery of Golgotha there were evil Mysteries in the West, especially in Mexico. Rudolf Steiner describes these Mexican Mysteries. How these Mexican Mysteries came about is quite complicated but I will try to summarize it.

The great spirit of the Atlantean period is known as Tao. Tao, also a tone, had sounded throughout the whole world and brought with it a certain harmony. Much later, a cult arose, a cultus of an ahrimanic counter-image personified by a spiritual being that had no physical body. The name of this ahrimanic spiritual being was derived phonetically from Tao; it was called 'Taotl'—an ahrimanic counter-image, an elemental body with a sub-earthly nature. Taotl's aim was to make earthly culture mechanistic, to harden it by means of the electric and magnetic forces of the earth, the subterranean forces of the earth, so that human bodies would no longer be capable of carrying an ego. That was the goal. Taotl Mysteries arose and the initiates of the counter-Sun Mysteries were present in them.

On the one hand, there were the Sun Mysteries with the Christ and Michael; on the other hand, there were the ahrimanic counter-Sun Mysteries. In order to increase their strength, these initiates in the counter-Sun Mysteries were taught to perform what was actually ritualized murder. Through this murder—during which the stomach of the sacrifice was cut out—the powers of the individual were spiritually increased in an evil sense. This murder was to be so horrifying to those sacrificed that they would never again want to return to earth, never again want to enter into an incarnation. Thus a sphere would be created that would be populated by these evil spirits—the so-called eighth sphere.

Then the divine Providence of the world founded a good Mystery to counter this Taotl cult and also sent a Being not embodied in a physical body, one spiritually related to Jehovah—Tezkatlipoka. Tezkatlipoka had the task of spreading love as a spiritual being in order to create a counter-balance to the Taotl cult. Ahriman set up a very strong force against Tezkatlipoka, namely, a spirit that was not incarnate but was connected with Mephistopheles, a devilish spirit. This mephistophelean spirit was called Quetzalcoatl—Rudolf Steiner mentioned that the sound of the name indicates that this was a spiritual being. Here I must note that there are various traditions connected with Quetzalcoatl. Many of them indicate that he was seen as a quite significant Toltec god, and that the Indians believed Cortéz to be Quetzalcoatl. That is a whole subject in itself. Familiarity with the research and the fundamental literature—for example, Bernardo de Sahagún's history of these Mexican relationships—will bring us closer to the view set forth by Rudolf Steiner that Quetzalcoatl was a mephistophelean spirit.

Now we see another aspect. A virgin is overshadowed by a spiritual being often represented as a bird; she brings a son into the world. At the same time—Rudolf Steiner dates this around the time of the Mystery of Golgotha—a black magician is also incarnated in Mexico. I am now describing two incarnated individualities—the first is the son of the virgin, and the second is the great initiate of the evil Taotl Mysteries. Rudolf Steiner describes this initiate as follows: 'This was one of the greatest, if not the greatest black magician to ever walk the earth; thus the black magician who had acquired the greatest secrets . . .'[4] Around AD 30, this black magician was to have brought humanity into a terrible state by means of his arts, but the son of the virgin did battle with him. The son of the virgin was called Vitzliputzli/Uitzilpochtli. Rudolf Steiner says that this name—Vitzliputzli/Uitzilpochtli—is spelled phonetically, which is interesting in light of the evidence provided by Bernardo of Sahagún. Although it is not certain, I believe that Rudolf Steiner did not have access to these resources. The document was published only after Rudolf Steiner's time, but the name is spelled phonetically with only a small variation from Rudolf Steiner: Vitzliopochtli. The 'Song of Uitzilo-pochtli' from this manuscript by Bernardo of Sahagún contains a description: 'Uitzilopochtli, the warrior. No one is my equal. Not without cause do I wear the cloak of yellow feathers because I made the sun to rise . . .'[5]

Around the time of the Mystery of Golgotha—from AD 31 to 34—Vitzliputzli carried on a three-year battle with this black magician. What would have happened if the black magician had not been defeated? He would have seized control of the fundamental secrets of the fourth as well as those of the fifth post-Atlantean cultural epochs. What does that mean? The secret of the fourth epoch is the secret of death and birth. Had he seized control of it, he would have claimed it for himself. The secret of the fifth epoch, the secret of evil and good, could have been appropriated by him as well. The black magician would have exercised total power, not only over humanity but over all creation through these two secrets. However, Vitzliputzli conquered him and crucified him. The body of the black magician was destroyed and his soul banned so that even it could no longer be active.

The result of this was that many, many souls who had been exposed to these ritualized murders, and thus lacked the courage or the desire to incarnate, learned through this deed that the earth was again free. Vitzliputzli created the possibility that these souls could descend again into an earthy incarnation. What had existed as ritual for such a long time—for centuries, almost a millennium—was suddenly set right through a deed enacted by Vitzliputzli around AD 34. However, the tradition lived on and some of these evil cultic activities continued as the first Europeans were arriving. The tradition also continued in cultic art, and depictions of it can still be seen.

The Franciscans in Mexico and California

All of this existed in Mexico and north into southern California as cruelty of the worst kind. Then the Franciscans came to this region, arriving first in Mexico. Later—in the eighteenth century—a Franciscan by the name of Junipero Serra came to the area north of Mexico along with his 'padres'. The Franciscans moved northwards; they lived and worked with the descendants of the Indians and also spoke with them about Christ. Who was the spirit behind these Franciscans? Francis of Assisi, this great personality, was already working with the Buddha in the region of Mars when the Franciscans under the leadership of Junipero Serra were moving north from Mexico into California. And Francis of Assisi continues his work with the Buddha in the region of Mars even today.

I mentioned that aspersions are now frequently cast on these padres, the Franciscan missionaries. However, they did enormous good for the Indian population; for example, they taught the Indians various skills so that the Indians had warmth in winter. Quite significant advances were brought by the Franciscan missionaries, who lived their lives in devotion, dedication, in love and compassion. They carried on the tradition of Francis of Assisi as living examples, and implanted these qualities through innu-merable deeds in this part of the world where the cruelest Mysteries had been practised. It might be said that they renewed and transformed the ether sphere in this part of the world. All of these missionaries were extremely well educated. For example, Junipero Serra—born in Mallorca in 1713—was quite talented; as a child, he learned many languages, Greek, Latin, Aramaic, Hebrew. He was offered a professorship at the University of Palma at 20, but he was a Franciscan who had experienced an inner conversion or calling and thought that he had to go to the New World where he was to work to bring the Indians to Christianity. He left everything behind. Had he remained in Europe, I am convinced the whole world would have known his name because he was such an outstanding personality.

Junipero Serra left Mexico in 1769, moving north into California with other Franciscan missionaries in order to found missions in California. He travelled up the coast year after year, gathering the Indians around him. Earlier these missions had been held privately by the Church, but more recently they belong to the state of California. They have undergone heavy renovation and can still be visited. This means that they have been restored, as can be readily seen. A gentle echo of the Franciscans' intent can still be experienced there. They lived in the spirit of Francis of Assisi, in the spirit of what Francis of Assisi and his fellow monks—there were many of them—had taken up in the Colchian Mysteries in the seventh and eighth centuries. They not only took up the Buddha qualities, but also joined them with the deepest qualities of Christianity, with the Christ-being. This continued. It developed up to the time of Francis, continued on through Bonaventure, then through Joachim of Fiore, and further as an echo through others who felt themselves connected to it; it then worked its way into the Templar movement. We can sense this as a strong influence in Christopher Columbus—the hidden side of him—and it makes its way over into the New World in a mighty stream. This marks the beginning of the modern age.

The Dawn of the Consciousness Soul—The Historical Figure of Faust and His Contemporaries

Manfred Schmidt-Brabant

Every period in time might be described as a period of transition. But many historians—Rudolf Steiner among them—agree that 1500 is a significant year, even a cosmic turning point in the history of humanity. We will observe that many factors characteristic of the modern age enter either through particular personalities or through events around this year, 1500. We think here of several biographies—I will look at a series of them from that time—or events that began then and continue into the future. We have discussed the discovery of America around 1492 and its consequences; the simultaneous expulsion of the Jews from Spain which creates a huge population wave that moves to Middle Europe, bringing with it the whole of Jewish culture and experience; and the conquest of Granada, and the final expulsion of Islam from Spain. Before we look further into what took place around the year 1500 we must first recall two significant aspects, both of which we have already touched upon.

The Secrets of the Seven Stages of Life

Hidden within esotericism and occultism and long held in secret was the fact that there are extensive time periods, each with its own specific motif—the so-called seven stages of life. The life stages encompass the idea that in every—every!—sevenfold development, a certain sequence occurs. The first stage is always connected with the secret of the abyss; the second with the secret of number; the third with the secret of elective affinities or alchemy; the fourth stage with birth and death; the fifth stage with the secret of evil or the encounter with evil; the sixth with the Logos, with the Word; and the seventh stage—quite general at first and almost impossible to clothe in words—the secret of divine bliss.

This sequence always takes place where a configuration of seven occurs. Thus even the great planetary developments of the earth can be characterized in this way. The so-called Old Saturn was the secret of the abyss, Old Sun was the secret of number, and Old Moon was the secret of elective affinities. The whole earth stands under the signature of birth and death, the next stage of planetary development will have the secret of evil as an entire planetary condition, and so on.

The earth also undergoes the separation into what were once called the root races. The first, the Polar period, the secret of the abyss; the Hyperborean period, the secret of number; the Lemurian period, the secret of alchemy or elective affinities; the Atlantean period, the secret of birth and death. The fifth root race—the entire post-Atlantean period—stands under the signature of the secret of evil. The smaller post-Atlantean cultural epochs take place under this general signature of the secret of evil: the Indian epoch, the secret of the abyss; the Persian, the secret of number; the Egypto-Babylonian-Chaldean culture, the secret of elective affinities; the Graeco-Roman period, the secret of birth and death. In the period we are examining—from 1413 on to be exact, but really beginning in 1500—it is the secret of evil as well as the secret of evil within the larger post-Atlantean period. The effect of the major impulse doubles the effect of the encounter the human being has with evil at this time.

The second aspect we must consider is that the human being gradually develops the elements of his soul during these post-Atlantean cultural epochs. This was the case with the sentient soul during the old Egypto-Babylonian-Chaldean period. The entire culture at that time, everything that was created in terms of culture, can only be grasped if we understand that the human being lived with his whole moral-aesthetic sense as though immersed in the perception of sensory experience, thus in the sentient soul. The sentient soul was formed when the ego was supported by the astral body. Then comes the Greek period. The intellectual soul arises within the human being. Philosophy begins; the creation of a heart-permeated mental activity begins; the ego is now supported by the etheric body. Then the period of the consciousness soul begins during which the human being develops the highest element of his soul, while his ego is supported by the lowest bodily element, his physical body, thus by the physical world.

During the period under discussion—around 1500—the human being enters the physical world, learns about the forces of the physical world and how to master them; materialism begins to blossom. However, in this physical world he also encounters what in esotericism is called the sphere of Ahriman, because that is where Ahriman is at home.

Luther

At the beginning of this period, we see two almost parallel biographies: Martin Luther and Georg Faust, the historical Faust. We will hear how both confront the devil, confront evil, each in his own way.

Martin Luther was born in Eisleben in 1483; he died there in 1546. He first studied philosophy and law with the intent of becoming a scholar. Martin Luther was extremely well educated, a fact that can easily be overlooked if we remember only his railings and vituperation. He used coarse and vulgar language, often so coarse that Rudolf Steiner says Luther could not be quoted in the presence of ladies. Then as a young man he had an experience. He found himself in a terrible storm; lightning flashed around him and he was gripped by an overwhelming shock. He made a promise that he would become a monk if his life were spared. To the astonishment and displeasure of his entire family, this highly talented young scholar enters the Augustinian monastery and becomes an Augustinian monk.

Of course, the higher-ups in the monastery discover his talent right away and send him to the university in Wittenberg to acquire a doctorate in theology—which he did. During his theological studies at Wittenberg he begins his encounter with the prevailing condition of the Church, particularly with a fundamental question that occupied him intensely: Is the human being actually punished or rewarded based on his guilt or innocence? Isn't it all a question of God's grace? This became a burning question because of a dreadful practice of his time, the so-called selling of indulgences. Indulgences began innocently enough during the First Crusade when people said: These poor knights will die somewhere without confession, without the last rites; so we will say ahead of time that they are free of all sins. The decision to send the knight off with an indulgence began as a good-hearted one.

But in the centuries that followed, this practice degenerated terribly, and finally led Luther to nail his famous 95 theses to the door of Wittenberg's castle church in 1517, inviting everyone to take part in discussing them. His theses were opposed to indulgences. Practically all 95 of them centre on the question: Can someone buy freedom from sin with money? You may recall from your studies that the selling of indulgences had grown completely out of hand. Rome turned their sale over to dealers in indulgences who travelled the country with money chests and certificates of indulgence, and these dealers received a commission from the sales. Luther himself cites the following satirical lines in his 95 theses: 'When a coin into the coffer drops, a soul into heaven hops'; or 'When coin into the coffer drops, a soul from purgatory hops'. This degeneration ran deep—grace, freedom from sin for cash. Luther fulminated against this in his own way and demanded a reformation of the whole Church. He circulated great and renowned pamphlets: *To the Christian Nobility of the German Nation*; another was called *Concerning Christian Liberty*; and a third was entitled *On the Babylonian Captivity of the Church*.

It was inevitable that he would be attacked. There were trials, especially the famous Imperial Diet of Worms, where Luther concludes, 'Here I stand; I cannot do otherwise. God help me.' Luther's excommunication had already been pronounced. He was given protection by the German nobility he had addressed, and they came to side more and more with him because they were also dissatisfied with the authority of the pope and the Church. They hid Luther away in the Wartburg where he first translates the New Testament and then, later, the Old Testament, ultimately the entire Bible. Following his re-emergence, the Reformation gradually unfolds. We do not have to go into the details, but we will instead consider what occurred inwardly.

Why did Luther have such an effect? It is undeniable that he set off an avalanche that still determines the religious landscape. According to Rudolf Steiner, the source of Luther's powerful effect is found in his earlier incarnation as one of the loftiest participants in the pre-Christian Mysteries, as a lofty initiate.[1] After his next incarnation came yet another incarnation, this time as Martin Luther.

There is an erroneous belief that an initiate who develops the capacity to see into the spiritual world in one incarnation maintains that capacity in subsequent lives. In fact that capacity is lost at the time of death, but its effect on the individuality remains. Thus Luther had no conscious memory of his time in the Mysteries before Christ, but these effects continued in his soul. They enabled him to enter into a perceptive, clairvoyant relationship with the spiritual world.

He now perceives that during his own time humanity is drifting into the realm of the devil—we would say, into Ahriman's realm. Again and again, the human being will be led through inner soul experiences of a thoroughly supersensible nature to an encounter with Ahriman, whom Luther calls the devil. Rudolf Steiner says Luther actually experiences the devil. He looks the devil in the eye. Luther himself spoke about this frequently, even in his *Table Talk*. Here, he comes to speak about Faust—Luther was very aware of Faust—and about the devil:

He had me quite often by the head but he had nevertheless to let me go. I tried hard to find out what kind of fellow he is. He often attacked me so violently that I no longer knew if I was alive or dead. He also brought me well into doubt so that I did not know if God existed, and I became completely downhearted about our beloved Father God. But with God's Word I warded him off. There is no help nor advice other than what God offers (through a little word spoken through a human being . . .)²

There is a whole series of such statements in which Luther openly speaks about his experience of the devil. One example of these encounters is when he threw the inkwell at the devil in the Wartburg—the ink stain has been replaced again and again over the centuries because visitors there keep chipping off pieces of it.

According to Rudolf Steiner, Luther naturally had to express in imaginations what he experienced spiritually. But what emerged from Luther was 'no mere doctrine';³ it was instead a result of the fact that he cultivated his connection with the spiritual world. What did he want in light of the fact that he saw humanity drifting slowly into Ahriman's sphere of influence? Today we would formulate it differently—drifting into materialism and so forth. Luther still saw this quite graphically. He sought out a way to rescue a view of Christianity that had not been infected by ahrimanic influences. Because he saw that people could no longer perceive anything spiritual and could not perceive the devil—which he continued to experience as an echo of his time in the Mysteries—Luther saw no other possibility than this: Human beings have to hang onto the sole record of the spiritual world, the one given by the evangelists in the Gospels.

The [German] term 'evangelical [Lutheran] Church' and the phrase 'I am an evangelical [a Lutheran]' arise from this. On the other hand, the Catholics said: Those are the Protestants who protest against everything, against the pope, against indulgences, and so forth. Both designations remained, notwithstanding the splits undergone by the evangelical Churches. The evangelical Churches set forth the Gospels as their source of strength in holding their own in the struggle against Ahriman.

Luther characterizes the whole soul mood of his time which we are only summarizing here. Rudolf Steiner asks, 'Who is a Lutheran today?—Actually, every person is a Lutheran!' and 'modern Catholic theology is, in fact, also Lutheran'.⁴ Luther thus represents the beginning of the age of the consciousness soul during which humanity will be confronted by Ahriman and must clarify for itself which direction to take. Luther proposes the path of the Gospels; the Scriptures can offer strength. He relies on the Scriptures.

Even in the pre-Reformation era—Wycliff and others are recognized by Protestant historians as precursors—it is said, as Hus did: The Holy Scriptures alone must impart the truth and structure of the Church.

Faust

Now we turn our attention to Luther's contemporary, Dr Johann Georg Faust (1480–1540). The biographies of both are chronologically almost parallel. Faust was also a participant in the old Mysteries, although in a completely different way. Luther stood in a Mystery stream that Rudolf Steiner describes as one of 'those Mysteries that prepared the way for Christianity'[5] and led to everything that was anticipated in Christianity. But this other individuality lived in a Mystery context that was entirely dedicated to a pagan experience of nature. The soul of Empedocles lived in the historical Faust. As Empedocles, he had sought to connect himself with nature as though in a misunderstood final stage of initiation, plunging himself into Mount Etna. But because he was led to the Mystery of Golgotha without preparation, he—and others whom Rudolf Steiner also mentions—enter into all manner of questionable practices. In his biography we find the life of an adventurer, the life of a magician. His opponents say he was a quack and a charlatan; those who appreciate him say he was a human being who struggles with the spiritual world, who also becomes aware of the devil and chooses a different path than Luther. He seeks to make a pact with the devil.

Later chapbooks quite reliably depict what lived in the figure of Georg Faust. Here is a person who connects himself with evil in order to acquire knowledge. The puppet play indicates that he had to connect himself with hell in order to fathom the deepest secrets of nature. In my book on Goethe's *Faust*,[6] I pointed out how deeply that shocked his whole world. He, like Luther, saw the devil; this is something others have also experienced, less intensely perhaps. It is the signature of the age of the consciousness soul that a wakeful consciousness might say: I will join with the devil in order to acquire knowledge. At that time, this still frightened people terribly.

His contemporaries thought that such a pact could not end well, that it had to lead to the person's downfall whereupon he would be snared by the devil. When, during his *Table Talk*, Luther came to speak of Faust—who was, of course, familiar to him as a contemporary—Luther also says: This cannot end well. This will be his ruin, and the devil will take him. It was the devil Luther knew so well, and he knew: No one can enter into a pact with this fellow.

Nevertheless, the figure of the historical Faust now gives rise to the creation of a great wave of imagination in Europe. The chapbook appears; it makes its way over to England where Marlowe writes a brilliant Faust drama, the first. The drama returns to Middle Europe, changes into puppet plays until, finally, the young Goethe sees this puppet play in Frankfurt in the middle of the eighteenth century and is inspired to come to a true understanding of the figure of Faust as representative of the age of the consciousness soul: The human being has to confront evil; he cannot run away from it. If he confronts evil in the right way, 'always striving',[7] then he will not succumb to the devil.

Thus two great streams emerge from Luther and Faust that are still active today. We need only recall everything non-Roman Catholic: the Protestant as well as the Calvinist Church; the whole western world and all that the figure of Faust became for modern-day human beings, not just in the German-speaking world—the riddle of the human being making a pact with evil in order to acquire spiritual powers and going about it in such an honest way that he is not snared by the devil.

The Witch Trials

There is something else that takes place around these events. In 1484, Innocent VIII issues a papal bull concerning the institution of witch trials. It is often thought that witch trials were something from the more distant past, perhaps the Middle Ages. But this is not at all the case. These witch trials were first set in motion relatively late, in 1484. They then continue into the sixteenth and seventeenth centuries. In his bull entitled *Summis desiderantes affectibus*, the pope says for the first time: With great concern it has come to our attention that there are people, men and women, who 'heedless of their own salvation ... have given themselves over ... to devils.' There follows a long accounting of everything these people do, how they curse and cause to perish 'infants and the offspring of animals ... as well as vineyards ...' and orchards. It is a long list—everything evil in which a person could be engaged; that is what they do. Therefore, says the pope, we commission inquisitors to find out what these sorcerers do and then, together with the secular branch, we destroy them. He adds: If anyone presumes to be an impediment to this, no matter who it may be, no matter by what right he may contradict this, he will incur 'the wrath of almighty God and of the blessed apostles Peter and Paul'.[8]

Then the period of witch trials begins, one that is rightly described as unholy. We immediately encounter something strange. Lists have been left behind by the executioners—several of them—where everyone they have burned at the stake is precisely recorded. Then they calculate the price of the wood for the pyre and the ropes at so many florins, and coolly add up the total. We can read this in the lists of condemned witches and sorcerers. They are, of course, people from all walks of life: clergymen, noblemen, aldermen, simple craftsmen. Then, suddenly, as we read through the lists something jumps out: there are always children among them—a little five-year-old girl; a seven-year-old boy. The reader stops and notes: This is completely different from the earlier trials of heretics. Those were people who stood for their convictions and went to the pyre or were thrown on the fire for them. But to accuse a five-year-old girl, a seven-year old-boy of witchcraft! Then there are officials, a spiritual advisor and so forth; these lists run right through the whole society and include all age groups. What was this about? How can a child be suspected of witchcraft?

Rudolf Steiner offers a unique explanation that throws a lot of light on these witch trials, especially if we are familiar with them and the literature about them. He says: They persecuted anyone who was suspected of being clairvoyant. Naturally, clairvoyance could arise quite soon in a child; people noticed when a child spoke about things other people did not see. At this time—and it is a matter of this time, not an earlier time—things were not to be revealed through clairvoyance that should be kept hidden and held in secret.

Philip the Fair

Something else also plays into this. We must look again at Philip IV, the Fair, who gave specific instructions about how to torture the Templars so that they would admit to all sorts of things in the agony of torture. The individuality known as Philip the Fair also comes out of earlier Mysteries—the black magic Mysteries in Mexico we have already discussed. In these Mysteries he had an experience of what happens to the human soul before, during and after death when people are hideously mutilated—as they were in the Mexican Mysteries. The pyramids of the Mexican Mysteries had enormous channels for the blood of the hundreds of slaves and prisoners of war who were slaughtered there, one after the other, so many that their blood streamed down the channels. Philip brings with him an experience—transformed—of what happens when a person is tortured: the victim first confesses to things he had actually just over-come, which was what happened with the Templars who had gone through the various levels of schooling described by Dante in his *Divine Comedy*. This torture was really horrifying; one graphic example describes a person outstretched and naked while glowing coals were placed on his abdomen. In anguish he confesses the sins he overcame and also reveals what resulted as spiritual vision from having overcome sin. He speaks of spiritual secrets.

These Mexican Mysteries had offshoots, and these offshoots found their way into the Indian culture in North America. We know the history of how the Indians tied a captured enemy to the stake and how he was then tortured to death over a long period of time. First came the children who pricked the prisoner with little knives; then came the women who poked at him with large knives. This went on for hours until the victim died at the stake. What did he do during this time? He began to speak. As the pain increased, he revealed everything he had experienced in regard to the wisdom of nature, nature initiation, nature secrets. When an enemy then died after being tied to the stake under these conditions, he was buried with great honour.

This is a cross between an almost black magic way of working and a nature magic way of working. Philip the Fair employed it with the Templars, thus inaugurating something that still exists today. Rudolf Steiner notes this explicitly, although it was before we knew everything we have learned during the last century about brainwashing, about the fact that during weeks-long torture—no longer with glowing coals, but almost—people are pressured to confess something they do not believe, to say something they actually do not want to say. This evil stream was instigated by Philip the Fair and his henchman Nogaret along with others, a camarilla that has returned in the twentieth century. Even today we can find this stream of causing people pain so that they say things they do not want to say and confess things they absolutely do not want to confess.

The Jesuit Order

Another event around the year 1500 is the founding of the Jesuit Order by Ignatius of Loyola. He lived from 1491 until 1556. After an injury, he decides to found an order that intervenes in a militant way for Catholic Christianity. Of course, on the one hand, there is the beginning of the Counter-Reformation, and the Jesuit Order takes a strong stand to reverse the rise of Protestantism. When we look at maps in Church histories, it is astonishing how vast regions that are today staunchly Catholic—like Austria and Bavaria and so forth—were largely Protestant in the sixteenth century. This was naturally a terrible source of concern for Rome. Thus the Jesuit Order was established in order to reverse this. But the Order has characteristics that also make it a spiritual problem and a spiritual force even today. Not without reason is it referred to by its shortened name, the Jesuits; only the human figure of Jesus carries any weight for them. They ignore everything we call Christ Jesus. There is a large theological work by a Jesuit expressly titled *Jesus der Christus* [Jesus the Christ]. Jesus is the Christ; there is no other Christ. It is a thick volume that sets out to prove this, in the course of which the author naturally falls into confusion when he comes to Paul. Paul was the first to say: The human being Jesus, and the god Christ.

This view was practised in great militaristic imaginations. The novice had to imagine two encampments. In the most vivid imaginations possible there is the camp of the army of Christ—Christ with His banner and His saints; the other is the army of the devil—the devil with his banners and his helpers. The individual was to have a strong inner experience of the fact that two great camps stand opposite one another; he was, of course, to turn towards the Christian camp. Then there is something that is always referred to in connection to the Jesuits, and rightfully so: the strictest spiritual exercises. The soul is drilled by means of these prescribed exercises until it has come so far that it says—and this is a literal formulation from Ignatius of Loyola that can be found in his book *Spiritual Exercises*—'When the Church says to me that black is white then, for me, black is white; and when the Church says that white is black then, for me, white is black.'

This gave rise to a concept attributed to the Jesuit Order, the concept of blind obedience. The member of the Order is to be available like a cadaver, like a corpse in the hands of an old man, without a will of its own. The goal is to eliminate any freedom in initiative and, above all, to turn entirely to the earthly character of Christianity in one's inner, meditative activity. Rudolf Steiner says that this results in the Jesuits becoming outstanding scientists; the Jesuit Order always excelled in educating their members to be the very best materialistic scientists.

Thus another stream enters at this time through the gate of the consciousness soul, a stream that we—in the anthroposophical movement—have always had to confront. Jesuitism is the complete opposite of Goetheanism. Although we can value the accomplishments of individual Jesuits, the intent of Jesuitism is the reverse of what anthroposophy intends. We can say this not as a personal or moral judgement, but objectively.

Agrippa von Nettesheim

The theme of this discussion is the historical figure of Faust and his contemporaries—we have already discussed a few of these great contemporaries, some of the great figures of the time. Agrippa von Nettesheim (1487–1535) is also part of this circle. If I were to make a chart or a diagram of all this, we would see that these lives run parallel to one another. Agrippa published several books on magic through which he brought into the consciousness soul age what had surfaced from various cultural realms in the past—Islam, Judaism, and so on. He was a mediator of the old occultism in the present day. For example, he took up the ten Sefiroth. Enumerating them—Kether, Hokmah, Binah, Hesed, Gevurah, Tifereth, Netsah, Hod, Yesod and Malkuth—he said: These are also an expression of all the hierarchies. For the seraphim, of course, Kether; the cherubim for Hokmah; and for Binah the thrones. It continues downwards through the kyriotetes, the dynamis, the exusiai, the archai, archangels and angels. And Malkuth, the realm—those are the blessed spirits of human beings.

He brings many such relationships, but I will only mention a few more. He assigns angelic names to the hierarchies: Michael to the archangels; Gabriel to the angels. And who belongs to Malkuth, the realm, the blessed spirits? The soul of the Messiah. It continues this way. The plants, organs, and, finally, the inhabitants of hell are illuminated, so to speak, by the ten Sefiroth. This is only one facet. As if through a lens, Agrippa von Nettesheim brings into focus this occult knowledge that entered through various streams. He bundles them together and guides them over into the present. We live in an age of occultism; and there are many people who frequent so-called occult bookshops where traces of Agrippa of Nettesheim can be found in very modern books on occultism, always newly formulated, always different.

Rudolf Steiner thoroughly appreciated Agrippa. He says that he fought to see '*only* what is natural in nature; and what is spiritual in the spirit'.[9] Of course, during Agrippa's time, nature was still understood to be something essentially living, elemental, a bit as it was understood by another great contemporary, Paracelsus.

Paracelsus

Paracelsus lived parallel to the others, from 1493 to 1541. He travelled widely throughout the countries of Europe and into the Orient. As a doctor, he wanted to learn to read in the Book of Nature. He tells that he learned things from everyone—from shepherds, itinerants and learned people; he learned everywhere. How does nature speak of the essence of the human being? How do I arrive at a view of the spirit from reading in nature? If we examine the works of Paracelsus, we realize that he identified what we call the members of the human being. He describes them somewhat differently; but that is not so important. He identifies the ether body, the astral body, the spiritual element of the human being. Above all, he arrives at the elemental forces in nature through his study of nature and his reading in the Book of Nature. He comes to how these elemental forces in nature are connected with the human organs; how the human organs are connected with the activity of the heavens. He learns to grasp the natural appearance of the human being as a microcosm of the macrocosm.

Based on serious reports about him, we should not wonder that Paracelsus was really a great doctor. I know from anthroposophical doctors—and Rudolf Steiner says this about himself, as well—that doctors today often like to look to Paracelsus if they are unable to do more for a patient. The work of Paracelsus is vast and encompasses not only medicine but also philosophy, philology and theology. Agrippa von Nettesheim works into the present like a conduit for old occultism. Through Paracelsus a second great conduit appears alongside Agrippa von Nettesheim—a spiritual understanding of nature, a capacity to read in the phenomena of nature. Rudolf Steiner discusses both of these individualities together in one chapter of his book *Die Mystik im Aufgange des neuzeitlichen Geisteslebens* [Mysticism at the dawn of modern spiritual life].[10]

Raimund of Sabunda

Another individual made these claims before Paracelsus—here again I am going backwards in time a bit—someone highly valued by Rudolf Steiner: Raimund of Sabunda. He was born in Barcelona and died in 1436. Raimund was the first to set forth the great doctrine of the two books: a book of nature and a book of spirit. He says the truth of the Holy Scriptures can be verified only if what is written in the ancient book of creation—the Book of Nature—is first understood. I first have to read in the Book of Nature; when I have done so correctly, I become capable of reading in the Book of Spirit. This is so fundamental that Rudolf Steiner calls the doctrines of Raimund of Sabunda an earthly reflection of the supersensible teaching of Michael.[11]

We are now gradually finding our way into the present, into the anthroposophical present as well. But Raimund also says: The human being who has sinned can no longer read in the Book of Nature; therefore he must first read in the Book of Revelation. As if in a prophetic pre-figuring of the dawning age of the consciousness soul, he demands the following of the future: Human beings must again learn to read in the Book of Nature so that they can correctly read in the Book of Spirit.

The Anglican Church

All sorts of terrible things happen to the Catholic Church during this time. Thu once again—around the year 1500, from 1491 to 1547—the whole Church of England separated from Rome. Here we come across the infamous Henry VIII. He had numerous wives; he divorced one, had another executed, and then divorced again. Since the pope and the Church were unwilling to play along with the drama of his many wives, Henry said: I will found my own Church! Perhaps it sounds a bit casual, but this is what lay behind it. Rudolf Steiner depicts it in this way as well. In order to free himself from the relentless dominance of Rome in his dealings with his wives, Henry founded the Anglican Church. He believed it was his business alone if he wanted to have one wife executed in order to take another.

Thus, during this period we find the Anglican Church in England and in the colonies influenced by England. But there was someone who spoke against this, who upbraided the king, a pupil of Pico della Mirandola and chancellor to Henry the VIII: Thomas Moore. He did not go along; he remained Catholic, for which he was executed. Today he is a Catholic saint. Through Thomas Moore, the whole of modern development experienced a moment of protest against protest. This is perhaps a para-doxical way of expressing it. Today protesting is quite in vogue. There are people who are against everything; people who are anti-authority. But there are also people who are against anti-authoritarianism, as though for a moment they step back and say: Wait a minute! Protest is not a given; protesting against protesting is also possible. That is a true sign of the consciousness soul.

Protesting could also come out of the intellectual soul; but when we also develop consciousness of consciousness, when we look at ourselves critically or look upon the critique critically—it is a pure consciousness soul activity that the intellectual soul cannot manage. That is a capacity that only gradually develops.

The Rosicrucian Stream

We will now consider something else that will lead us into the present. Another stream begins in 1484, the Rosicrucian stream in the narrower sense. There had been an earlier incarnation of Christian Rosenkreutz during which, as a young boy, he experienced a great initiation through twelve initiates. There he brought together everything they had to offer in the way of initiation knowledge, each from a different major cultural epoch; he internalized it and then, in a completely new form, he rayed it back to the twelve so that the wisdom each had was gathered together in a new way and received from him. This is then passed on to the pupils of these initiates. The youth died, but this wisdom is passed on to the pupils in forms we see later as the so-called Rosicrucian writings with their diagrams, images, and so forth. Two such diagrams can be found in a lecture Virginia Sease gave in Compostela, later published in *Paths of the Christian Mysteries*. For example, the Sophia is shown, and how the world develops out of her.[12] These are wonderful diagrams with which we could spend an entire lifetime if we were so inclined.

From the middle of the twelfth century on, a small stream flows for a while through these pupils. I have pointed this out; naturally they are all connected with one another—the Templars, the Cistercians. It was not as it is today. The world was manageable; above all, it was a world in which there was a shared understanding among people who sought out what was spiritual, people who generally criticized and distanced themselves from Rome.

Then this youth is reborn as the actual Christian Rosenkreutz, Father Rosenkreutz. He grows to be quite old, living from 1378 to 1484. Once again he undergoes vast experiences, travels through the Orient, and has something like a Damascus experience. He sees how the etheric Being of the Christ is connected to evolution—the Damascus experience is seeing how the Christ-being is related to the whole of earth and human evolution. Then he meets the pupils and descendants of his old teachers and the actual Rosicrucian Order now arises, still small in number. After his death in 1484 it begins to unfold across Europe; again, this is around the year 1500 and beyond.

Christian Rosenkreutz has always accompanied his Order from the spiritual world. He also incarnated later, a fact that can give rise to sensationalized ideas and speculation; but these speculations are not so important. What is significant is that a spiritual being like Christian Rosenkreutz is present in the evolution of humanity.

A problem arose for the Rosicrucians who then entered into the consciousness soul age with an awake consciousness. They saw a great danger coming—the danger of two great kinds of imbalance. I have already explained that the human being ascended from the sentient soul to the intellectual soul, and then to the consciousness soul. The latter rests on the physical body but its uppermost soul member simultaneously borders on the spiritual, on the developing Spirit Self. It is an enormous tension, one not encountered by the soul at any other stage. On the basis of this tension, the danger arises that the human being could tear himself asunder or lose himself in one of two extremes. He could lose himself fully in matter and become a technocrat in his constitution. Or he could lose himself to what is spiritual and succumb to flight from the world.

What does this mean? It means that what had previously been the historical problem we discussed—emperor and pope—becomes a problem in the very constitution of the human being during the consciousness soul age. Every person in the consciousness soul age is vulnerable to the problems of technocracy, of the material, of entering into a purely materialistic relationship to the world; or is vulnerable to the problem of withdrawing into the spiritual, retreating from the world. We have seen this with the great religious orders.

For the Rosicrucians—who are always correctly identified as descendants of the Templars—the Templar's goal now arises as a new ideal. Every man is his own emperor and pope; every human being becomes so powerful in his soul that he has the sovereignty to handle the physical world as well as the spiritual world without being torn apart. The ideal arises that we call the true modern path of schooling, Rosicrucian schooling. It is a path of schooling the human being can undertake in daily life. The Rosicrucian pupil does not need to flee the world, to withdraw into a monastery. He can be a locomotive engineer, a pilot, a businessman; standing in life, he does justice to all the demands of life yet pursues a spiritual path. This was what the Rosicrucians want to make possible, and what they made possible—which meant that something else had to take place.

The Buddha on Mars

The human being goes from one earth life to another; he goes through the planetary spheres. He has an after-death experience. People have always known this; even in antiquity there are descriptions of the path the soul takes after death. The human being goes through the planetary spheres until he reaches a point called the cosmic midnight hour; then he

turns back to a new incarnation, taking new capacities with him. He
passes again through the planetary spheres and prepares himself for the
next incarnation. During this whole time, the karma of his old life has
transformed into the karma of the new, and spiritual beings have
approached the human being. But one sphere is particularly important for
life on earth and life in the spirit. Spiritual beings are connected with these
planetary spheres: the angels with the moon; the archangels with Mercury; the archai with Venus; the elohim, the exusiai with the Sun; and in
the Mars sphere live the spirits of movement, the dynamis. This is to be
understood spiritually. The dynamis participate everywhere the human
being acts; whether he is doing something physically or spiritually, he
always requires strength, the cosmic strength of the dynamis. However,
Mars had come to the point where impulses of a strongly materialistic
nature were active in it; one can also say they had a contentious and
warlike nature, but they were an extension of materialistic impulses.

The initiates around Christian Rosenkreuz recognized the necessity for
one of them to go to Mars and create new conditions there. This becomes
the famous journey of the Buddha to Mars. Rudolf Steiner describes how
Christian Rosenkreutz sends the Buddha, his closest friend and pupil, to
Mars where he takes on a mission similar to the mission of Christ on the
earth. He brings with him a spiritualization of the conditions on Mars. For
all the souls who afterwards pass through the Mars sphere again on their
way back to earth, he becomes a teacher of a certain capacity—if they
have prepared themselves for it.

This capacity is described only inadequately if we say it is the capacity
for meditation, although it concerns meditation. The Buddha on Mars is
our greatest teacher of meditation, but more than just meditation; it is a
practice of turning inwards while standing in the outer world. There are
always indications within the anthroposophical path of schooling that it
does no good to withdraw to a quiet cabin or a monastery—strength
cannot be acquired there at all. It is much more appropriate to find
concentration in the hustle and bustle of life and to face the spirit
inwardly, through its inner movement and based on our own sovereignty.

If we were to take a course on meditation and exercises, there could
certainly be an extensive discussion about the many interesting attempts
people make. Travelling on a bus or car or on a train, we might suddenly
say: I want to forget all about the world out there. I want to concentrate
on myself, to pull myself together. Then we have the experience that this
is not so easy, that we are continually distracted. But we also have the
experience that certain forces begin to become active in us which we have
never noticed before. In a solitary cloister cell today—during the Middle

Ages it was different—what else is there to do but concentrate? Gathering yourself together in the midst of outer life, that is the Rosicrucian impulse, the great impulse that came through the Buddha as he went to Mars in 1604 as the result of a Rosicrucian initiative.

Rosicrucian writings begin to appear in 1603; first was the manuscript of the *Chymical Wedding*, then came the published works, among them the *Fama fraternitatis*. Rosicrucianism spreads, but because of the outbreak of the Thirty Years War it is suppressed as it tries to spread further. Instigated by the Jesuits, as is asserted today, this conflict was the great war that decimated Middle Europe right to its foundations—just where Rosicrucianism would have blossomed. Cities were burned to the ground, people murdered; 30 years of war left a cultural wasteland in its wake. This was the first great blow against Roscrucianism, one from which it only slowly recovered.

Anthroposophy

In fact—and I say this not to boast, but in a purely factual way—Rosicrucianism does not resurface fully until the appearance of anthroposophy. It was always a stream; the traditions had always existed. But what now creates the bridge between the Middle Ages and the present— as well as other bridges—did not really become active as a mighty cultural and historical impulse until anthroposophy.

Anthroposophy seeks to accomplish what Dante describes as the goal of the Templar initiation—the appropriate goal for the modern age. It places human beings spiritually on their own two feet; it even places them politically on their own two feet. When the goal is socio-political, it is called threefolding the social organism. When it is spiritual, it is called anthroposophy. What anthroposophy wants and what the Templars failed to achieve back then—because Europe was not yet ripe for it, according to Rudolf Steiner—is sovereignty, autonomy, the possibility for individual self-determination to awaken in human beings.

We must conclude our look at the Middle Ages with this image, although it asks us to make giant leaps. Much takes place after 1500, not the least of which was the French Revolution, again a significant turning point. Earlier, Paracelsus had been connected to the Rosicrucians, as was Agrippa von Nettesheim; in modern terms, I would say it was a club comprised of those who knew the spirit and understood the spirit, and had many contacts with one another. And if we look at the destiny of the Rosicrucian stream that flows through all of this, we see the continuation of the great Templar impulse that reaches into the present.

I have spoken to you about the cults that arose at the turn of the first century through Markus and Ormuz; about the transformed old Isis cults. These then flowed into the enigmatic Templar cults which are again transformed for the present time by the Rosicrucian masters. Rudolf Steiner, for example, learned about them in the twentieth century. They will continue to have an effect as a cultic experience of the human being between spirit and nature.

The School for Spiritual Science, as we call it, was created towards the end of his life by Rudolf Steiner and forms the central core of anthroposophy. Membership of the School has a greater sense of obligation attached to it than membership of the Anthroposophical Society. Anyone who becomes a member of the School is faced with two requirements: to open himself to the spiritual world through meditation, *Vita contemplativa*, and to be active in the world as a representative of what is spiritual, *Vita activa*—in other words, to be his own emperor and pope as a unity without being torn apart. All of us who are active in this know that it is only a beginning. We have just arrived at or are still standing at the gate to where a true Rosicrucian schooling will lead in the future, in the next centuries, in the next millennium. But we also know that we are accompanied in this by all those who have wrestled with these questions in the past. Rudolf Steiner once said: 'Brunetto Latini ... is there ... he can be found if he is sought spiritually.'[13]

Whether people have returned in physical incarnation as Platonists, as Aristotelians, as pupils of Chartres, as members of the Dominican Order, as Templars, as Cathars, or whether spiritual beings, the dead, are accompanying us and will perhaps incarnate during the next century, we have considered here a stream of spiritual continuity that flows through human history beginning in the year 1000. Anthroposophy wants nothing else but to be part of and engaged with this stream.

Notes

Editor's note: The references to Rudolf Steiner's works listed below are to the original German editions, with a literal English translation of the title shown in brackets. The passages quoted in the text have been translated directly from the original German. The 'GA' numbers given refer to the catalogue number of the *Gesamtausgabe* or Collected Works in the original German as published by Rudolf Steiner Verlag, Switzerland. The dates of the cited lectures are also given. To facilitate the identification of English-language editions of the cited lectures, a bibliography follows on page 207.

Citations are given in full the first time they appear in each lecture. Works cited only by title and GA number are by Rudolf Steiner.

Lecture 1

1. Jan Hus, *Schriften zur Glaubensreform und Briefe der Jahre 1414–1415* [Writings on the reform of thinking and letters 1414–1415], ed. Walter Schamschula (Insel Verlag: Frankfurt, 1969), p. 95.
2. *Dictatus Papae*, cited in: *Fischer Weltgeschichte* [Fischer world history], Jacques Le Goff, *Das Hochmittelalter* [The High Middle Ages] (Fischer Bücherei: Frankfurt, 1965), Vol. 11, pp. 90f.
3. *Lexikon des Mittelalters* [Lexicon of the Middle Ages], ed. Bruno Mariacher (Artemis Verlag: Munich/Zürich, 1989), vol. 4, p. 1934.
4. *Die Erneuerung der pädagogisch-didaktischen Kunst durch Geisteswissenschaft* [The renewal of the pedagogical-didactic art by means of spiritual science] (GA 301), lecture of 7 May 1920.
5. *Jeanne d'Arc, Die Akten der Verurteilung* [Joan of Arc, the acts of condemnation], trans. Josef Butler (Einsiedeln: Cologne, 1943), p. 216ff.
6. A reference to Johann Wolfgang von Goethe, *Faust, Erster Teil* [Faust, Part One], l. 2836.
7. Published as *Paths of the Christian Mysteries: From Compostela to the New World*, Virginia Sease and Manfred Schmidt-Brabant, trans. M. Miller and D. Miller (Temple Lodge: Forest Row, 2003).
8. *Vier Mysteriendramen* [The four Mystery dramas] (GA 14), *Die Prüfung der Seele* [The soul's probation], Scene 2.
9. Virginia Sease, ed., *Esoterik der Weltreligionen* [The esotericism of world religions] (Verlag am Goetheanum: Dornach, 2001).

10. *Esoterische Betrachtungen karmischer Zusammenhänge* [Esoteric studies of karmic connections], vol. 3 (GA 237), lecture of 13 July 1924.

Lecture 2

1. See www.gallica.co.uk/celts/torc.htm for photographs of the Treasure of Vix.
2. *Erdensterben und Welterleben. Anthroposophische Lebensgaben. Bewusstseins-Notwendigkeiten für Gegenwart und Zukunft* [Earthly death and cosmic life. Anthroposophical gifts. Necessities for consciousness in the present and the future] (GA 181), lecture of 2 April 1918.
3. *Esoterische Betrachtungen karmischer Zusammenhänge* [Esoteric observations on karmic connections], vol. 6 (GA 240), lecture of 27 August 1924.
4. Walter Johannes Stein, *Weltgeschichte im Lichte des heiligen Gral. Das neunte Jahrhundert* [World history in the light of the Holy Grail. The ninth century] (J. Ch. Mellinger: Stuttgart, 1977), p. 6f. (Available in English as *The Ninth Century and the Holy Grail*, Temple Lodge: Forest Row, 2001.)
5. Ibid., p. 166.
6. *Erdensterben und Welterleben* (GA 181), lecture of 21 August 1924.

Lecture 3

1. Virginia Sease and Manfred Schmidt-Brabant, *Paths of the Christian Mysteries, From Compostela to the New World* (Temple Lodge: Forest Row, 2003).
2. Markus Osterrieder, *Sonnenkreuz und Lebensbaum. Irland, der Schwarzmeer-Raum und die Christianisierung der europäischen Mitte* [Sun cross and tree of life. Ireland, the area of the Black Sea, and the Christianization of central Europe] (Urachhaus: Stuttgart, 1995).
3. *Okkulte Untersuchungen über das Leben zwischen Tod und neuer Geburt* [Occult research on life between death and a new birth] (GA 140), lecture of 12 March 1913.
4. *Das esoterische Christentum und die geistige Führung der Menschheit* [Esoteric Christianity and the spiritual leadership of humanity] (GA 130), lecture of 18 December 1912.
5. *Okkulte Untersuchungen* (GA 140), lecture of 12 March 1913.

Lecture 4

1. Karl Heyer, *Das Wunder von Chartres* [The wonder of Chartres] (R. Geering: Basel, 1926); Gottfried Richter, *Chartres* (Verlag Urachhaus: Stuttgart,

1982); Frank Teichmann, *Der Mensch und sein Tempel, Chartres, Kathedrale und Schule* [The human being and his temple. Chartres, cathedral and school] (Verlag Urachhaus: Stuttgart, 1991); Michael Ladwein, *Chartres, Ein Führer durch die Kathedrale* [Chartres, a guide through the cathedral] (Verlag Urachhaus: Stuttgart, 2000).

2. Heinz Kaminsky, *Sternstrassen der Vorzeit* [Star paths of prehistory] (Herbig: Munich, 1996).

3. Heyer, p. 59.

4. *Esoterische Betrachtungen karmischer Zusammenhänge* [Esoteric studies of karmic connections], vol. 3 (GA 237), lecture of 13 July 1924.

5. Ibid.

6. *Fischer Weltgeschichte* [Fischer world history], vol. 11, p. 90.

7. *Das Initiaten-Bewusstsein* [Initiate consciousness] (GA 243), lecture of 14 August 1924.

8. Heyer, p. 63.

9. *Das Initiaten-Bewusstsein* (GA 243), lecture of 14 August 1924.

10. *Esoterische Betrachtungen karmischer Zusammenhänge* [Esoteric studies of karmic connections], vol. 3 (GA 237), lecture of 13 July 1924.

11. Gen. 1:2.

12. *Erdensterben und Welterleben. Anthroposophische Lebensgaben. Bewusstseins-Notwendigkeiten für Gegenwart und Zukunft* [Earthly death and cosmic life. Anthroposophical gifts. Necessities for consciousness in the present and the future] (GA 181), lecture of 16 July 1918.

Lecture 5

1. Karl Heyer, 'Martianus Capella und die Sieben Freien Künste' [Martianus Capella and the seven liberal arts], cited in: *Die Drei* [The three], vol. 4, no. 12, March 1925.

2. Ibid.

3. *Das Geheimnis der Trinität* [The secret of the Trinity] (GA 214), lecture of 23 July 1922.

4. Raymond Klibansky, cited in: David L. Wagner (ed.), *The Seven Liberal Arts in the Middle Ages* (Indiana University Press: Bloomington, 1983), p. 24.

5. In: Lynn Thorndike, 'Elementary and Secondary Education in the Middle Ages', *Speculum* 15 (1940), 405, p. 59 from: *Vatican Fondo Palatino, Codex Latinus 1252* (translated by M. and D. Miller from the German trans. by V. Sease).

6. *Esoterische Betrachtungen karmischer Zusammenhänge* [Esoteric observations on karmic connections], vol. 3, lecture of 13 July 1924.

7. Ibid.

8. Ibid.

9. Alanus ab Insulis, *Der Anticlaudian oder die Bücher von der himmlischen*

Erschaffung des Neuen Menschen [The anticlaudian or the books on the divine creation of the new human being], trans. and intr. by Wilhelm Rath (Mellinger: Stuttgart, 1966), p. 134.

Lecture 6

1. Henry Charles Lea, *Geschichte der Inquisition im Mittelalter* [History of the Inquisition in the Middle Ages], 3 vols., vol. 1 *Ursprung und Organisation der Inquisition* [Origin and organization of the Inquisition] (Greno Verlag: Nördlingen, 1987), p. 60f.
2. Ibid.
3. Emil Bock, '2. Brief des Paulus an die Thessalonicher 2, 2–9' [Second Letter of Paul to the Thessalonians 2:2–9] (Stuttgart, 1930), cited in: *Beiträge zur Übersetzung des Neuen Testaments* [Contributions on the translation of the New Testament], p. 10f.
4. *Über Philosophie, Geschichte und Literatur* [On philosophy, history and literature] (GA 51), lecture of 28 December 1904.
5. Ibid.
6. *Vorträge und Kurse über christlich-religiöses Wirken* [Lectures and courses on Christian religious work], vol. 5 (GA 346), lecture of 10 September 1924.
7. *Die Grundimpulse des weltgeschichtlichen Werdens der Menschheit* [The fundamental impulses of the world-historical evolution of humanity] (GA 216), lecture of 1 October 1922.
8. *Vorträge und Kurse über christlich-religiöses Wirken* [Lectures and courses on Christian religious work], vol. 2 (GA 343), lecture of 3 October 1921.
9. *Exkurse in das Gebiet des Markus-Evangeliums* [Excursus into the realm of the Gospel of Mark] (GA 124), lecture of 13 March 1911.
10. Sigrid Hunke, *Allahs Sonne über dem Abendland: Unser arabisches Erbe* [Allah's sun over Europe: Our Arabic heritage] (Fischer: Frankfurt a. M., 1997), p. 305f.
11. Rainer Maria Rilke, *Das Stundenbuch* [The book of hours], Book Three: 'Das Buch von der Armut und vom Tode' [The book of poverty and death] (Insel: Frankfurt a. M., 1962).
12. Lea, p. 134.
13. *Die Mission einzelner Volksseelen im Zusammenhang mit der germanisch-nordischen Mythologie* [The mission of individual folk souls in connection with Germanic-Nordic mythology] (GA 121), lecture of 17 June 1910.
14. *Wege der geistigen Erkenntnis und der Erneuerung künstlerischer Weltanschauung,* [Paths of spiritual discovery and of the renewal of an artistic world view] (GA 161), lecture of 1 May 1915; *Menschliche und menschheitliche Entwicklungswahrheiten. Das Karma des Materialismus* [Evolutionary truths about the human being and humanity. The karma of materialism] (GA 176), lecture of 11 September 1917.

15. *Die Philosophie des Thomas von Aquino* [The philosophy of Thomas Aquinas] (GA 74), Dornach, 1993, lectures of 22 and 24 May 1920.

Lecture 7

1. 1 John 4:16.
2. *Wie erlangt man Erkenntnisse der höheren Welten?* [How to attain knowledge of higher worlds] (GA 10).
3. Meister Eckhart, 'Reden der Unterweisung 13' [Instructional talks 13], (ed. Quint, *Predigten* [sermons], p. 73), cited in: Arnold Angenendt, *Die Geschichte der Religiosität im Mittelalter* [The history of religiosity in the Middle Ages] (Primus Verlag: Darmstadt, 1997), p. 99.
4. *Die Geheimwissenschaft im Umriss* [Occult science in outline] (GA 13), chapter: Die Weltentwickelung und der Mensch [World evolution and the human being].
5. Hildegard von Bingen, *Scivias*, II, 7, cited in: Angenendt, p. 151f.
6. *Vier Mysteriendramen* [The four Mystery dramas], *Die Pforte der Einweihung* [The portal of initiation], Scene 2.
7. Luke 23:46.
8. *Muspilli*, cited in: Angenendt, p. 671.
9. 'Nikodemus-Evangelium' [Gospel of Nicodemus], cited in: Erich Weidinger, *Die Apokryphen. Verborgene Bücher der Bibel* [The apocrypha. Hidden books of the Bible] (Bechtermünz Verlag: Augsburg, 1988), p. 485.
10. Ibid., p. 487.
11. *Vita Anskarii*, cited in: Angenendt, p. 728.
12. *Von Jesus zu Christus* [From Jesus to Christ] (GA 131), lecture of 11 October 1911, pp. 167–8.
13. Gottfried Richter, *Chartres* (Verlag Urachhaus: Stuttgart, 1982), p. 132.

Lecture 8

1. Gershom Scholem, *Major Trends in Jewish Mysticism* (Schocken Books: New York, 1995).
2. *Die Geheimwissenschaft im Umriss* [Occult science in outline], chapter: Die Erkenntnis der höheren Welten [Knowledge of higher worlds].
3. *Die Geschichte der Menschheit und die Weltanschauungen der Kulturvölker* [The history of humanity and the world views of civilized nations] (GA 353), Dornach, 1988, lecture of 10 May 1924.
4. Martin Buber, *Die Legende des Baalschem* [Legend of Baal-Shem], Frankfurt a. M., 1920; Christian Knorr v. Rosenroth, *Kabbalah denudata*, 3 vols. (Frankfurt, 1677 and 1684).

5. Karl Heyer, p. 65.

6. *Esoterische Betrachtungen karmischer Zusammenhänge* [Esoteric studies of karmic connections], vol. 3 (GA 237), lectures of 8 and 10 July 1924.

7. *Wie erlangt man Erkenntnisse der höheren Welten?* [How to attain knowledge of higher worlds] (GA 10), chapter: Die Weltentwickelung und der Mensch [World evolution and the human being].

8. Hanns Bächtold Stäubli, *Handwörterbuch des deutschen Aberglaubens* [The concise dictionary of German superstition] (W. de Gruyter: Berlin and Leipzig, 1927–42).

Lecture 9

1. *Das Initiaten-Bewusstsein* [Initiation consciousness], lecture of 14 August 1924.

2. Ibid.

3. Ibid.

4. Joachim of Fiore, 'Expositio in Apocalypsim', Venice 1527, cited in: Bernard McGinn, *Die Mystik im Abendland* [Mysticism in the West], vol. 2 (Herder: Freiburg, 1996), p. 516.

5. Joachim of Fiore, 'Psalterium decem chordarum', Venice 1527, cited in: Bernard McGinn, p. 517.

6. Virginia Sease and Manfred Schmidt-Brabant, *Paths of the Christian Mysteries: From Compostela to the New World*, pp. 118, 120.

7. Delno C. West and Sandra Zimdars-Swartz, *Joachim of Fiore. A Study in Spiritual Perception and History* (Indiana University Press: Bloomington, 1983).

8. 1 Cor. 12:12.

9. West and Zimdars-Swartz, p. 17.

Lecture 10

1. *Die Tempellegende und die Goldene Legende* [The temple legend and the golden legend] (GA 93), lecture of 22 May 1905.

2. *Innere Entwicklungsimpulse der Menschheit. Goethe und die Krisis des neunzehnten Jahrhunerts* [Inner impulses in the development of humanity: Goethe and the crisis of the nineteenth century] (GA 171), lecture of 25 September 1916.

3. *Zur Geschichte und aus den Inhalten der erkenntniskultischen Abteilung der Esoterischen Schule von 1904 bis 1914* [On the history of the cognitive-cultic section of the Esoteric School 1904–1914, and from its contents] (GA 265), Dornach, 1987, p. 95.

4. *Über Philosophie, Geschichte und Literatur* [On philosophy, history and literature] (GA 51), lecture of 28 December 1904.

5. Dora Baker, *Tesoretto* (Stuttgart, 1979), p. 21.

6. *Esoterische Betrachtungen karmischer Zusammenhänge* [Esoteric studies of karmic connections], vol. 3 (GA 237), lecture of 13 July 1924.

7. Dante Alighieri, *Die Göttliche Komödie* [The divine comedy], trans. Karl Witte (Berlin, 1921), *Inferno*, Canto 15, ll. 82–85.

8. *Naturbeobachtung, Experiment, Mathematik und die Erkenntnisstufen der Geistesforschung* [Nature observation, experiment, mathematics, and the levels of knowledge in spiritual research] (GA 324), lecture of 23 March 1921.

9. Dante, *Inferno*, Canto 1, ll. 1f.

10. Ibid., Canto 3, l. 96.

11. *Naturbeobachtung,* (GA 324), lecture of 23 March 1921.

12. Dante, *Inferno*, Canto 15, ll. 82–85.

13. Ibid., *Purgatorio*, Canto 27, ll. 140ff.

14. C. Englert-Faye, *Vom Mythos zur Idee der Schweiz* [From mythos to the idea of Switzerland] (Zürich, 1940).

15. Dante, *Purgatorio*, Canto 28, l. 142.

16. Ibid., Canto 33, l. 145.

17. *Mythen und Sagen. Okkulte Zeichen und Symbole* [Myths and sagas: Occult signs and symbols] (GA 101), lecture of 28 December 1907.

18. Ibid., lecture of 14 September 1907.

19. *Die Sendung Michaels* [The mission of Michael] (GA 194), lecture of 13 December 1919.

20. Helmut Gebelein, *Alchemie* [Alchemy] (Diederichs: Munich, 1991), p. 1121.

21. *Das esoterische Christentum und die geistige Führung der Menschheit* [Esoteric Christianity and the spiritual leadership of humanity], lecture of 28 September 1911.

22. Ibid., lecture of 27 September 1911.

Lecture 11

1. See *Die Offenbarungen des Karma* [The revelations of karma] (GA 120), lecture of 16 May 1910.

2. Cited in John Leddy Phelan, *The Millennial Kingdom of the Franciscans in the New World. A Study of the Writings of Gerónimo de Mendieta (1525–1604)* (University of California Press: Berkeley and New York, 1956), p. 26 (translated by M. and D. Miller from the German trans. by V. Sease).

3. Ibid.

4. *Innere Entwicklungsimpulse der Menschheit. Goethe und die Krisis des neunzehnten Jahrhunderts* [Inner impulses in the development of humanity: Goethe and the crisis of the nineteenth century], lecture of 18 September 1916, p. 62.

5. Manuscript by Bernardo de Sahagún, *Aus dem Aztekischen* [From the Aztec], trans. Eduard Seler, in: Konrad Theodor Preuss, *Die Eingeborenen Amerikas* [The indigenous peoples of America] (Mohr: Tübingen, 1926), p. 49.

Lecture 12

1. *Menschliche und menschheitliche Entwicklungswahrheiten. Das Karma des Materialismus* [Evolutionary truths about the human being and humanity. The karma of materialism] (GA 176), lecture of 11 September 1917.

2. Karl Kiesewetter, *Faust in der Geschichte und Tradition. Mit besonderer Berücksichtigung des okkulten Phänomenalismus und des mittelalterlichen Zauberwesens* [Faust in history and tradition. With particular emphasis on occult phenomenalism and medieval magic], vol. 1 (H. Barsdorf: Berlin, 1921), p. 21 (from Luther's *Tischreden* [Table talks]).

3. *Menschliche und menschheitliche Entwicklungswahrheiten* (GA 176), lecture of 11. September 1917.

4. Ibid., lecture of 18 September 1917.

5. Ibid.

6. Manfred Schmidt-Brabant, *Die sieben Stufen der Einweihung. Goethes 'Faust' als Urbild der modernen Initiation* [The seven stages of initiation. Goethe's Faust as a primal image of modern initiation] (Verlag am Goetheanum: Dornach, 1996).

7. Goethe, *Faust* II, Act 5, Bergschluchten [Mountain gorges], l. 11936.

8. In: Roland Fröhlich, *Grundkurs Kirchengeschichte* [Basic course in Church history] (Herder Verlag: Freiburg, 1980), p. 114f.

9. *Die Mystik im Aufgange des neuzeitlichen Geisteslebens und ihr Verhältnis zur modernen Weltanschauung* [Mysticism at the dawn of modern spiritual life and its relationship to a modern world view] (GA 7), p. 102f.

10. Ibid., p. 100ff.

11. *Mysterienstätten des Mittelalters* [Mystery sites of the Middle Ages] (GA 233a), lecture of 6 January 1924.

12. Virginia Sease and Manfred Schmidt-Brabant, *Paths of the Christian Mysteries: From Compostela to the New World*, p. 178f.

13. *Esoterische Betrachtungen karmischer Zusammenhänge* [Esoteric studies of karmic connections], vol. 3 (GA 237), lecture of 12 September 1924.

Bibliography of Cited Materials from the Collected Works of Rudolf Steiner

Publishers:
RSP   Rudolf Steiner Press (England)
AP/SB   Anthroposophic Press/SteinerBooks (USA)

7   *Mystics After Modernism* (AP)
10   *Knowledge of the Higher Worlds* (RSP)
13   *Occult Science, An Outline* (RSP)
14   *Four Mystery Dramas* (SB)
51   not translated
74   *The Redemption of Thinking* (AP)
93   *The Temple Legend* (RSP)
101   not translated
120   *Manifestations of Karma* (RSP)
121   *The Mission of the Individual Folk Souls* (RSP)
124   *Background to the Gospel of St Mark* (RSP)
131   *From Jesus to Christ* (RSP)
140   *Life Between Death and Rebirth* (AP)
161   not translated
171   *Inner Impulses of Evolution* (AP)
176   *The Karma of Materialism* (AP)
181   *Earthly Death and Cosmic Life* (AP)
194   *The Mission of the Archangel Michael* (AP)
214   *The Mystery of the Trinity* (AP)
216   *Supersensible Influences in the History of Mankind* (Rudolf Steiner Pub. Co.)
233a   *Rosicrucianism and Modern Initiation* (RSP)
237   *Karmic Relationships*, Vol. III (RSP)
240   *Karmic Relationships*, Vols VI + VIII (RSP)
243   *True and False Paths in Spiritual Investigation* (RSP)
265   *'Freemasonry' and Occult Work* (SB)
301   *The Renewal of Education* (SB)
324   *Anthroposophy and Science* (Mercury Press)
343   not translated
346   *Book of Revelation and the Work of the Priest* (RSP)
353   *From Beetroot to Buddhism* (RSP)

Diagam of the Right Tympanum, West Portal, Chartres Cathedral   From: Roland Halfen, *Chartres, Schöpfungsbau und Ideenwelt im Herzen Europas* [Chartres, creative architecture and the world of ideas in Europe's heart] (Mayer Verlag: Stuttgart, 2001)

Illustrations 1 and 2   The Death of Lazarus. Depicted on a capital in Vézelay. From: François Vogade, *Vézelay, Histoire, Iconographie, Symbolisme* [Vézelay, history, iconography, symbolism] (Vézelay, 1996)

Illustrations 3 and 4   Master Bertram. Detail from the Petri Altar, from Grabow, Hamburg, Kunsthalle

Illustration 5   The Temptation of Adam. Depicted on a capital in Vézelay. From: François Vogade, *Vézelay, Histoire, Iconographie, Symbolisme* [Vézelay, history, iconography, symbolism] (Vézelay, 1996)

Illustration 6   Head of a demon. Depicted on a capital in Vézelay. From: François Vogade, *Vézelay, Histoire, Iconographie, Symbolisme* [Vézelay, history, iconography, symbolism] (Vézelay, 1996)

Illustrations 7 and 8   Battle between two demons. Depicted on a capital in Vézelay. From: François Vogade, *Vézelay, Histoire, Iconographie, Symbolisme* [Vézelay, history, iconography, symbolism] (Vézelay, 1996)

Illustration 9   The Temptation of St Benedict. Depicted on a capital in Vézelay. From: François Vogade, *Vézelay, Histoire, Iconographie, Symbolisme* [Vézelay, history, iconography, symbolism] (Vézelay, 1996)

Illustration 10   The Basilisk. Depicted on a capital in Vézelay. From: François Vogade, *Vézelay, Histoire, Iconographie, Symbolisme* [Vézelay, history, iconography, symbolism] (Vézelay, 1996)

Illustration 11   The Devil of Lust. Depicted on a capital in Vézelay. From: Gottfried Richter, *Romanisches Burgund* [Romanesque Burgundy] (Stuttgart, 1979)

Illustration 12   Elemental Being. Depicted on a capital in Saulieu. From: Kate A. ter Horst-Arriëns, *Zwischen Gut und Böse* [Between good and evil] (Dornach, 1982)

Illustration 13   Gargoyle, Nôtre Dame de Paris. (Archive V. S.)

Illustration 14   The Descent of Christ into Hell. Illustration from the Stuttgart Psalter. From: Herbert Vorgrimler, *Geschichte der Hölle* [The history of hell] (Munich, 1994)

Illustration 15   An Angel Closes Hell. Illustration from the Psalter of St Swithin's Priory, *c.* 1150. From: Herbert Vorgrimler, *Geschichte der Hölle* [The history of hell] (Munich, 1994)

Illustration 16   The Fourth Tone. Depicted on a capital in Autun. From:

Gottfried Richter, *Romanisches Burgund* [Romanesque Burgundy] (Stuttgart, 1979)

Illustration 17   Paul, Servant of Jesus Christ; Romans 1:1. Illustration from: *The Bible* (Stuttgart, 1996)

Illustration 18   Beginning of Revelation, Rev. 1:9ff. Illustration from: *The Bible* (Stuttgart, 1996)

Illustration 19   Illustration from the Ingeborg-Psalter, Matt. 24:1–25, 46. Illustration from: *The Bible* (Stuttgart, 1996)

Illustration 20   The Mystical Mill. Depicted on a capital in Vézelay. From: François Vogade, *Vézelay, Histoire, Iconographie, Symbolisme* [Vézelay, history, iconography, symbolism] (Vézelay, 1996)

Paths of the Christian Mysteries

From Compostela to the New World

Virginia Sease and Manfred Schmidt-Brabant

Over the past decades there has been an upsurge of interest in 'the Camino', the pilgrim's route to Santiago de Compostela in northern Spain. But where does this fascination in the spiritual exploration of the Middle Ages come from, and what is its significance? Virginia Sease and Manfred Schmidt-Brabant attest that we live in a time of spiritual quest, discovery and change. Humanity is becoming increasingly sensitive, and primal memories are beginning to emerge in people's consciousness. Within this dynamic context of inner transformation, the Camino's historic importance is being re-echoed in many human souls.

Rudolf Steiner stated that people have a need to live not only with external history but also with the esoteric, hidden narrative which lies behind it: the history of 'the Mysteries'. Now at the beginning of the twenty-first century, the authors suggest that it is increasingly necessary for us to live consciously with this veiled history of humanity's continual search for communion with the divine world.

Based on lifelong researches and contemplations, the authors present a survey of extraordinary breadth and depth. Focusing on the spiritual history of mankind, they begin with the cosmic origin of the Grail Mysteries and culminate with the Supersensible Michael Cultus and the Being of Anthroposophia. In the intervening chapters they study the School of Athens, early Christian art and its Gnostic impulses, the Grail Initiation in northern Spain, the role of the Cathars and Troubadours in the Manichaean stream, the Camino to Santiago de Compostela and the esoteric aspect of music for the pilgrims, the Music of the Spheres and the Elders of the Apocalypse, the Templars as emissaries of the Holy Grail, the initiations of Christian Rosenkreutz and his relation to anthroposophical art, the early Rosicrucian impulses in America and Europe, and much more.

256pp; 23.5 × 15.5 cm; paperback; £14.95; ISBN: 978 1 902636 43 6

The New Mysteries
and the Wisdom of Christ
Virginia Sease and Manfred Schmidt-Brabant

In the old Mystery cultures the human being experienced himself as a child of the gods, or even an instrument of them. According to Rudolf Steiner's spiritual-scientific research, the birth of independent thinking came only with our present state of consciousness—through becoming aware of the individual self. But who is this self? Who am I? Virginia Sease and Manfred Schmidt-Brabant maintain that real self-knowledge is intimately connected with knowledge of the central being of world evolution: the Christ, or the 'I AM'.

Focusing on the being of Christ and on Christianity, *The New Mysteries* presents a series of engaging lectures on the developing Mystery wisdom of our age. Having given an overview of the history of the Mysteries in their book *Paths of the Christian Mysteries*, the authors deepen and further their study by paying special attention to the effect of the Christ Mysteries. Among the essential themes of this new volume are the transformation of conscience, the place of prayer and meditation, and the significance of sacrifice today.

208pp; 23.5 × 15.5 cm; paperback; £14.95; ISBN: 978 1 902636 74 0